"In *Calling the Circle*, Christina Baldwin lovingly guides us to a new way of perceiving ourselves and the world. By taking us to the center of the circle, she leads us not only to our innermost selves but to a way of seeing that could save the planet."
—Jerry Snider
Editor/Publisher
Magical Blend Magazine

"*Calling the Circle* addresses the longing within each of us to build a new world, and it offers a basic and immediate tool with which to begin. This warmly written book, which reads like a letter from a wise and caring friend, offers a lucid vision of cultural transformation through the activities of our daily lives."
—Shoshana Alexander
Author of *In Praise of Single Parents* and
Editor of *The FindhornGarden*

Calling the Circle "...really distills and makes very accessible the principles to maximize growth fulfillment."
—Dr. Elizabeth Roebuck, psychologist
Cambridge, MA

"*Calling the Circle* presents a practical road map which can be used by both corporations and families to clarify intent, develop consensus, and commit action. Through well chosen examples, it describes a process built on human values that unleashes a peer group's collective wisdom and experience. *Calling the Circle* defines what teaming is all about."
—Ric Rudman
Senior Vice-President, Corporate Services

CALLING THE CIRCLE

The First and Future Culture

CALLING THE CIRCLE

The First and Future Culture

Christina Baldwin

Swan•Raven & Co.
P.O. Box 726
Newberg, Oregon 97132

Library of Congress Cataloging-in-Publication Data
     Baldwin, Christina
     Calling the Circle: The First and Future Culture
                  p. cm.
     Includes bibliographical references.
                 I. Title.
BF1623.R6B35   1994
302.3'4--dc20
                     94-21483 CIP

ISBN 0-9632310-8-1 : $14.95
         1. Ritual.
         2. Circle--religious aspects.
         3. Communication in small groups.
         4. Decision-making, Group--Religious aspects.

COVER ART: Susan Boulet
COVER DESIGN: Marcia Berrentine
DESIGN IMPLEMENTATION: Carlene Lynch

Printed in the United States of America
Address all inquiries   Swan•Raven Co.,
                               P. O. Box 726,
                               Newberg, Oregon, 97132
                               U.S.A.

Printed on recycled paper.

This book is dedicated to that
Pure Spirit
upon which peer spirit
radically depends
and
to all who hold the rim.

Table of Contents

...LET US NOW LEARN HOW TO BE A PEOPLE
      WHO SEEK THE WISDOM OF ORDERED COUNCIL.

LET US REMEMBER
      HOW QUICKLY ONE WHO LEADS
         MAY BE TAKEN FROM US.

LET US UNDERSTAND
      THAT WHAT MAY BE IMPOSSIBLE FOR ONE
      MAY BE POSSIBLE FOR MANY.

AND IF ALL THIS ESCAPES YOUR MEMORY
      REMEMBER ONLY THIS:
         SEEK THE WISDOM OF ORDERED COUNCIL—

      HOWEVER MANY
         HOWEVER FEW
            HOWEVER OLD
               HOWEVER YOUNG

      SEEK THE WISDOM OF ORDERED COUNCIL.

Paula Underwood, *The Walking People*

Preface

The Power of the Circle

There is a river cottage I visit which has been in my friend's family for several generations, a summer home for the city folks built by this family of Wisconsin German farmers.

There is a ritual for getting here—circuitous routes from town, down one county road and then another, routes they all know by blood, and I only by acquaintance and a lucky sense of direction.

There is a ritual for getting here—the driveway unmarked, a quarter mile of two sandy parallel tire tracks between Grandpa Zimmer's cornfield and the scrub oak he cut for firewood before central heating came to the white frame farmhouse.

There is a ritual for getting here—because in the middle of this drive there hides the remains of a granite boulder and everyone who comes, be they family or friend, must ease their car over this slab rock without gutting the mechanics and bleeding oil or gasoline on the sand. The rock is part of the ritual for visiting; you learn to turn at the white flag and go slow over that rock or you'll be getting the tow truck to take you back to town.

The boulder is navigable now, though I've watched my friend drop down on her knees in an auto showroom and gauge the distance from floor to chassis, seeing this heirloom rock in her mind and not buying a new car that couldn't make it to the cottage.

The boulder is navigable now because, summer after summer, when it was the size of a bathtub, as long and as high, Grandpa Zimmer spent his evenings straddling rock and working away at the surface with a diamond-headed auger, drilling small round circles into the surface of the stone. And autumn after autumn, when the freeze came, Grandpa Zimmer filled those holes with buckets of river water. And winter after winter, the ice did its work and blew up more of his boulder. Bit by bit. Water set on stone.

Water crystals expanding against granite, no match for each other; the soft, burbling river set to its winter task: persistent, changing *form to meet the need. The need here, in the bowels of the rock, is to bore within, to be the circle in the center of the stone.*

It is autumn on our planet. The twentieth century is over. We stand in the middle of great change and cannot see what transformation is coming any more than the river can see itself cooling at the end of summer.

The boulder is the patriarchal way, and the auger is the energy of circling bored into granite, and you and I are the water at work. You and I are the water, willing to set ourselves to the next task.

You and I are the water, H_2O, the molecular heart of the planet. Eighty percent of everything on earth is water. You and I are the water. We are the majority of everything. We can be steam, be river, be rain and rainbow. We can be ice, talking to the granite one molecule at a time, convincing the rock to let go, to let itself be shivered: to be slivered small enough to be carried by water, to become sand, to rest on the banks of a river.

Come sit with me on this boulder. We will take turns boring the auger into stone. It is not such hard work when more than one is working. We will tell each other stories. We will help each other do the tasks of our lives. We will wear this stone away without violence. There has been enough violence.

We will talk to the granite.

We will not give up.

We will be like drops of water falling on a stone...

There is no one but us.
There is no one to send,
nor a clean hand nor a pure heart
on the face of the earth, nor in the earth,
but only us,
a generation comforting ourselves
with the notion that we have come at an awkward time,
that our innocent fathers are all dead
—as if innocence had ever been—
and our children busy and troubled,
and we ourselves unfit, not yet ready,
having each of us chosen wrongly,
made a false start, failed,
yielded to impulse and the tangled comfort of pleasures,
and grown exhausted, unable to seek the thread, weak, and
involved.
But there is no one but us.
There never has been.

Annie Dillard
Holy the Firm

CHAPTER ONE

The Awakening

*J*come from the middle. I grew up in Indiana and Minnesota, in the matrix of two families: my mother's Scandinavian farming background, and my father's Scotch-Irish-English bee-keeping background. I have spent most of my adult life, thus far, living in the middle of the country, in the middle of the middle class. On the suburban edge of Minneapolis, the air is still breathable, trees grow, and children cluster brightly on street corners to wait for the school bus. People lock their houses, but don't fortress them. Six blocks in one direction, a major highway connects this neighborhood to the arterial system that carries on the life of the city. Six blocks in another direction is a park, and between here and there, one summer dawn not long ago, a deer stepped daintily among the petunias and geraniums and surprised the dog and me. It is as gentle an urban environment as exists these days.

I venture out across the continent to teach but have always returned to center. To rest here among the oaks and rolling farmlands, the lake-studded city with its drastic seasons, to be surrounded again by the moderate people, the nice people, the folks who collectively represent the American Dream—the dream of a decent and comfortable life. This is the environment we were taught to aspire to: the scene that shows up in a thousand variations on television, in movies and books to reinforce the collective fantasy about modern life. It is a fantasy that is falling apart.

While life in the middle has incredible stamina, it seems to me to lack adaptability. As our aspirations are threatened, we try harder and harder to maintain the status quo. But the topics at dinner parties are radically changing. We reach across our still bountiful tables, grappling with the awareness that our personal lives cannot be separated from the life of our times. Over the drone of the television, we admit we don't know what is really happening—let alone have any idea what needs to happen. Ready or not, (please pass the salad), we are reconsidering the assumptions, expectations, and values that have guided our lives thus far. As our view of life is challenged, we live with a persistent suspicion that we are on the verge of immense change. How will we live through this much change? *How will our children and grandchildren live? From what sources will we draw our values? What will have meaning? What will offer stability? How will we take care of ourselves, our loved ones, and all the world's strangers? How will we care for the planet which sustains us?*

I believe we *can* address and answer these questions. I know the power to do so lies within us. What has been missing is the mechanism for organizing this power. I believe this mechanism of self-empowerment and focus is *the circle*.

The kind of circle this book addresses is a council of ordinary people who convene to accomplish a specific task and to support each other. In this circle, leadership rotates, responsibility is shared, and a sense of invisible wisdom provides the cohesion of the group.

Calling the circle is a simple idea—any one of us can do it. The circle can emerge anywhere that it is invited. Let's define a common need, goal, or course of action. Let's meet and agree upon the direction of the group and how individual needs will be supported within this overall direction. Let's state certain guidelines for respectful behavior to govern the circle meetings. Let's admit the presence of heart connection as well as intellect, and acknowledge spiritual energy as a guiding force.

Calling a circle doesn't have to be a huge risk or lengthy experiment. We can start small, start with one evening—start with a dinner party. My friend, Michael, called two buddies he's known since high school; the three men went off for the weekend together at a cabin. They gathered around the wood stove and got to know each other in ways they hadn't even realized they were missing. My mother, Connie, experienced a Croning Ceremony when she came to my brother's house one Christmas. Since then she has been helping other older women design Coming of Age ceremonies for themselves, and using the circle to garner support for spouse caregivers. When another friend, Mary Love, moved to Missouri and wanted a spirituality group, she called one, and helped the leadership step forward so that it is now self-sustaining. Whenever I want to have a serious conversation, even over the phone, I ask my friends to "enter into council" with me. We each light a candle to create a sense of connection to a source beyond the ego, settle in to listen and respond carefully.

Circles appear wherever we call them. I called a circle as part of my twenty-fifth college reunion. Circling was still such a new concept, I wanted to see if the readiness I felt in other groups was also present among women who had mostly grown up in the middle of the Midwest. One early evening in June of 1993, we closed the doors to the girls' dorm, and twenty women from Macalester College, Class of '68, looked at each other anew. On a coffee table, I laid out a Balinese cloth, candles, and a basket that travels with me. To this centerpiece, each woman contributed an object that symbolically represented her life now: photos of family, a favorite book, an identification badge from work, a running shoe, a rock from Lake Superior. We lit the candles and looked at each other in the flickering light, seeing remembered twenty-year-old faces in our forty-seven-year-old eyes. We opened the discussion and began sharing all the things we don't always take time to speak about in the busyness of our days. It had been a quarter of a century since we came of age: now what? As we went around the group, each woman held her object, said what she had come to say. It took three hours of close attention.

The specific issues brought forward may be different, but in circle after circle, a kind of communal consciousness occurs. When we stop to admit it, we *do* understand the immensity of the task we face. These women, who had flown in from Montreal, Hollywood, Iowa City, Cincinnati, from little towns and big ones, all knew what the problems were. We acknowledged that they are real and unavoidable, that they will consume the rest of our lives and our children's lives, whether we want them to or not.

We teetered on despair, but kept asking: "What can we do? How can we imagine responding?" Soon we were thinking together.

By midnight, this group of near strangers, with no set agenda, had come up with twenty suggestions and comments for activating values in their own lives.

"We pledge to be consistent with our children, to not lie, to utilize stability and unconditional love, wherever we find it. • We keep in mind that our lifetime goals and dreams are bigger than we are and cannot really be finished. • We know that the level of sharing and intimacy among midlife women is unprecedented in human history. We are trying to figure out what it means and what gifts it brings us. • We know that our children are watching. Our mothers are watching. Our husbands and brothers are watching. • We have learned that ultimately all politicians and systems will disappoint. The 1960s demonstrated, through charismatic leadership, what it is now possible for the ordinary individual to do. • We acknowledge that with all our freedoms, we seem to have lost our outrage, and our willingness to limit other people's behavior when it infringes on our values. • To address the problems facing us, we resolve to become a vocal majority. • We will consider how every decision impacts the next seven generations. • We will trust spirit. Put our lives into a larger context. • We will cleave to joy. • We will keep praying; it is positive energy going out into the world. We open our hearts to loving kindness. • We will create circles among those who pray with us and for us."

I know these women are doing something differently in their lives as a result of this circle. How do I know? Because I am doing something differently, and change in a circle is circular.

When people gather in circles, when we reveal ourselves by speaking from the heart, we discover common threads, common concerns, common longings. More and more, people tell me that they cannot make rational sense out of the questions they feel compelled to ask or the changes they have to make, and they cannot put off making them: it is simply time. Here in the middle of the modern world, tucked away where we are hardly noticed, something is happening. Not just in my life, but in the lives of many people. We have the incredible opportunity to dream a new dream and to fashion a renewed social order that can carry out our dreams.

THE SHATTERING OF THE COLLECTIVE DREAM

Part of the time I was writing this book I lived with my brother, Carl, and his family. Carl owns his own business installing electronic doors. He works too hard. He wants his business to succeed so he can sell it and make a career shift while he still has the energy to try something else. He needs money to live now, to save for his daughter Erin's college expenses, to plan for retirement. He is up at 5:00 A.M., at the office by 6:30 to get paperwork done before the phone starts ringing. My sister-in-law, Colleen, works a mixture of at-home and on-site jobs as a technical writer. She aspires to being an essayist and practices creative writing in snatched moments late at night. It is a sporadic commitment of time, though the dream travels with her consistently. Erin attends public school and Brownie Scouts, plays hockey in winter, softball in summer, and loves horses. A very bright child, she thinks about things, including what she will do when she grows up and what the world will be like.

In the mornings, Colleen gets Erin off to school, carpooling several children through the neighborhood. Even though this is the suburbs, a child was murdered in the local park and conscientious mothers don't let their children walk very far unescorted. At 3:30, she hurriedly leaves the office or turns off the home computer to pick up Erin, take her to the day's activities. While I am here, I help. Carl coaches the hockey team and shows up to take Erin to practice. In high school, he was a star skater himself. His knees are shot, but he still skates with the kids, still plays ball with his daughter, likes to go bowling, watches sports. In the evenings he romps with Erin and the dogs. We have supper. Carl falls asleep on the couch folding laundry and watching the Discovery channel. I share the cooking, do dishes, read, or write in my journal, handle my own business paperwork. We like to play Skipbo and Boggle. We listen to Erin, see that she practices piano, gets her homework done, and goes to bed on time. One by one, she summons us down the hall to her room for a tuck-in chat and hugs. "Send in Daddy," her dulcet voice rings through the upper level of the house. "Send in Mommy... Send in Auntie Christina." We are America.

Something is happening here in the middle. My work beyond the house is different than theirs. I travel to teach seminars based on earlier books: journal writing courses and spirituality workshops. With my teaching partner, Ann Linnea, we offer women's empowerment circles and consultation on council-bond change. Whatever the topic and focus of the group, and whoever attends, these experiences all have something in common: they call people into circle.

And then I come home to my apartment, or to my brother's house, to the suburbs and the city and life in mid-America. Even though the status quo is falling apart underneath us, there is microwave popcorn and a good video to watch and the time-consuming tasks of daily life. A dozen times a day we face a choice: to maintain the familiarity of what is—or what we pretend about what is—or to open ourselves to change, to practice how we might let go and see other possibilities.

Carl and I grew up in a house with two parents who were thoughtful about the state of the world. We all ate supper together and talked—about everything from how school was going to politics to history and art. Not heady intellectual discussion, that's pretty hard with four children gathered around, but a consistent attempt to get through to us, to bring the world to our attention, to show us that things mattered, to instill values.

We were taken to the local art museums, to plays and concerts, and quizzed on events. "What do *you* think? Are you going to have a mind of your own," I remember my father asking us over and over again, "or are you going to do what everyone else is doing and not ask why?" When I graduated from college he told me, "I don't know where you're going to end up... I've tried to raise you to be adaptable, to live on the moon if you have to."

I don't know if I'll ever live on the moon; I hope not, for I find this planet awesomely beautiful. And since we seem to be living in a reprieve from the notion that we ought to blow it up, what my generation may have to do is even harder: learn to live on the earth again. Learn to re-vision a world that is not the apocalypse.

The evidence is everywhere: *the twentieth century is over*. The life plan laid out by the World War II generation is not going to hold for the Vietnam generation, let alone for the children of today. This life plan did an incredible job rebuilding after the devastation of the 1930s and 1940s. In the industrial world, it provided booming employment, prosperity, and a contented retirement for many. In the course of this recovery, it also did incredible, perhaps irreversible, damage to people, cultures, resources and the environment on a global scale. The system which currently runs the world *has* to change if human beings are to survive, and nobody seems to know how to change it. *How may we carry on with our personal needs and dreams and, at the same time, see that the next generations have a chance to fulfill their personal needs and dreams?*

Systemic change is terrifying. We watch one section of the world after another fall into chaos and violence and we don't want that level of disruption to happen in our own lives, communities and countries. Yet, we need systemic change. We try to fix problems on an isolated basis, shuffling money and social attention back and forth, and our approach is not fixing anything. We keep trying to find the middle of the road, the moderate response, a way to hold our lives together. We cling to middle ground yet something is happening.

While the status quo is being bulldozed out from under us, we are coming awake.

AWAKENING: WHERE WE ARE NOW

We are living in the middle of an experiment in how to be human. Since 1970—with the invention of popular psychology—hundreds of thousands of people have gone through some form of awakening to *consciousness*. Tumbled along with everything else that is happening in the culture and in our personal lives, there is this added ingredient: consciousness. Throughout human history there have always been lonely visionaries, but never before has the call to awaken been heeded by so many. We do not know what long-term impact this will have on the species—to have so many people alive at the same time who have entered into some form of greater consciousness.

One level of consciousness is the ability to watch ourselves act at the same time that we are acting, to simultaneously think and feel and do. Consciousness is the mind's capacity to observe the self in reality, and to be thoughtful about our actions.

I remember the day I really "got" consciousness. I remember it because I was twenty-four years old, living in Europe, on the first leg of my post-college quest to find my life's direction. I was old enough to know that something was missing. Some hidden aspect to my own thought process needed to be revealed in order for me to progress.

I was living in England that early spring of 1970, working part-time and actively seeking something unknown to me. I wandered around London, especially the Soho district, the focal point of the counterculture. There was a head shop I hung around, soaking up the atmosphere, the incense and many cups of Jasmine tea. One day a man joined the conversation circle of tea cups and groovy attitudes. He leaned toward me and said, "I have a message for you. What you seek you will find in the Chalice Gardens. Go to Glastonbury." Before I could question him, he was gone.

Two days later I took the train to Bath and the autobus over to Glastonbury. I visited the local abbey where Gwenivere and Arthur are buried, wandered around the town looking for gardens. Two hours later, following directions, I was wandering the hillsides of mythical Camelot. The Chalice Gardens turned out to be a large cemetery. In early April, these hillsides were covered with daffodils nodding under a changeable sky. "What am I doing here?" I kept asking. "Who is trying to guide me? What do you want?" As no insight or answers came, I grew nearly frantic: here I was at the beginning of my quest and I was failing it. Missing the signals. I felt stupid, naive, alone, misled.

To rest and think this over I went into a small chapel. Thumbing through a Bible on the altar, I closed my eyes, let the book fall open wherever it willed. My finger came to rest on Isaiah 55:12:

> *Ye shall go out with joy and be led forth in peace;*
> *the mountains and the hills before you shall burst into singing*
> *and all the trees of the field shall clap their hands.*

Suddenly I was crying. I lay down on a long cart at the back of the chapel (only later did I realize it was a casket cart) and tried to calm myself as best I could. Taking long, slow breaths, I recited the phrase over and over: "I shall go out with joy... I shall go out with joy."

I think I napped briefly and when I woke, the sun, which had been clouded over all day, was flooding through the chapel window, the beam of light moving up my body in the waning of the afternoon. Warmth. I lay there accepting the caress. When the light reached my head, something changed: the light seemed to enter my mind—to turn my whole being to light. I was, literally and metaphorically, illumined. A capacity opened in my mind that allowed me to observe myself as I never had before. I was conscious at both a psychological and spiritual level. I "came home" inside myself—I arrived.

Many people can tell stories about coming awake—a click that occurs in the mind which enables us to witness ourselves in the midst of our own actions. In consciousness, the larger Self and the smaller self become aware that they are accompanying each other. The ego has a consultant, an inner voice of guidance—the Soul's voice joins the journey.

By the mid-1970s, I was back in Minneapolis teaching journal writing classes and working as a freelance magazine writer. In those days, I would put up a few posters, send out several dozen announcements, and rent a room at the back of a bookstore, a women's center, a church basement, or someone would volunteer their home. Little groups would gather—eight, ten, fourteen people at a time. I charged fifteen dollars tuition for eight class sessions; you could pay two dollars a night if you wanted. Mostly women came, carrying spiral notebooks from the drugstore, loose-leaf binders, office ledger books converted from accounting to diary keeping. Sometimes a few male poets or gentle introverts would venture to join the circle. Even then, instinctively, we made a circle. At the time, we couldn't quite explain why we were writing, what kept us at it, what the drive was. I called people into writing circles, suggested an informal curriculum, designed exercises we could do together and then discuss. Discussion—to hear ourselves think out loud—seemed the greatest gift.

Looking back, I realize these early journal classes and the writing itself were a gate—a gateway into consciousness. Consciousness is essential to the circle, to where the circle has the potential to take us. Consciousness is the foundation for making our own dreams real, and making a society which can support our values and dreams.

It doesn't matter how we wake up: perhaps it's through journal writing, meditation, therapy, or some life event that shakes and startles us. *Something* is happening to millions of people in the last decades of the twentieth century: we are experiencing an arousal of collective Mind. Whether consciousness comes like a lightning strike or surfaces through gentle persuasion, millions of people are shifting into a frame of mind where we are able to stand in the middle of our lives, observe ourselves in the world, and question. *We are awake* and it is our ability to be awake that also gives us the ability to dream—to envision, to create, to make happen. We are a tremendously powerful life force, and many of us aren't sure how to activate this force in our personal lives or in the larger culture.

Out on the seminar circuit at the beginning of the 1990s, I was teaching at Omega Institute in Rhinebeck, NY, when questions arose that became the foundation of this book. Omega Institute is a former boy's camp converted into an adult retreat center. Each week of summer a community of learners—consisting of about 450 students, 125 staff, and a dozen faculty at a time—gathers to study an eclectic curriculum of new thought.

It was August, a week of country heat with no air conditioning. I was teaching in a little building on the hill. I'd gone over on Sunday evening with a young staff assistant to get my bearings, placed a mix of pillows and chairs in a circle, turned over a cardboard box and draped it with a scarf and a candlestick. I laid out handouts and registration materials. I thought I was prepared. I thought eighteen people had signed up.

The next morning, more than forty journal writers crammed into the room. The circle disappeared in the chaos of simply finding a place to sit. A hodgepodge of rows began to develop. Laughing at the unexpected influx, I blurted out, "What are you all doing here?" People looked up, looked around, laughed back with me. We settled down to sweat and write together, but the question wouldn't go away. The question grew into a metaphoric theme for the week:

- What *are* we all doing here?
- Where has all this seeking come from?
- Why now?
- What for?
- What are we supposed to do with this experience called "self-actualization?"
- How does the drive to heal the self relate to the need to heal the world?

The forty people at Omega, and thousands of others I have met in my teaching travels, are a new kind of human being. We are a diverse group of people who have taken seriously the personal, psychological, and spiritual agenda. We have invested great amounts of time, energy, and money in self-healing. We have used ourselves in a living experiment to refashion the ways our minds work, to review our beliefs about who we are and how the world is, and to redefine our relationship to Spirit. This is our foundation: a sturdy sense of self, a willingness to review and change what we believe and how we act, acknowledgment that we need spiritual guidance and presence, even—or especially—in a secularly defined world.

FINDING CENTER: WHAT WE NEED NEXT

In Alex Haley's *Roots*, the father of Kunte Kinte takes his newborn son to a river near their African village, dips his small body into the stream, anoints the baby with mud from his birthplace, and then raises the child high to the sky. "Behold," he says, "Behold the only thing greater than yourself."

What is greater than the self? This is an imperative question in the modern world. What we believe to be greater than the self is what we put at the center of our lives.

When people live in a culture that has forgotten its relationship to mystery, a number of things go awry. We cease to regard life as sacred because we don't hear it described this way. We forget we are the sisters and brothers of all life because we are told we are the "masters" of creation. We revel in fantasies of specialness, and are tormented by our sense of isolation. And having lost our understanding that center serves as our point of interaction with the sacred, we fill the hole with substitutions. In modern culture, these substitutions include: status, class, ethnic and racial divisions, celebrity, violence, and personal power.

We all have rituals in our lives; we have simply forgotten that in our original way of living on the earth, these rituals were sacred, not secular. These rituals were designed to remind us over and over and over again of our true relationship to life: that of a grateful, amazed supplicant at the feet of mystery.

The rituals at my brother's house are typical of our confusion. My brother rises early and puts out the dog, makes a cup of coffee, lights a cigarette and leaves for work. In a sacred context, he would do the same things with intention. Putting out the dog would grant him the opportunity to greet the day in ritualized manner. His first cup of liquid would be treated as a libation, a drop spilled on the earth in thankfulness, then the rest swallowed. His drive to work would be a time of reflection, to make "holy smoke" and set his course for the day's activities. He would call upon spiritual power to help him make good decisions, listen wisely, practice fair business based on spiritual principles.

My sister-in-law rises and showers and brings in the newspaper to read at the kitchen table. In a sacred context, she would wash herself as a cleansing ritual, washing off the old life, taking up the life of the new day. Her morning reading would offer spiritual insight for the work awaiting her.

I rise, slip on clothes, forget my dreams, ignore my journal. In my mind, the litany of the day's duties begins to recite itself. Being self-employed, only I know what I am up to, only I can keep myself on track. Sometimes I manage this with grace, sometimes with nagging. In a sacred context, my duties would become a mantra, or I could sit in meditation, bow down before my day, light incense and think about the holiness of the present moment.

My niece is wakened at 7:30 by her dog and my puppy clambering over the covers, licking her face exuberantly. She smooths the tangle of long blond hair out of her eyes and greets the day. In a sacred context, the dogs might be seen as messengers of the day's possibilities. We would gather around, help her recall dreams, tell her our own night visions, treat these stories and images as important.

Instead, we muddle through. The newspaper does not provide inspiration; it simply frightens us with reminders of how much trouble the world is in. Colleen quizzes Erin on her spelling words. I edit a piece of manuscript. Erin leaves for school where there is no mention of the sacredness of the day, where any such reference would be challenged, fought over, denied. We are busy people. In the evenings we ask each other, "Did you have a good day," but what do we mean by this question? We have forgotten.

Among indigenous peoples—from the Arctic circle to the Australian outback—the common element of life is a daily relationship to sacred center. What is missing for most of us in the modern world is an understanding of how to live as an act of worship. We don't know what to revere. We don't know how to experience or show reverence.

In the summer of 1991, a Native American man came to participate in a writing course I was teaching in northern Minnesota. He was the only person of color in the class. He struggled to create the safety he needed to share his experiences, to believe he would be heard. After the first session he phoned me at my room. "If you are going to be my teacher," he said, "I want to approach you in the traditional way. I need to bring you a pouch of tobacco. Do you know what this means among my people?"

I had been reading about spirituality and native traditions and had several friends in the native community in Minneapolis. "I think I understand," I told him. "Tobacco is a sign of respect, that you come for teaching. If I accept the tobacco, it means I take seriously the request. The exchange creates an obligation between us, a kind of covenant." I expected a little bag of Bull Durham, the kind of offering I had made myself when approaching a Native teacher. He brought me an elaborately beaded deerskin pouch, a gift of such beauty and significance I knew we needed to talk before I could accept this obligation.

When he left the class, we stood together outside on the grounds of the university. "I want you to continue to carry the pouch," he said. "I have received the teaching I needed. I have been treated with respect." At first I was hesitant to accept the gift, but I stood with him in the daylight and listened as deeply as I could. "If you keep the pouch, it comes with an obligation. Everyday you must go outside and pray with this pouch. It needs to be taken out to greet each day."

Now he was my teacher. I thought of my usual life, sitting at the computer and writing to the hum of the air conditioner. I thought of Minnesota winters when I dressed in wool socks and sweat pants and avoided going outdoors for days at a time. Every day was not an easy commitment to make. "You do not do this for yourself," he said. "You do it for the pouch, for what the pouch carries."

"When I'm outside," I asked him, "Then what? What do I do?"

"You open the pouch and sprinkle a little tobacco as an offering. You say your prayers." What prayers, I wondered? I knew the Lord's prayer. I knew the bedtime prayers my family had taught me.

They did not seem appropriate to this obligation. Gil must have seen the confusion in my face. "The pouch will teach you to pray," he reassured me.

It has. And this ritual, this obligation to get outside, to look at the day, to say something holy to the morning, has been my beginning, a bridge between the modern world and the natural world, a bridge to rediscovering my place.

What is greater than the self is the world. The natural world. The spiritual world. The universe. This home we are a minuscule part of. We have forgotten how to live in our real home: to relate the self to the mystery of the world. What is missing from the middle of modern life is relationship to the sacred. If we are to "save" our place in this world, we need to come home to it, even though we don't know how. We will discover *how* once we discover *where* it is we are going.

The days of our lives wait to be acknowledged as holy. Only we may not take the time or know how to invite holiness into the day. We may not remember why the sacred is so important, and feel embarrassed when somebody brings it up.

I had a friend in college who had been blind since birth. I read him our English assignments, literary passages rich with visual imagery, describing people and vistas in nature. He would say about the sighted world, "I know I'm missing something significant, but I don't know what it is." This is the exact wording people use to express their loss of sacred center. We don't have language for what is missing in our individual lives, what is missing in the community, in the culture and, now, what is nearly obliterated from the world. *How do we mourn what we have never known?* In the circle we have the opportunity to be very intentional about what we bring to the center—and to bring the sacred back to center.

When I was in the midst of book writing, a friend called and asked to come by. "If you can spare me even an hour," she said, "I'd appreciate it. I heard your speech last month. I need to know more about circles. I need to know *now*. I have an executive board meeting coming up and I want to do something different. Help."

It was 7:30 on a rainy Friday morning when she showed up with fruit and bagels and I poured us each a cup of strong coffee, steamed milk. Throughout my apartment I had lit candles in several rooms, turned a few lamps on low to brighten the corners. My writing space is mostly a large altar, the furniture snuggled around the real essence of the place, which is a collection of stones and driftwood, shells, low glass and wooden tables, several large pieces of art. "It feels good in here," Karen said, "What is it?"

"The circle," I told her. "Welcome home."

TAKING THE SELF INTO THE WORLD

I believe that my most significant achievement in the first half of my life has been to restore my personal sanity: I am a functioning human being. I know how to think. I know how to feel. I know how to solve problems. I know how to communicate. I am willing to hold myself accountable. I can be in relationship. I practice prayer. This is what I have to offer the world.

I first tiptoed into therapy when I was twenty-seven. A couple of older cousins began talking to me about the counseling they were doing. It was 1974, and I was writing in my journal fairly oblivious to the idea that my belief system and actual reality were not the same. "So," I ignorantly asked, "what's therapy...and do you think I need it?"

Ten years later I came out the other end of the psychological pastry tube feeling, over all, pretty sane. And this is what I learned: if I change my belief system, I can change my life. My belief system, and our collective belief systems, comprise reality. If we change what we believe, we change what is possible. We change reality. The mind changes the world. Consciousness is the tool of our liberation. What a miracle: you and I, bumbling through our personal issues, our pain and recovery, have discovered the tool of our liberation.

As we come to understand that we can, through our own efforts, change our beliefs, we also come to understand that we can, through our own efforts, change our lives. And when we change our lives, that is, as we become able to think for ourselves, we can imagine that through our own efforts we can change society. In my early forties I kept looking in the mirror and thinking, *"So, here I am. I have a mind. Now what? What do I want to do?"*

This isn't an unusual mid-life dilemma. We come to these crossroads by several paths. Some people have spent a great deal of time and energy in the first twenty-plus years of adult life figuring themselves out; others have spent a great deal of time making their mark in the world. Either way we end up asking—*Now what? What do I want to do?* Often, it seems to me, these two types may be partnered with each other and quietly, or openly, critical of how the other has spent his/her time, not realizing the mutuality of our quandary.

Each quandary poses its own dilemma. As seekers we face the challenge of taking our consciousness out into the world: fashioning a practical, pragmatic place that can incorporate who we are. As doers, we face the challenge of turning inward: learning how to listen for inner guidance and deciding to value the spiritual aspects of life. At least this is how I see us, sitting around the supper table at Carl and Colleen's, discussing our ideas of what's coming next for each of us.

A friend of mine with a good head for business and a heart for higher purpose became one of the players in a business group arranging international shipments of goods into eastern Europe, Russia and the Middle East. Most of this business was conducted by phone and fax, outlining deals and striking bargains which fell through again and again as information was reinterpreted through a dozen intermediaries. Twenty-four hours a day somebody's phone was ringing.

I couldn't help thinking that the circle could have made this process different. Within the circle, these people could have held "council," could have faced each other, speaking to the center so that everyone could hear what was going on. Within the circle they could have created communal accountability and coordination. In the absence of the circle, I watched my friend get sucked into the mire. Days and nights—since that's when the European faxes came in—were consumed with pressure, anxiety and angry telephone conversations in which she toughed it out with faceless colleagues around the world.

I kept saying, "What concerns me most is the unremitting stress you're living with. Isn't there some way you can trust Spirit in all this?"

My friend kept saying to me, "It's not about magic. That spiritual stuff isn't pertinent in this arena. I can't apply one to the other."

This is where our quandaries intersect—in situations where we may decide to apply one path to the other instead of seeing them as separate. We may apply Spirit in the business world and apply pragmatics to the spiritual path. I don't know how I will resolve this dilemma for myself, but I know I have skills in both areas and I am determined to integrate my work, my play, my living, my faith. My friend says her world is not about magic. Mine is.

I want to build a Third Culture in which I may apply the personal journey to the social journey. And I am going to devote the second half of my life to helping restore sanity in the world around me. I am going to translate the skills learned in journal writing, in therapy, in spiritual counseling, into skills that can operate in the world beyond the self. I am going to utilize the skills learned in corporate consulting, marketing, product design, and human resources and see how these skills can be spiritualized. *And the way I'm going to do this is through the circle.*

As I make this announcement to myself, I suspect I am just as naive about what will be required in the outer world as I once was about the requirements of exploring the inner world. And yet, it seems the only logical journey—taking the self into the world, offering myself to the world. I offer myself to the world that our collectively changed consciousness makes possible and work to bring that world into being.

THE SINGLE STEP

A journey begins with a single step.

Walking around and around the cushioned indoor track at the health club with my sister-in-law, I notice we are making circles, logging up several miles as we talk. We create a walking council, exchanging stories and ideas, thoughts we want each other's help in holding. "What I've learned from listening to you talk about the circle," Colleen says, "is the firm belief that we can change the direction we're going in, if we can get down to the level of empowerment. My despair is that I haven't a clue what the level of empowerment is and what that would mean...for me."

The circle begins at home. Begins at home if I am a single person living with a cat and two nervous parakeets; begins at home if I am a busy parent getting children out the door and working part-time at the mall; begins at home if I am a manager or business owner or a retired teacher who's bored with gardening and golf. The circle begins on Monday morning and Wednesday afternoon, on Saturday evening in April, July, October, February. The circle begins wherever we are, whoever we are, with whatever we're doing in the day-by-day routine of ordinary life.

•

The teenage son of a friend asks, "Mom, why do you always light a candle when you want to talk seriously with me?"

The mother says, "The candle sets the tone. I want you to know that this is going to be an important conversation and I want you to pay attention to me in a different way than when we're just passing each other in the house."

"Okay, cool," he says, and they are in circle.

•

Two friends are having a picnic in the middle of a hiking day. There is homemade bread and apple juice, cheese and fruit. They sit facing each other. One spontaneously picks up the bread and tears a piece off the end. Without saying a word he holds it up to the day. They look at it together. They feed each other. They do the same with the juice. Then they eat lunch.

•

A minister is meeting with two parishioners who have been involved in a long-standing argument. She joins them in the library where three comfortable chairs have been pulled around a coffee table. There is a Bible opened to one of her favorite passages for conflict resolution. There is a candle. She lights it, looks in the faces of the two men, "Are you ready to begin?" she asks. She waits for them to nod. She reads the scripture. She puts a palm-sized rock on the table. "There will be no casting of stones in this conversation, but whoever wishes to may hold the stone while he speaks, and we will listen."

•

A woman visits her parents to tell them she is getting divorced. This will be hard news for them. She spends two days bringing little things to their kitchen table: a feather, a piece of bark, photos of her husband and children taken last Christmas. Her mother adds a small vase of flowers. There is no acknowledgment that this is an altar, that is not a language common between these two generations. The actions of the mother and daughter are natural rituals of centering. When the woman also feels centered, she begins the conversation.

•

A woman is undergoing chemotherapy for breast cancer. A friend of hers who had a mastectomy three years earlier says, "I want you to meet my circle of survivors." The next Thursday, six women come to her house. They create a private space in front of the family room fireplace. They have brought a quilt, massage oils. The woman sits in the middle on the quilt. The women massage her hands and feet. They anoint her forehead. They sing to her, songs she knows, songs that are new. They ask if she will accept their energy for healing. She says yes. They take off their sweaters: each woman is one-breasted, naked to the waist. "We are beautiful," they whisper. "We are the tribe of one-breasted women." They extend their hands, palms up, toward her: she feels the heat

•

A man is called into personnel, given notice of immediate termination and told to clean out his desk. Humiliated and in shock, he carries an empty box back to his cubicle. His co-workers help him pack up personal belongings. One by one, spontaneously, they begin to recite everything they appreciate about him. "Stop, stop, please," the man says, "I don't want to lose it in front of you guys..."

"We just want you to know you'll be missed," another man says. They escort the man to his car like an honor guard. They decide to meet so they can talk about approaching management as a unified group, to see if management will let them influence how these layoffs are handled, to see if they can become part of the decision-making process, not its victims.

•

A church calls a circle to discuss the homeless people in their downtown parish, and how the church might respond. The homeless hear of the meeting and join it. "We know what our needs are," they tell the parishioners. "Do you want to listen?" The group expands the circle, holds a council in which everyone's voice is heard. The church moves out of its traditional position of "providing for the poor" into a position of participating with the homeless to empower change.

•

In a neighborhood stressed by changing populations, the children in an elementary school form a council to provide creative, nonviolent solutions to their everyday conflicts. The council members—fourth, fifth, and sixth graders—wear badges on the playground and intervene when trouble occurs. They call a circle when one is needed, so that each child gets heard and a solution is reached. One teacher sits in this circle as a witness. She doesn't interfere unless the children's process gets stuck and they call on her for assistance.

It is through these ordinary acts that the circle re-enters the world. It is through these ordinary acts that the world is changed. Day by day by day, we wear away the stone we have become. It's scary changing models, but our future will be determined by what we do.

The most important step we can take with the circle is use it. Use it now, today, especially if we are not in crisis. We can set this structure in place in our lives, in our work, in our neighborhoods, in our civic centers, in our religious or spiritual communities, in our families and friendship groups. We need these skills to recreate Third culture, and to stay sane in our culture as it is.

I pledge allegiance to the Earth
and to the flora, fauna
and human life that it supports,
one planet, indivisible,
with safe air, water and soil,
economic justice, equal rights
and peace for all.

Women's Environment
and Development Organization (WEDO)
of the Women's Foreign Policy Council

CHAPTER TWO

Circling: The First and Future Culture

So here we are in the middle of all our busyness and ordinariness. Here we are in the rush of days and weeks going by. The list keeps growing of things we never quite get to: paperwork, housework, little niceties we used to have time for. There's not even much time to notice what we have let go of, life propels us by these missed opportunities so fast.

Then something happens that threatens to interrupt the tenuous flow. This event could be anything—anything on the list of anxiety that runs through our minds after midnight, a list that begins, "Please don't let this happen to me..." But something *will* happen to us, something *will* hit us personally, because that is the nature of life. We do not escape; we live and do the best we can to cope.

My friend Carol calls. Teachers in her school district are threatening to strike. She's nearly frantic. "I feel helpless," she says over the phone. "I have to go to work, so does John, and if the kids suddenly need watching every day, I don't know what we'll do. John's company is already down-sizing. He's afraid to ask for any special adjustments to handle child care for fear they'll use it as an excuse to let him go. And I can't quit—we need the income..."

"Well, have you talked to anybody?" I ask, "Teachers? Other parents? The School Board?"

"I was up at school the other day and I know Jenny's teacher well enough to ask her what she thought. I've never seen Mrs. Ebble so tense. I got an earful about how the teachers think the Board is stonewalling. She says the Board's just concerned about budget cuts and not quality of education. At the last PTA meeting, the Board sent a representative to ask us to decide which extracurricular activities to cut. I think they want somebody else to take the flack. The whole situation seems near panic. Brandon says he's quitting soccer because his coach told him it's going to be cut anyway.

"Arlene, my next door neighbor, is the only parent on the block who's home days. We were watching some of the kids playing hide-and-go-seek last Saturday when she turned to me and said, 'Well, if the strike comes, I can't become den mother to everyone else's kids. You'll have to find some other way of coping.' There are so many aspects to this—everything from my overall concern about what's happening to education, to what am I going to do if I can't go to work because the kids would be home alone all day with the TV! What can I do?"

"You could call a circle," I suggest.

"We tried that. Last week the PTA officers hosted a meeting at the community center, invited teachers, parents, some of the Board members to come hear each other out on neutral ground. It turned into a shouting match. The women were complaining about how nobody cares about the kids anymore; the men got belligerent and started yelling at each other."

"No. I mean really *call a circle.*"

A circle is not just a meeting with the chairs rearranged. A circle is a way of doing things differently than we have become accustomed to. The circle is a return to our original form of community as well as a leap forward to create a new form of community. By calling the circle, we rediscover an ancient process of consultation and communion that, for tens of thousands of years, held the human community together and shaped its course.

DREAMTIME: THE FIRST CULTURE

In ancestral times, the circle flourished as the primary communal structure in richly diverse pockets of human community that spanned the globe. The Inuits of the Arctic Circle met in council and built their dwellings round. The Aborigines of Australia painted sacred spirals on cave walls and on their bodies and followed the energy of the earth across the vast expanses of the outback. The native tribes of the American plains constructed teepees and set them in circles. African tribes built circular villages. In all these variations of human adaptation, the circle was the common element. *The circle is our First Culture.*

First Culture was the flowering of human community based on the campfire, the council and the circle. It flourished for thousands of years in kinship-based tribal groups across the globe. First Culture was rooted in the development of agriculture, a skill about ten thousand years old, which necessitated that small bands of hunter/gatherers claim territory and stay in place long enough to plant seeds and harvest crops. In hundreds of variations, the human tribe adapted to climate, terrain, and natural resources. They developed social structures which helped sustain them on the land and spiritual myths which helped explain the mysteries of life. These structures and their spiritual base are evident in paintings, carvings, petroglyphs, runes, crafts and architecture. What seems to have been intact in all these settings were the concentric circles of interconnection—the campfire, the extended family, the tribe, humanity, nature and the mystery of Spirit. *And deep in my cells, I remember the first circle.*

Many, many thousands of years ago, when we captured the spark of fire and began to carry the embers of warmth and cooking and light along with us from site to site, fire brought a new experience into being. Coming in from the veldt where we had been wandering in small breeding groups, we found shelter in caves and crevasses and brought the safety of the light with us. The fire warded off predators, cooked the meats and roasted the roots and nuts that were our staple diet. With the flame, we could provide more food, extend the safety, sustain more people.

We made a circle around the flame and began to face each other. We came into circle because the fire led us there. Struggling to keep warm, struggling to keep safe, it made sense to put fire in the center. A circle allowed space for each person to face the flame, to take place. As a member of a fire circle, we each could claim a place of warmth and a piece of the food.

Out of this instinctive taking of place, the idea of community began to develop.

Socialization is not always a smooth process. Sometimes I can still hear the snarls of males vying for control, the fierce protective grunts of the females guarding their young, the squeals of little ones cuffed aside, the sighs of the old and vulnerable. The circle provided the basis for community, a format for working things out. As we refined social skills, the circle grew with us. With our faces animated by the flicker of flames, we began to recognize each other as kindred, as "like kind." Surrounded by familiar kin, with bodies fed and sheltered, the rules and taboos of community social conduct could be established.

When I see someone again and again in firelight, the fire becomes symbolic of our connection; I see a spark in the other. Perhaps as we first faced each other across the shimmering circle of light, we were able to envision the spark of the Sacred in each other's eyes. We wondered about our place in the larger circle of the earth and sky, in the community of creation. Around the campfire, a mythology arose about our creation and our reasons for being, and we told stories about our place in the scheme of life. The fire was a sacred symbol, the source that provided a cohesive center. And when we fell asleep around the fire's coals, we dreamed.

We felt small and vulnerable on the great natural skin of the planet. So many things were unexplainable. How could we be so hungry and when we cried out, one among us would find a berry bush, or a flock of birds would come within range of our slingshots? How could a woman's body swell and swell, and then, in the midst of crying and blood, push out another human being? Why did death come, and sometimes healing? Full of wonder, we developed rituals of thankfulness. Out of spontaneous gratitude, we believed ourselves to be in relationship with some Spirit Being who helped safeguard our lives.

We experienced a radical dependence upon all of nature. We were her daughters and sons, and so we named her—Mother. We carved images of the Mother goddess, crawled into womb-like caves, made offerings to the land, threw gifts of incense into the fire, built altars of cairn stones, notched the trunks of trees to mark our passage, danced and drummed and sang, and held council in the sacred shape of the circle. I remember. And so do you. Our cells recall another way to lead our lives. Our cells are leading us in a process of reclamation.

THE POWER OF ONE CIRCLE

It is dusk on a Saturday evening. Carol and John's house is quieted from its usual daily busyness. There is soft music playing as a group of teachers and parents enter. Lights are low. A cloth is spread on the coffee table in the center of the living room and objects depicting school life are laid out—a bowl of apples and cookies, pencils and small pads of paper, the Crestview Eagles emblem, school photos of the children whose parents have come to circle. These familar objects shimmer in the light of several candles. Arlene has come, so has Mrs. Ebble and several of her close colleagues. The president of the Parent Teacher Association is here, John and three other fathers, five mothers of Jenny and Brandon's friends. This time the circle has been called with intention.

It had taken Carol one whole evening to draft a paragraph statement asking people to participate:

"I am calling another meeting," she wrote, "to hold council about the issues facing us regarding the impending strike between the teachers of District 269 and the Board. The purpose of the meeting is to provide a forum in which teachers and parents together can develop a plan to approach the Board and advocate for resolutions that will be best for everyone. This meeting will be at our home and will be held as an intentional circle. We will use the structure of council to hear each other out, gather information, develop understanding and plan considered action. Circling may be new to us, but it is an ancient form. We will literally sit in a circle, open and close formally, pass a talking piece around to share the floor (Jenny's day-glo pink ruler ought to work well). We will design the outcome of the evening as we go. If you are willing to take this risk and explore a form that may really help us here, please let me know by Friday. I know this is short notice, but it's all the time we have."

In the entrance way, people greet and introduce themselves as they arrive. They take off coats and get a cup of tea or coffee before entering the living room. Even though it has not been articulated, there is a sense that this is consecrated space. People settle in, expectant and a little nervous about how to behave around the centerpiece and candles.

Carol and John live on a block where people hardly know each other except for the visiting that occurs between their children.

John works for a company where everyone spends the day in cubicles doing highly isolated tasks. Carol works at a software firm. Year after year, their children are educated by people they hardly know. They go to church, sit in rows and listen politely while someone else tells them what God is. The closest they get to governing council is the voting booth, and most of the time they vote without much sense of what the issues really are, or what this or that candidate can really do. We know this routine; we live it too. It's life in the middle.

John says, "Many of us are only bare acquaintances. If the circle works as Carol has explained it to me, we're going to get to know each other much better tonight. I'd like to suggest we start with a minute of silence. Whatever you want to do during that time is fine. Pray or meditate, breathe deeply, or do multiplication tables—it's all about focusing. We need to draw a line between the day and the circle. We need to make a space in which we can hear each other more accurately than we usually do and find a way to speak our own truth."

When people settle into silence for one minute, or three or five or ten, a sense of timelessness may occur. But in ordinary settings, silence in a group has become a signal of discomfort rather than contemplation. We fidget. Our minds race around looking for something to say. Silence between partners or friends may indicate anger or sullenness. Since silence has become a sign of social disapproval, we may need to retrain ourselves in order to feel comfortable. Breath helps. By concentrating on gentle, rhythmic breathing, we may slip into stillness, rest there, and then gently let the mental energy rise again. When John feels his own mental energy returning and senses that others in the room are also ready, he signals the end of silence by ringing a small brass bell. People open their eyes.

Opening a circle with ritual is essential to help people drop their expectations that the circle is just another name for a committee meeting, task force, or project team. People are often surprised to find themselves in a setting that includes ritual. And yet, they are also intrigued. Lighting a candle, creating even a small focal point in the center, following a time of silence by reciting a quote—whether it's a poem or a mission statement—all help us remember our roots in the circle.

After this evening's silence Carol begins. She is eager for the idea to work, her voice vibrant. "As convenor this evening, I welcome you to circle. I appreciate your coming, and your willingness to try a new form of meeting in order to resolve this problem. I've called this meeting, but in circle it's not mine to run—the circle belongs to all of us."

In holding a circle, leadership rotates, responsibility is shared, and each participant agrees to trust that there is something present that's larger than all of us. In building trust, group guidelines have proven very helpful in creating an agreed-upon environment inside which we can carry on the business of the circle. The purpose of Carol's called circle is to generate ideas to break the stalemate and show support for the teachers, the children, and the school system itself. To frame this discussion, Carol suggests the group observes basic guidelines: confidentiality, careful listening without interrupting, making statements that have to do with problem-solving, and calling for time out if people need to regroup and think through an issue. Carol and John are being very careful in how they introduce this circle: they want to invite people into council without scaring them.

Beverly Ebble starts by saying, "My biggest problem is isolation and lack of vision. I'm so busy coping with the twenty-four little beings right in front of me, I don't feel connected to the staff or the larger picture. Certainly I want my kids to pass their grade equivalencies, but I also want to help them grow up, ready for the world. You can't imagine the level of need some of these youngsters have. I get the sense nobody is raising kids anymore, that most of us are just passing them on and on in the system, and I get into despair about where they're going. And then, when the School Board says it's all about budget cutting—even my own salary—I get angry and defensive."

When the pink ruler is passed to her, Arlene says, "Well, I'm raising my kids! I'm the only mother here who's home when they get home." There is a flurry of murmured response among others in the circle, but they respect the talking piece and let Arlene finish her thought. "Okay, okay, just listen to me. I don't mean to say you're doing it wrong and I'm doing it right. I'm saying times have changed from how it was when we were kids. My question is, if we ask parents to do something more, will parents find the time to take an interest in what's happening? I'd like to suggest some kind of coalition between parents and teachers so that we can bring the Board a solution, rather than another demand. But I don't know how to design it..."

This is a complex discussion about a complex problem. People need to express their overall concerns and then break the problem down into small enough pieces to see how they can effect change. Of course there's tension, but it's creative tension. The circle is not always a group of like-minded souls who agree with each other about everything. There is room in the circle for many opinions, voices, views. Listening to Arlene, several parents feel themselves shift into guilt and defensiveness, but because they don't interrupt her, they hear the rest of her statement and relax again into problem solving.

A father named Tom takes his turn. "At work we're using Quality Control Circles to problem solve in several divisions. I'm wondering if we can adapt this concept to what's happening here. Maybe we could design teams that would take responsibility for different extracurricular activities, use volunteers and cut costs in that area so there'd be more money to negotiate salaries."

SECOND CULTURE: THE MODERN WORLD

This circle is not so strange that we cannot imagine ourselves within it. Opening with a moment of silence and passing a talking piece may be different than the last meeting you or I attended, but it's conceivable that the format helps. Certainly the tone of this gathering is more constructive than that of the community forum hosted by the PTA officers. What happened in the PTA meeting was a microcosm of what's happened to our culture as a whole. Our understanding of how to hold council has been replaced with the drive to maintain and control access to power. Controlling access to power creates a hierarchy model for society in which the powerful few maintain dominance over those who believe themselves deprived of power.

In this model it is the circle itself that we have lost. Through a re-examination of anthropological evidence, scholars are recovering the First Culture heritage which previously had been hidden in what was considered "prehistory." Until approximately five thousand years ago, there were thriving First Cultures throughout the world. Most of these cultures did not fortify or build defenses. They did not expect domination, and yet—in agrarian societies scattered throughout the Mediterranean, Europe and the Americas—domination occurred. Warrior cults began raiding these more pacifistic groups, and eventually the world turned from circle-based communities to the patriarchal and hierarchical societies that I call Second Culture.

When we understand the underlying beliefs functioning in Second Culture, and in our minds, it's easy to see why an event, even one as simple as a community meeting, is unable to achieve its stated purpose of communication.

Raised in Second Culture, we have been trained to believe in patriarchy-as-reality from the moment of birth. We inherit a culture that sees the world through the lens of domination and submission. In patriarchy, we have been taught to believe that some people are leaders and most people are followers; to believe that when someone assumes power and moves to the top of the heap, then the rest of us are knocked down a notch; to believe that overpowering is the only way to get our wants, desires and needs met; and to believe that only the weak, the losers, and the inept allow themselves to be pushed aside, to be marginalized at the rim of society.

When we think about the underlying beliefs driving Second Culture, it's easy to understand why an event as simple as a community meeting is unable to achieve its stated purpose of consulation. As the organizer of the meeting, the president of PTA, even though he is a well-meaning man, tried to maintain control in the ways he knew—by exerting his leadership and by expecting others to respect his position as leader of the meeting. He assumed people would follow format, would adhere to Roberts' Rules of Order, would let him guide the proceedings. But the situation was emotionally charged and others fought to wrest that control away, to establish their own point of view, to make the crowd follow their line of thinking. Ted Johnson could bang the gavel all he wanted and it wasn't going to stop Joe Smith from getting his two cents in, and it wasn't going to prevent the fourth grade teachers from walking out en mass, nor keep Pam Anderson from bursting into tears of frustration and again embarrassing her husband, who never understands why she can't control herself in public.

We've been in this scenario. We were schooled in it. We grew up in it in our families. We have experienced it in nearly every conflict situation we've ever lived through: at home, at work, in our churches and synagogues, in any group where power has become an issue. And in a society based on control and power, power will always, eventually, become the issue.

By hosting a meeting in a circle, Carol and John are challenging five thousand years of enculturation. They are saying: power will be shared, opened up, dealt with differently, so that we may find a new way of being together that can lead us to re-imagining what culture might be. Carol and John are just two folks in the middle—our neighbors, ourselves, and yet they are beginning to re-imagine culture.

For the most part, we believe in the patriarchy because it is the model that has been presented to us as reality. However, patriarchy is not reality. It is a *model*, a system, a construct that has been built and can be unbuilt. Enculturation—that which we have been taught to think of as reality—is how we see the world, but it is not necessarily how the world really is.

The human mind learns by comparing a present image with a previous image. This is both our source of genius, and of our conditioning. The baby sees a furry four-legged creature and asks, "What dat?"

The parent explains, "That's a doggie, honey. See the nice doggie?"

The next day the baby sees another furry, four-legged creature and says proudly, "Doggie!"

"No," says the parent, "That's a cat."

So the baby looks more closely. The baby begins to discern the subtle differences that make a dog or a cat. The baby gets so good at this discernment that no matter what color or size or hair-length is presented her, she can tell whether this is a dog or a cat. This process of discernment functions voraciously in the youngster's mind, which gobbles up and integrates information about concepts and ideas as well as about dogs and cats.

Once we have checked out that our categorical discernment is "right," we stop holding that part of reality in question. The baby trusts her parents' perceptions and incorporates their information. The student trusts the teacher. The adult trusts the government and religion. We begin to assume that our information about the world around us is intrinsically true.

Over time, we establish a matrix of understanding which so thoroughly frames how we see the world that we cannot imagine anything else. And this is our dilemma. To function as good members of society, we have learned to see the world through the lens of our collective conditioning. But what we have been taught to think of as reality is actually only our collective imagining of reality. For the most part, in patriarchy, what we have been taught to believe is not actually in our best interests socially, psychologically, or spiritually. And so, we must reteach ourselves.

The tool we have for training ourselves to see the world differently is consciousness. In those moments when we are really conscious, our conditioning is able to fall away and we see something anew. These are often ecstatic moments. We experience an internal "ah-ha" that revitalizes us and reframes how we connect with other people, situations, and the natural world. The lens falls away for a brief glimpse. Insight comes and goes, but these moments are enough. They provide breakthrough, and breakthrough provides a basis for new thinking. We who have had even one moment of consciousness—a moment when we have understood that how things are is not the way things have to be—hold the tool of our liberation.

Carol and John are inviting themselves and the others in the circle to gather with intention and to hold personal consciousness. When Arlene finishes her thoughts, when Mrs. Ebble articulates her frustration, when Tom sees the correlation between what's happening at work and its application at his children's school, liberation begins.

Liberation begins in circle by listening to each other. In a circle, the use of a talking piece, or comfortable reliance on moments of silence, allows us to listen differently. Interaction slows down. There is breathing space. Our minds downshift from the usual pace of thought. In circle, we may practice being bi-focused in our concentration: paying attention to what is being said, and letting other people's words and actions get through the usual social barriers. We shift from ego-centrism to circle consciousness.

I was raised in a typical family where "reality" was fought over on a minute-by-minute basis. We all knew that only one person's point of view would be proclaimed as the right one, and that this determination of "what really happened" was some kind of prize—was power. Carl and I and our two younger siblings engaged in constant squabbles to define reality—to be the one able to say what happened—to be believed. Coming in from play, Carl would say, "Mom, mom, I saw a tiger in the woods!"

And I would contradict him, "No you didn't, it was only a dog."

"He was a tiger...or maybe a lion!"

"No, stupid, there aren't any lions or tigers in Minnesota."

It never occurred to us to question whether or not this contest mattered; that maybe Carl's sense of magic could be validated along with my sense of realism; that maybe two views of what we saw in the woods were even preferable to one. In Second Culture context, enculturation had taught us that reality is a contest of power. If Carl won, he would proclaim that his perception was right and mine was wrong. This was often the same struggle our mother was having with our father and the same struggle our father was having with the world.

The circle reintroduces the idea that different perceptions are both valid and helpful, and that they do not have to compete with each other for dominance.

The circle is revolutionary because it removes this struggle for dominance and allows us to look at other issues. As long as we are vying for power, we have little energy genuinely available to solve problems, address concerns, or sustain common purpose. When we call the circle—with its potential for liberation—into the midst of Second Culture, we pave the way for a new amalgam of the past and present to emerge—a Third Culture.

THIRD CULTURE: THE CIRCLE AND THE TRIANGLE

Hierarchy is a triangular structure that locates leadership at the top and provides efficient means for organizing and carrying out tasks. Hierarchy is a useful structure for teaching, passing on information, organizing data, and mass producing goods.

The circle is an organizational structure that locates leadership along the rim and provides an inclusive means for consultation. Circling is a useful structure for learning, governance, creating community, providing services, and observing ritual.

Both the circle and the triangle have influenced each other. They work best when allowed to occur in combination. A council may be called in which every person has a voice and then a group of elders takes all these voices into consideration when they make a decision. A board of directors may be consulted to set the directions for a business. A school board may be approached by a coalition of parents and teachers with a plan for resolving budget deficits or other conflicts of interest.

What happened in the Second Culture that now makes the Third Culture necessary is that the circle and the triangle were separated. Their unique abilities to balance inclusivity and momentum were destroyed. Hierarchy, misapplied, became what we call "patriarchy" or "machine world," a system without soul or conscience that has even been willing to destroy the planet on which it stands. The circle, misapplied, has been treated as an archaic or ceremonial structure that doesn't have enough power to influence the real workings of the world. This imbalance is killing us, and any way we try to resolve it through the blinders of our conditioning leads only to another dead-end.

So when Carol and John call a circle, they cannot expect the circle to work if they simply read the circle guidelines, pass around a talking piece, and stay in the same frame of mind in which they usually function. They are challenged to leave their conditioning behind and listen to each other in a different way. To listen for the soul of the dilemma we are all in. To listen for the core of the problem to reveal itself. To experience power in community with each other, and to celebrate this power by sharing responsibility with each other and for their task. To invite the Sacred to rejoin the circle and provide a context of wisdom and guidance larger than the wisdom and guidance of any single person—no matter how wise. On a Saturday night, in the middle of somewhere, they, and we, begin.

To pray you open your whole self
To sky, to earth, to sun, to moon
To one whole voice that is you.
And know there is more
That you can't see, can't hear
Can't know except in moments
Steadily growing, and in languages
That aren't always sound but other
Circles of motion
Like eagle that Sunday morning
Over Salt River. Circled in blue sky
In wind, swept our hearts clean
With sacred wings.
We see you, see ourselves and know
That we must take the utmost care
And kindness in all things.
Breathe in, knowing we are made of
All this, and Breathe, knowing
We are truly blessed because we
Were born, and die soon, within a
True circle of motion,
Like eagle rounding out the morning
Inside us.
We pray that it will be done
In beauty
In beauty.

Joy Harjo
Eagle Poem

CHAPTER THREE

The Sacred in Everyday Life

While I am at my brother's house preparing to move to the Pacific Northwest, every night my family sits down to eat supper around a circular table. With the dogs circling underfoot, looking for a spot to lie out of the way, Carl, Colleen, Erin and I sit in a circle that is not a circle. A circle that is gutted of its ritual, its ceremony, its sacred center, gutted of our ability to hold council. Thankfully, the television is off, but there is no moment of gathering among ourselves, no grace said over the food.

To bring the Sacred back into our lives, we need to notice that it's missing. We need to open ourselves to longing. There is a longing loose in many of us for which we have no name, or all the names we apply to it cover over the true nature of what we seek.

In our family of four, we represent the spectrum of the culture we live in. Carl, the pragmatist, works hard trying to hold together a decent life for himself and his family. I see his frustration, trying to make the system work for him. He is a man among millions like himself, not wanting to think about their entrapment, their lost dreams and goals, feeling the weight of getting through circumstances as best they can. Colleen, the loyal mate and awakening woman, is caught between wanting to utterly support her husband, and the role of advocacy she needs for herself and her child to survive as women. As an officer of the Parent Teacher Association, she takes a stand on issues at school, but there is no structure in place to help carry out her ideas. She is curious about matters of the spirit, curious about the circle. She wants to try out the things I talk about, outside the home. Erin absorbs the culture presented to her on television, in school, at home—and by her aunt. And for a brief while during my transit, I am living downstairs writing my way into the creation of Third Culture. Here, in the middle, we each live our lives in the ways we think are available to us.

I bow my head at the table for just a second and silently pray one sentence, "Please help us be open to the heart of our own lives. Amen."

DESCENT INTO LONGING

When I was an adolescent, each evening at dusk I would sneak out of the dining room, stand on the house steps for a few moments of solitude, and stare up at the night sky. "Star light, star bright," I whispered into the revolving seasons, "I wish I may I wish I might have the wish I wish tonight..." And then I would stand there, the sounds of family life threatening to intrude and ridicule my little ritual, the coldness of most Minnesota nights causing me to shiver and hug my arms around my torso. What was that wish? That deepest wish that drew me outdoors?

It was sheer longing—that staring humans do when the soul rests in the eye and we take a long look inward, mesmerized by the depths of sky within. "I want..." we whisper, pause, breathe, stare. "I want... something."

In group after group, individual by individual, you tell me you catch yourself in the middle of the day, staring out the window wondering what you have been doing all these years. You tell me you hate your job, but you need the money. You tell me you are lonely. You tell me you aren't sure you're really a grownup because there is no rite of passage that makes you feel that way. Maybe you'll get married. Maybe you'll get married again. You tell me your husband is in the den watching World War II or Vietnam videos, sorting something he cannot name. Or you tell me your wife's side of the bedroom looks like a library of the occult, books on angels and goddesses, Tarot cards, drums and rattles, and candles. You are not privy to each other's thoughts, and have forgotten how to talk intimately somewhere along the line. You tell me that it is midnight when you get the paperwork done, or the laundry folded, and you still have dishes to wash before bed so that you can get up early and get everyone out the door for another day. You tell me you don't know what kind of relationship you want with a man or a woman, that all the rules have shifted and your passion feels like a small unturned stone in the pit of your belly. Nothing moves you. You stare at the body count on television and forget whether this is programming or news. You are afraid of your deadness. You are afraid of your aliveness. You eat too much. You are waking in the middle of the night and the only breath you hear is your own. Sometimes you feel like screaming—how long has it been since you made such a sound? Sometimes you put your head on the windowsill and pray for help.

For a long time during the descent into longing, we don't know what we want or what is trying to come alive in us. The culture yells its distractions in our faces: eat, buy, consume, throw out, exercise, so that you may eat, buy, consume more. I remember my incoherent confusion for years before I could put a name to longing. I remember my mother's longing, the aura of frustration that surrounded her, the implosion of all her desires. I remember my father's longing, the rage he batted at the world.

Something is happening. Our longing leads us down an unknown path.

In every path that leads to maturity, there is some form of dark night, a readiness finally to enter into shadow, to explore what we have kept hidden. We enter into darkness by dealing with the wounding we have endured and the wounding we have caused. We enter the darkness by admitting the level of crisis we are in. We enter the darkness by walking off the edge of our life maps into unknown territory. In the descent, we face the spiritual tasks of grief, forgiveness, compassion, and—eventually—transformation. The energy that gets us through the descent is our longing. And the place we are aiming toward, whether we have named it or not, is sacred center.

In 1991, I gave a speech to two hundred rural and small town women in the hills of western Wisconsin. These were not big city career women. They were women who stayed home and raised children, women who worked the farm with their families, women who held small town jobs in local businesses, who were nurses in the local hospital, who taught at the local branch of the state university system. Gathered for a one-day "Focus on Women" retreat, I'd been asked to give an address titled, "Journey into the World." On a snowy March Saturday, we gathered to find out what this might mean to us—to journey into the world. We talked of our awakening as a gender: women who had been asleep, compliant, busy with children and family tasks. About twenty minutes into the talk I asked them to raise their hands if they would answer "yes" to the following questions:

- Do you have the feeling that you are already, or are becoming, somebody different than you were raised to be?
- Have you made choices about marriage, family, and career that are different than the choices your mother made?

With each question, hands went up and down. People were thoughtful, bits of our lives flashing before the inner eye.

- Are you actively healing from your past, perhaps through therapy, recovery programs, spiritual counseling?
- Do you consider yourself in a life-long self-education process?
- Do you have a sense that you are doing all this for a reason, even if the reason isn't clear?

Tension was rising in the room; the questions were unusual, discomforting. Lastly I asked:

- Is there a dream or sense of purpose that haunts you, something you want to do with your life?

Ninety-eight percent of the hands waved in the air. The crust broke and each person's longing flew out of her body, creating a great communal energy field, a passionate "YES! I thought this was my secret, but YES!" Relief swept through the room, relief to be asked, to hold up our hands, to let tears form in our eyes, to turn around and look at the crowd, to see our neighbor's arms waving, and to know that we are not alone. Something got turned on in our minds. We accessed something. Women stood up, reached around for each other, looked in each other's eyes, laughed and talked all at once. Pandemonium broke loose. Women stood around in small spontaneous clusters and talked to each other. When we reconvened, we wrote statements of our visions on blank name tags —where we wanted to be in five years—and wore these proclamations to lunch.

I learned much in this gathering: if the longing is here in the back country of the heartland, it must be everywhere, in all of us. A seed lying dormant, waiting for something to call forth its sprouting.

Do YOU believe you were born for a purpose?

This is a life-changing question to ask because if we answer YES, then we must eventually ask: *Will we do it then? Will we discover our purpose and carry out our part?* And if we answer YES to that question, we rip ourselves open to the descent in order to bring our lives into alignment with our longing.

Active, changeable spiritual forces influence our lives, whether or not we pay attention to them, whether or not we take responsibility for them. In the circle, people share stories of crisis and leaps of faith. We learn that we are not alone, that others on another coast, in another land, express similar questions, anguish, confusion, determination, faith, and hope. *Something is happening.* We are breaking open our longing and undergoing both an individual and collective descent.

Many of the *Dreamtime* caves, known for their magnificent Paleolithic paintings, for their evidence of our earliest circles and spirituality, are reached by crawling on the belly half a mile into the earth in utter darkness. Half a mile. In utter darkness. The limestone walls damp and close. The tunnel smelling of earth and fear. Most of us make this spiritual journey in other ways, but the intent—the willingness to descend—must be the same. To admit. To acknowledge. To stand in our incomprehension of how to cope. To lament for our age and come through.

If we are going to be capable of using the circle to build Third Culture, we have to admit how much trouble our present culture is in. We say we know that change is necessary, but we put off initiating that change as long as possible. This is human nature. We want to stand our ground, and we want the ground we are standing on not to shake.

"Chaos," says the Random House dictionary, "is a state of utter confusion or disorder, a total lack of organization." It's the words *utter* and *total* that frighten me the most in this definition. I like my confusion in manageable doses. Chaos isn't manageable. I can't get out of my own descent.

Star light, star bright…Night. Rest. Darkness. Descent is passing a man standing by the freeway exit holding a sign that reads, "I need an operation. I need work. Please help me," and bursting into tears at our helplessness. Descent is being afraid to open the car door when a woman runs up to the window yelling, "Some guy is chasing me!" because this is a "bad" neighborhood, because it's late, because with all the drug violence this could be a set-up for robbery. Descent is reading the newspaper, any newspaper, any day of the week, looking at the small stories, the paragraphs of human anguish. Descent is remembering that somewhere a woman is raped every few minutes; sometimes a nation of women is raped. Somewhere a troop of young men stands and shoots at another troop of young men because they are told to. Grieve.

Night. Rest. Stars. Your father abused you. Your mother didn't protect you. Your brother died of AIDS. Your sister has breast cancer. Your work holds no meaning. You can't remember if you and your partner still really love each other, or if you are merely an habitual presence in each other's lives. You want something, but you don't know what it is. Your longing is elusive, a dream that escapes you as soon as you open your eyes. Your alarm clock carries it away. Time is passing. You are getting older. Descend. Descend. Descend. It is Monday, you start another week. There are too many cars on the highway. Forgive.

Some scientists say that if we don't reverse our ecological course in the 1990s, it will be too late. Many popular movies depict the violent end of our culture, the terminators on the other side of chaos, the space aliens who rescue or devour us. Many young people are nihilistic and violent. They shave their heads and pierce holes in strange places in their bodies. We, too, are numbing out. Television programming is full of fake images, hyped sports, dreadful news, sound-bite docudramas. Dial 911. Dial 911, now. Open your eyes. Look at this. Have compassion.

We gather in circles in order to acknowledge the spiritual journey. We bring our chaos, and use the circle to ask *how are we ever, ever,*

ever going to create a culture in which we want to live, in which our children and grandchildren will want to live? It is night. Darkness. We are fragile. We are confused. We want to spare ourselves too much disruption. We don't know what to do. Chaos: a state of utter confusion or disorder, a total lack of organization.

When I can, I like to start a circle in darkness. It shakes us up a little, gets us into our bodies, aware that we are breathing, aware that we are surrounded by the bodily presence of other people we don't know. Now that we can turn on the lights almost everywhere we go, we are strangers to darkness. So I like to start in shadow and invoke the mythic memory of the cave and the campfire. I like to call up the hypersensitivity that darkness brings. We learn from our alertness in the night. The descent teaches us to endure, to make room for what is coming. We learn to live in creative tension, to tolerate increasing amounts of change.

Just be here. Don't be afraid of the night. If we won't open our hearts, we cannot heal. We can only repair that which we have allowed to be broken, opened, wounded by caring, by trying, by getting involved. Only the broken heart has the ghost of a chance to grieve, to forgive, to long, to transform. Life is change. If we will be in the dark, in our fear and confusion, life will change. We will ascend. We will come up out of the caves and find something marvelous to cling to—like a flower.

Sometimes the journey of descent contains a grand gesture to which much story may be attached, or a catastrophic event that is used for transformation. Ann solo kayaked around Lake Superior. Bob and Harry and Leslie are HIV positive and living each day to its fullest. Connie, Elizabeth, and Mary are women willing to come fully alive since reaching their seventies. Barbara flew to Venezuela and adopted a child. David chose to leave the business he started. Patt has survived Chronic Fatigue Syndrome. Cathy's house burned down in twenty minutes with everything in it—except her husband, her children, herself.

These events may be used as anchors—a way to explain the level and significance of our change to others. The actual work of transformation is not really explainable; it's a subtle mystery. But events we can talk about help us peg the process and convey story.

And sometimes, for many of us, the journey of descent contains only small incremental lessons that are hard to explain: an eagle that flies alongside the car on a day we are crying in anguish, a dream that brings new insight, a child's voice telling us simple truth. Our path toward transformation is based on the decision to use any-thing—and everything—to wedge open the heart. In my spiritual journey there have been no burning bushes hovering before me, no falling down on the road to Damascus, no grand gestures, but there have been uncountable moments when the opportunity was present to see in the ordinary something extra-ordinary.

And this is exactly how we may put the sacred back in our everyday lives: by acknowledging the extraordinary within the ordi-nary.

Chaos is the great catalyst. The socio-politico-psycho-spiritual system is not, overall, in very good shape. The system *needs* chaotic disintegration. The system is falling apart; something new will emerge. The self, as defined by society, is not in very good shape either. We are used as little more than mechanisms of consumption to keep the economy functioning. We *need* to fall apart and wake up so that the new may emerge. Growth occurs when something breaks open, moves over, and makes room. Perhaps there is nothing the mat-ter. Perhaps we are individually and collectively moving through our descent.

ASCENT

At age sixteen, reading the Transcendental poets in high school English and riding my horse on the suburban edge of Minneapolis, I first began to understand what I was longing for. I had thought I was longing for John McDonald to like me. I had thought I was longing to prove myself to the popular crowd at school. I had thought I was longing to become an actress like Hayley Mills or a writer like Anne Frank. Until one day I rode my horse over to a small, local cemetery, let her graze among the headstones and sweet spring grasses while I sat on her back reading my Walt Whitman assign-ment. One couplet from "Song of Myself" electrified my mind:

"Failing to fetch me at first, keep encouraged,

Missing me one place, seek another;

I pause somewhere, waiting for you."

I read these lines again and again. This was a promise. Who was making this promise? What voice spoke through the poet's hand

and left this line for me?

"Please," I say to my brother, my sister-in-law, my niece, "could we just hold hands a moment before we eat?"

"Why?" asks Erin. She is not being flippant; she simply wants to know.

"Because this is the first time all day we've been together. It's a chance for us to talk with each other, to find out how we are, to share what's been happening, to keep getting to know each other better. Pausing and touching help us all really get here." They reach their palms compliantly around the table.

"You say it," says Erin, "say something."

We are silent a moment. I can feel my brother's discomfort. What am I trying to do to his family? He acquiesces, but that's all I know of his reaction. He clears his throat, strokes the hairs of his mustache aside, and does not look directly at me. I am hesitant. I want to respect where he is in his journey. I do not want to coerce him. *And* I want to bring who I am to the table too. I say, "Thank you for this day, for all the blessings we have received. Thank you for safety, that we are all here at the table again. Help us watch over our dreams. Help us lead our lives with love in our hearts." We squeeze hands and pass the food. It's a beginning—here in the middle.

Longing is energy. We do not *have* energy—we *are* energy. The mass culture deadens us. We have to struggle to reclaim and *be* our energy. Energy is not so easily controlled.

I galloped my horse most of the way home, both of us gulping in wind, my heart excited. "I am alive!" I shouted. "I am going to be really alive!" That's what I wanted. I wanted my life—the fullness of my life. As long as I believed there was *Something* out there waiting for me, I would search. I would seek one place and then another. I would not fail my life.

To live life at full voltage, to let our spirits shine brightly, is perhaps the greatest taboo. We run into this taboo over and over again. Sometimes it is taboo to mention Spirit at all. Sometimes it is taboo to veer away from standard religious forms—the sense that we had better be talking to Jesus or Jehovah or not talk at all. We are so confused. We are so polarized.

Later that evening of our first family prayer, Erin comes into my room, where a candle is lit on an altar I've made on the corner desk. She asks if we can come into circle. She knows we talk more deeply, that we make a commitment to listen to each other with greater attention when the circle is named and called forth. She brings in a little plastic carrying case that holds her altar things: rocks and feathers, a string of tinsel stars, the jawbone of a seal I brought her from British Columbia. She comes for teaching, and to teach: that is how the circle works.

In the middle of a meandering council of our thoughts she says, "I don't think my daddy understands you."

"No," I agree, "I don't think he does, not all the time." This is my brother, who, at age eleven, took all his paper route money and bought me a saddle so I could ride in style on the horse I had bought with all my baby-sitting savings. "What your daddy is thinking about in his life right now and what I'm thinking about are different, but we've known each other since we were babies. We love each other, and we can wait for the understanding to come." This conversation isn't just about us—it's universal. *What view of life are we holding? What have we done with our longing for the fullness of our lives? What do we put in the center?* "It's all right, sweetie," I say, "You're growing up in a strong family that's teaching you lots of different ways to see the world."

"I know," she nods wisely. "I like to play hockey with daddy, and I like to be in circle with you."

We are all waiting for understanding to come, for our hearts to open to our own lives. Hopefully, we wait with love. In the midst of all our differences, the important thing is that we seek. That we keep ourselves alive. That in the night we look for stars. Move on.

THE SACRED IN EVERYDAY LIFE

When I first met my friend Ann, she was a woman in training. Shaken by the swift death of her closest friend, Betty, she and a colleague, Paul, had decided to fulfill their longing for mid-life adventure by taking a kayak trip around 1,200 shoreline miles of Lake Superior—the largest and most dangerously changeable inland body of water on the planet. They honed their paddling skills for three

years, and by the time they shoved off in four foot waves from
Duluth, Minnesota, on a June day in 1992, both were aware that they
did not understand what was really driving them on this journey.

"I knew I needed to radically change my life," says Ann. "I
knew I had to get so far away from my usual routines, the demands
of my family, the pull of my own inner conditioning, that I would be
able—finally—to discover who I really am and how I could live the
life my true self would require. The only way I knew how to do this
was through wilderness, by turning myself over to the natural
world."

For sixty-five days in the coldest, stormiest summer in 150
years, Ann and Paul fought the lake for survival. It was an heroic
journey, the kind most of us will not choose to undertake. She survived, becoming the first woman to circumnavigate the lake by
kayak. And the years since her return have been the greatest test of
the journey.

To me, the most interesting aspect of any heroic feat is what
change it allows spiritually. When Ann came off the lake, she had
stripped down to the barest core self. For a brief while, she had no
assumptions—the world was new to her, her life was new to her, she
could choose anything—and so she was obligated to choose very
carefully.

"The grand gesture is only temporary grace," she says. "The
paddler, the mountain climber, the cancer survivor, we each come
back to the framework of the lives we left, and if we do not *do* something with our experience it dwindles. Our awakening becomes a
sentimental journey, a good story. And that's what many people hope
we will do—tell the story but not rock the boat, not proclaim that we
are forever changed or set out to sustain that change."

In the act of sustaining the change, those who make the grand
gesture that opens them and those who cope with incremental opening find our commonality. "Oh, I see," I say to her, "on the lake you
went through the same kind of process I did by writing *Life's
Companion.*"

"And what was that?"

"Allowing myself to be stripped down," I say. "I had to hum-
ble myself, submit to the flow. I was in an invisible lake, battling
invisible weather that no one else could see. I cried a lot in frustration, gratitude, prayer. I pleaded with God to help me, to give me the

next sentence, and the next. I had no way to say what happened to me until you came back from the lake and began telling me what happened to you. I had to break free—just as you did—and I had to do it while staying right in the middle of my life."

Incremental opening is a process of accumulation. Over time we become aware of all the things that have been holding us down in our lethargy and we are challenged day-by-day to shed first one thing and another. Finally we begin to see that we are breaking through. We break through our conditioning to the real longing—the real purpose—the dream that haunts us. Breakthrough does not need to be grand or grandiose; it just needs to be authentic. And the only way *I* can sustain the authenticity is to turn my life over to spirit.

Spiritual connection and direction don't always come easily—sometimes we go through periods where it doesn't feel as though direction is coming at all. Living the sacred is simply not a skill that 99% of us are taught. Even if we are religious, we live in a secular culture that effectively removes connection to the Sacred from the heart of important consultation, decision-making, education and most of our personal lives. We face the task of exploring our skills and habits, noticing the changes of heart, mind, and activity which foster connection to Spirit. To live this experiment we need perseverance, ritual, and community.

Perseverance is the commitment to stay awake, to battle our inertia, our lethargy, our desire for avoidance. There is both a dreamer and a sleepwalker in each of us. The dreamer longs for moments of ecstatic knowing and connection to spiritual task. The sleepwalker longs for safety and status quo. The dreamer prays to fulfill our lives at the deepest level. The sleepwalker counter-prays that the trip is not too costly, too risky, too threatening. We know the tide has turned within us when it is more frightening to be separated from the soul than to be separated from the status quo. We practice spiritual perseverance through ritual.

Ritual is any action we do with intent to keep the channel open. Ritual is the transformation of ordinary action into symbolic action. As I said in *Life's Companion*, "We can light a candle because we need the light, or light a candle because it represents the light we need." We can go jogging because we need the exercise, or because we need to touch the earth in a real, prayerful way to begin or end the day. Either way, we get the light, we get the exercise, and when we add the layer of ritual, we also have the opportunity to connect our ordinary actions to spiritual intent. Perseverance and ritual work in tandem. On days when the mind and heart have closed down, ritual gives us a way of signaling our persistence: "I am not giving up. I am still saying—come find me Spirit, help me open up again."

Community is where we find "like kind," where we find the support, challenge, and accountability to hold to the path. Without community, doubt and lethargy overwhelm us. The community of the circle is how we keep ourselves alive. The circle is where we develop the skills that keep the Sacred in our lives. Perseverance in the circle is the commitment to stay focused on our dreams and to dedicate ourselves to being thoughtful, active participants in council. Ritual in the circle is the way we invite collective wisdom and acknowledge spiritual center. When these elements are present, the circle is a tool that can help us do almost anything—and that is its brilliant gift.

Living with the Sacred in everyday life is not a formula. It's a radical shift in attitude. The challenge for each of us is how to let this shift occur in the middle of the week, in the middle of our busyness and ordinariness. Since we were not raised in a culture which integrates the Sacred with daily life, we have to teach ourselves this reintegration.

By the time Ann came back off the lake she was a woman gone wild. There was something "feral" about her. She was no longer a domesticated human being. Animals swam with her. She could read and interpret the vibrations of rocks and trees. She was—and still is—profoundly moved by acts in nature that the rest of us are unlikely to even notice. A moonrise stuns her.

Ann is different from other people I know. She has permanently opened the connection between herself and nature. She keeps house, raises children, jogs, swims, skis, teaches seminars, writes books, makes a living, takes great risks, stays connected, tastes the wind. She is a natural ecstatic. In our friendship and working partnership, I have had to learn how to be around this energy, to honor it and not be embarrassed. To be with her on the water or in the woods is to know there is a way of being human that is mystery in the modern world. I do not need to travel to study with some native shaman or find a tribe of isolated original people in order to understand how to live on the planet—I see all this alive in Ann. I see that our First Culture connection to Spirit-in-the-World is alive in her—and so I assume that it must also be alive in me.

Every morning, unless they were trapped by wind and storm, Ann and Paul got up at dawn, broke camp and headed out in seventeen foot sea kayaks to brave the lake. Hour after hour they paddled: 3,000 strokes an hour. Twelve hundred miles at an average speed of three miles an hour is four hundred paddling hours. The body takes over in this kind of repetitive movement, the way it does when we jog, or do dishes, or drive a car. Unless there's sudden change or crisis, the body goes on automatic pilot, leaving the mind free.

Endless hours of paddling gave Ann the opportunity to review her whole life, to visit and revisit scenes, choices, relationships, decisions, outcomes. She underwent the kind of total mental clearing that few people accomplish. Sometimes Paul was a quarter-mile away, sometimes they disappeared from each other's sight in the long troughs of waves. Many times they took days of solo time apart from each other. Alone on the lake, totally responsible for her physical, mental, emotional, and spiritual survival, Ann entered into direct connection with the Sacred.

In First Culture communities, members go through an initiation process when they come of age, and often again in mid-life when they come into wisdom. For tens of thousands of years people have danced, sung, drummed and sweated, smoked holy pipe, ingested psychotropic plants, entered trance, and gone into the wilderness to experience initiation. Initiation means to begin. Spiritual initiation is the beginning of connection between the self and the World—the natural world, the mystical world, multi-dimensional reality. Initiation opens the door, creates an internal space where meeting may occur.

In our secular, ego-based culture, *personal* drive, *personal* power, *personal* stamina are all that are revered. This emphasis on the personal denies the richness of what is really present: the mystical, magical, mysterious spiritual realm within which the personal makes its way. We may be initiated through ceremony, or by accumulation of awareness. Once initiated, we move beyond fixation on the personal to live our life in spiritual context. Once initiated, we move beyond the five ordinary senses to an awareness that we are being somehow sustained and guided by forces beyond the comprehension of the ego-self.

COMING HOME

What I didn't say about my trip to Glastonbury on the day my consciousness blinked open is that I crossed over the line between the ordinary world and the spiritual realm. There was, in the Chalice Gardens, a chapel with an oil painting of the Virgin Mary hung in the back of a small stone grotto. The walls were chilly and the room half-lit by the flickering light of many votive candles. There was a presence of prayer. I stood there, waiting. Lit a candle. The painting began to cry. One tear, then another, rolled down her cheeks. Shocked and open, I also began to cry. I reached out with the tip of my finger and lifted a droplet of wetness off the bottom rim of the frame, tasted it: salty water. With my other hand, I wiped a tear off my own cheek, tasted it: salty water.

For a Protestant girl from Minnesota this was—and still is—unexplainable. Was it a hoax? An hallucination? It doesn't matter; it was mystery. And to accept the moment of initiation, we have to accept the mystery. There is *Something* which promises that "failing to fetch me at first, keep encouraged; missing me one place, seek another." There is *Something* that pauses somewhere waiting for you and me.

I am doubled in age from the twenty-four-year-old who went to Glastonbury. I live smack in the middle of our modern, mystery-denying culture. I have endured long periods of closed-heartedness and confusion when I didn't even feel enough connection to pray upon waking, or to pause before eating, but I know the unexplainable still resides within me and it is my only hope of living an honorable life.

It is significant that in moments of re-centering, I do something physical—tapping my chest, sitting down to breathe or getting up to run, to dance, to leap on my bicycle and head out over the side streets, to find someplace to flop on the earth again, to lie back and look up at the sky, or to find a lake or ocean and dive in. When we are disconnected, mystery reaches for us again through the body. And by moving into the physical, by dropping into the body, we make ourselves available.

The body is a trustworthy source for bringing the Sacred into everyday life. And I believe we cannot really live the Sacred until we trust the body and allow the body to teach us openness. Sacred mystery resides in the body. To explain the mystery of Jesus or Buddha or Mohammed, we say that they were God incarnate—God made flesh—God embodied. We believe these were human beings who were literally inhabited by the Sacred. In our own connection to mystery, we also embody Spirit, we house the Sacred. We are also inhabited by God.

I don't know what my Methodist minister grandfather would have said to this idea, but I think he knew embodiment. Besides serving as a rural pastor, he was also a farmer and a bee-keeper, a sensual, sexual man who loved his wife and fathered eight children. His sermons were full of references to the life of the land, the rigors of homesteading, the glories of the buttes and foothills that surrounded his Montana valley. And there were times—not in the pulpit, but out in his garden or standing transfixed among the bees—that he appeared lost in mystery. Listening. There were times he touched my cheek or hair with his roughened, gnarled hands and our eyes held while some message passed between us, a message that I was too young to hear in any other way and he was too shy to say. The last time I saw him was the morning he died. I awoke on the other side of the world from Montana and there was his face, just for an instant, shimmering in the sunlight at the end of the bed—that same gentle, piercing look now embodied before me.

What we embody is the heart's desire to be an equal presence in the world. The heart resides within the body, and the body responds when heart energy is released. When the "heart"—not the physical muscle, but the sacred muscle, the heart center—is open, the body vibrates with energy. The intellect drops and our thoughts, feelings, decisions, and choices about action are accompanied by physical sensation. Heart energy flooding the body occurs as a sensation of expansiveness throughout the chest, as though the heart is not encased, as though our bones have dissolved and there is no block between our "self" and the world—the world of nature, or the presence of another person.

This is not an unknown experience. In the middle of February, Colleen calls from the kitchen, "Listen, a cardinal is singing." Alone in the living room, Erin dances with the puppy in her arms. Carl checks through the house at night, pauses at Erin's door, tucks her foot back under the covers. There are many ways to allow the heart to open in the middle of ordinary action.

When we allow heart/mind/body/spirit to meld, the torso feels warm, vivified. We may feel a "fire in the belly," as though the pelvis is a bowl filled with comforting, smoldering warmth. This is not sexual energy; it is spiritual flame. Unconditional love, agape, the eternal light, *prana, ch'i, kundalini*—every spiritual tradition has named this sensation, trying to explain it, trying to find ways to talk about it, to admit it into the realm of knowledge we share. Life force, pooled and ready, holds us centered. When we are dropped into the body and the body is enlivened with spiritual energy, the door is open to the listening point.

Spiritual connection is a listening point between the small self and the Sacred; a constantly shifting balance between receptivity and action. I have come to trust this integration so much that all my relationships, even business ones, contain something of this element. The heart-based relationship is different from a meeting of minds: we can "drop" together. We are able to connect at the heart level, to experience communion with each other beyond words. When I meet someone new and experience dropping, I pay attention. I look for spirit, look for the potential, go into a spiritual alertness about what is being offered and what my right relationship to this offering might be.

When we disassociate from our bodies, we disassociate from the capacity to house Spirit. These are hard times, when we are suddenly left alone again with the rampaging of the personal. Even after we make solid spiritual connection, periods of disconnection happen when we are stressed, afraid, in the midst of significant change. Of course, these are also the times we most need connection. So we cycle back to perseverance, ritual, and community, finding our way back into the flow. Each period of disconnection helps us discover our resilience, and learn more about how we reconnect.

Spiritual connection, or disconnection, begins at the level of thought, in how we react to situations, to other people, to interruptions, distractions, requests for action and changes in plan. Instead of assuming we (ego) have to figure out what to do, we may slow down internally and ask: *What is trying to happen here? How might I support the spiritual possibility? Where do I put my energy? What action, or refraining from action, would help the spiritual forces that are at work?* When we pause to ask these questions, everything that happens becomes an opportunity to stay connected to Spirit rather than an excuse to disconnect.

Living at Carl and Colleen's, every morning when they are gone to work and Erin is in school, I take my tobacco pouch into the back yard, put my arms around the nearest tree and pray into its bark. *"Thank you, Sacred One, for this day. For the sun that rises and sets. For the air that I breathe, the food that I eat, the sustenance which you provide. May all that I do today be for the healing of the world. To this end I ask your help in how I spend my time, energy, focus and love."*

I pray for all the people I hold dear, for help in the projects I'm working on, the decisions I face. I pray for guidance in the interactions the day will contain by phone and in person. I pray for those I don't know who need a sense of Holy Presence to be with them. And I pray that my temporary presence in the shared space of this family be a blessing I know how to offer and also receive. I leave a pinch of tobacco in the crook of a branch and round up the dogs. I come inside and get about my business. To pray is to state our openness, our intention to notice and sustain the flow. When we pray, everything that happens occurs within spiritual context. We know where we are. We are held in the circle of life.

God/Us

It's only recently that I've begun to understand what it means to have a relationship to Spirit. A relationship is based on *exchange, interaction,* and *mutual acknowledgment* of each other's presence.

If you and I pass each other on the street and do not look up or say hello—even if we notice each other out of the corner of our eyes—we are not in relationship. If I say hello and ask you for the time or change for a dollar and you don't respond—we are not in relationship. Relationship is greeting, meeting, opening to the next possibility between us, building on memories, working things through, trusting the connection and recreating it day by day.

How audacious to think we might be in relationship with God, and yet that is what the sacred writings and teachings really tell us: that we may know and be known by God. *Something* watches, interacts, provides, sustains. And to be in relationship requires that we also watch, interact, provide and sustain.

The relationship I'm suggesting is mystic: the ability to be at-one-with. We have many experiences of mysticism—the unity-moment that is one of the natural states of the brain. Scientists have studied the brain wave activity of people who have been willing to live for a few days with electrodes attached to their temples. They have shown that mystical experience is measurable; it occurs daily. Yet when asked, these people often have not registered their communion consciously. Researchers theorize that "unity" is an experience the ego cannot comprehend and so it hits "erase" and we snap back to ordinary attention, not realizing time has been lost, that we've been tripping into connection with the Sacred.

My third grade teacher called it "daydreaming." It was a bad attribute. She rapped her ruler sharply on the flat of her desk, or knocked her knuckles on the top of my head. "Chrissie is a bright enough child," my report card said, "but she has a tendency toward dreaminess. She is not always paying attention." Oh yes, I was paying attention, Mrs. Daubenspeck; the world was exploding in upon me, coming through the open windows, taking me away from the multiplication tables and out into the miracle of an Indiana spring.

Perhaps the ego erases communion because the culture we live in denies our common experience. Culture denies mystery and our relationship to mystery, and so do we.

One evening when we are in circle, using a small brass goddess figure as our talking piece, Erin asks me, "So, do you think God is a man or a woman?"

"I think God is spirit," I say, "God is energy, God is love."

"But then He doesn't have any hands! How can God help people if He doesn't have a body?"

"*We* have bodies," I tell her. "God counts on us to be Its body, to be God's hands and hearts in the world. You know how sometimes your mom or dad will say just the right thing, or hug you when you really need it and you didn't ask?" She nods. "And you do this too, for us. You say the right thing, or hug us before we know we need it."

"Or like how Pudsey and Willow wake me up in the morning licking me all over?"

"Yeah. When exactly the right thing happens that makes our hearts whole again, well, maybe that's more than just people being together. Maybe God is helping us know what to do. Maybe God is asking us to do something..."

She looks thoughtful. "But what about when people do bad things or hurt my feelings, is that God too?"

"I don't think so. I think that's our own confusion, the times we stop listening and get in God's way."

Later, when I am tucking her in, after the usual snuggles and good-nights, she whispers softly in my ear, "Goodnight, God-in-there." I can barely hear her tiny voice, but then the message isn't addressed to me. I lift my head to look back at her, but she is already asleep.

"Goodnight, God-in-you," I whisper in return. The dogs take up their sentinel posts by her bed and the night is still.

Community.
Somewhere, there are people
to whom we can speak with passion
without having the words catch in our throats.
Somewhere a circle of hands will open to receive us,
eyes will light up as we enter, voices will celebrate with us
whenever we come into our own power.
Community means strength that joins our strength
to do the work that needs to be done.
Arms to hold us when we falter.
A circle of healing. A circle of friends.
Someplace where
we can be free.

Starhawk
Dreaming the Dark

CHAPTER FOUR

Journey Into the World

*a*nd then, it is morning. We waken and see the world around us, the ordinary view outside our windows imbued again with the possibility that we may be connected to all this—the weather, the birds, a tree growing through its seasons. We awaken and see the world close up, the people and animals who share our space are our neighbors.

For if we are creatures imbued with spirit in a world imbued with spirit, then we are connected to everything. We are, literally, everything. Wake up and behold. We are the world and the world is us—the natural world, the spiritual world, the inner world. Behold. We have been lied to, have been told we are separate from the rest of creation, that humankind is set apart. We are not. The atoms of this planet are all the same. If we break ourselves down, break our cells down—the skin, the bones, the muscles, the soft tissues—at the atomic level we cannot tell ourselves apart. We are every body: the bird's tail, the oak tree's leaf, the rock in the roadway, the dog's fur, the water running in a brook. My body is the same as your body. Behold—we are one. We know this. Behold and come into community. Come home.

So many mornings I have stumbled out into the day, blinking, and tried to relocate myself in the world. Making my way into the day's breath, sensing what kind of weather will hold me, what's happening in the natural realm. When I am on the highway at that time of day, I am awed by people's faces glimpsed through car windows, walking the sidewalk, waiting for a bus. The modern world requires that we "put ourselves together" and head off to work—groomed and dressed, usually in ways that are not the most comfortable for us—forcing us into early sociability and removing us from contemplation. And yet, a vulnerability remains behind the veneer. If we look quickly enough at each other coming out of sleep, coming out of our houses, we can still glimpse the soul, with its wonderment at our connection and bewilderment at its loss in the modern world.

What I see, and what I mourn—in my own face in the mirror and the faces mirrored back at me—is the toll of our isolation.

ISOLATING CIRCUMSTANCES

Community is the baseline reality, the communion that naturally exists in the deepest design of the world. Invisible circles of atoms cluster into molecules, combining in marvelous diversity to create all that is. Things group together by attraction and affinity. One molecule of water seeks another and runs out the tap, goes into the teapot, its metals holding together even in heat. And one human being seeks another. We are mammals, creatures that move in herds, packs, prides, families and tribes. We thrive best in the company of others. We evolved while living in small, sustainable communities that shared in raising children, growing food, building shelter, designing work, making crafts, worshipping and celebrating. This is our social-genetic inheritance, passed down as surely as the color of our skin and eyes.

Isolation is an imposed reality, a false separation foisted upon us by the structure of modern society. Isolation convinces us of our singularity. Isolation convinces us to compete instead of cooperate. This overlay of isolation is a virus which infects our natural way of life. By creating the illusion of separation, by highlighting differences, by making ideology, religion, color, gender, and affection things to fight over, isolation fosters war, famine, violence, and hatred.

We have become so isolated from the world that we think we can destroy our own life-support system and ignore the consequences. We have become so isolated from each other that we think we can ignore the needs of billions of children, and the anger of the generations which have grown up without even rudimentary support and socialization.

We work in assembly lines and cubicles. We look at the world through plate glass windows. The carpool lanes on the freeway are nearly empty compared to the congested lanes with one person to a car. When we come home from work, we push the button on the garage door opener and go into the cocoon of our individual houses. Weeks go by when we do not see or speak to our neighbors.

Colleen comes home from a school meeting and sets a stack of papers on the kitchen table. She makes a cup of tea and tells me, "I get so tired of being the lone voice, the 'crazy woman' who impedes the process of what everyone else seems to think is normal. The PTA has a little extra money and the administration wants to spend it on walkie-talkies so the principal can talk to his staff without leaving his office. And I'm saying, what about the kids? Let's do something that makes their experience here richer. Let's bring in six weeks of writers and artists. Let's build a natural sciences lab. Is this such a strange or difficult thing to understand?"

Isolation is the thing we struggle against, time and time again, in order to create a few moments of connection. When the barrier drops even for an instant, we feel encircled and elated. Shopping for fish, I notice that the woman behind the butcher's counter is wearing beautiful earrings. "Wow, what great earrings," I say.

Her face lights up. "My father sent these to me...can you believe it? I was so touched that he'd understand my taste and buy me something this beautiful. I don't have any place to wear them but at work. Are they too much?"

"They're perfect." I say, "The colors enhance everything in the case...and I'll have a pound of halibut." We laugh. We are friends for this moment. Then the barrier falls back into place. It falls back into place because isolation is schooled into us until we see the world through the lens of aloneness, difference, competition, challenge, threat, control, and domination. What do this woman and I have in common besides our taste in earrings? Unless we come into community, we will never know.

Isolation is a policy to which we unconsciously acquiesce. Most of the time we don't see how our sense of aloneness has been constructed, how it is maintained by the machine-based society around us. The sense of isolation imbedded in our culture becomes imbedded in the family, and even in the self. After a while, we can no longer tell whether isolation is something extruding from the self thereby creating a society of isolation or something intruding upon the self from an isolating society. We expend great amounts of energy trying to feel connected when the system has no interest in fostering this experience. We get angry at ourselves—but not at our oppression. We are, by and large, a lonely bunch.

Isolation inhibits us from taking our places and trusting ourselves to really be here. The greatest evil of isolation is the passivity it engenders—the belief that there is little we can do to change our own circumstances, and certainly not much we can do to change the circumstances of others. Once we believe we are helpless, our only option is cling to our isolation, trying to create enclaves of safety. An enclave is not the same as a community. A fortress is not the same as a neighborhood.

I understand the yearning for ordinary life, for safety, for assurance that my way through will not be too great a task. I want safety, too. I want to die of old age, sitting on the porch of the Old Friends Home, reading my journals and looking into a world that I have helped sustain. I want safety, but I don't know if this is a reasonable expectation at the turning of the twenty-first century. I want safety and I am a woman. I have been afraid often and raped once. I have stood by, letting myself be threatened and abused and not even recognizing it, or knowing what to do. I have stood by, watching another woman or child or gentle man be attacked because I didn't have the support or clarity to intervene. I have felt incredibly, searingly alone. And I have felt ecstatically connected to the beauty of the world, touched by other people, in love with my life.

There are two things I have always understood about my relationship to the world: I love it passionately and, just as passionately, I want to change it.

I was eleven years old when I came up with my first sweeping plan to save the world. That particular afternoon I was sprawled over the pages of the *Minneapolis Star*, reading Ann Landers and Peanuts and scanning headlines for my Weekly Reader quiz on world events. There was a famine in India. A photographed face of a brown-skinned girl stared from the page at me. She looked hungry and far away. Our eyes locked—hers black and intense with need, mine brown and intense with idealism. I read the accompanying story. The monsoons were late, the crops had failed. On another part of the page there was a story about grain surpluses that year. The elevators and silos of America were full to bursting. Farmers didn't want to sell at glut prices and the government had bought all it could: there was simply too much crop. I made an arc in my mind. It seemed so simple, why hadn't the grownups thought of this? We could send our extra grain to India. Surely the government would be glad to see it put to good use. Surely the government did not want to waste food any more than my parents wanted me to waste food. The good use of food was universally understood. We prayed our thankfulness for it every night before eating. *Come Lord Jesus, be our guest and may this food to us be blessed. Amen.*

I studied both articles thoroughly until I was sure I understood the problem and the solution. I was so excited with my plan I could hardly wait for my father to get home. He was, in my eyes, a powerful man. He had connections. I would tell him my idea. He would think it was wonderful. We would write President Eisenhower. We would call our Congressman. They would all agree to ship the grain to India. They would be able to pay the American farmers a fair price now that someone wanted to buy. The politicians would ask among themselves, "Who is this Chrissie Baldwin who thought up such a good plan for the grain?" My family would be proud of me, and I would go to bed in the blue-and-white flowered room I shared with my sister, surrounded by my collection of horse figurines, my record player and dolls, and know that the dark-eyed girl would live.

I don't think he had his coat off before I showed my father the newspaper and announced my plan. He laughed ironically. "It won't work, hon," he said. "That's not how things are done."

"But *we have* the food, and *they need* the food. Why won't the government sell it to them?"

"India is a poor country. They can't pay for it."

"Then let's give it to them, like a present. Like sharing…" He shook his head. "What is the government doing with it then, with all that extra grain?"

"They're dumping it," my father informed me, tossing the newspaper onto the couch. "Pushing it off piers with bulldozers into the ocean to rot."

"But it's food! They could make bread."

"It's not bread. It's politics and power and there's nothing you or I can do about it."

I heard the brown-skinned girl cry out at the back of my mind. I saw her go down, folding over her empty stomach. And I could not believe my rage. How could my father get up and go to work and come home and take off his shoes and wait for me to set the table and wait for my mother to put food before him in a world where they dumped grain into the sea? I had been innocent. I had been ignorant. But now I knew what was going on. How was I going to go to school and study long division and chase Billy Jensen on the playground? How was I supposed to eat supper and make peanut-butter graham crackers for my blond and blue-eyed little brother to smear across the highchair tray? I stood in the hollowed-out center of my awakening and wanted to scream, but at whom?

Two things I *still* understand about my relationship with the world—I love it passionately. And just as passionately, I want to change it. And one thing more I have come to understand about myself: I, too, am a person who can come home from work and take off my shoes and make supper while the brown-skinned girl is still folded over her empty stomach. Sometimes I hear myself mouthing my father's defeatism. It does not make me feel proud. But some-times I am capable of standing in the middle of the tension of our times and questioning my assumptions until I am awake again.

My impulse to respond compassionately is still alive and I am determined to find ways to respond effectively—my life, your life, and life itself depends upon us. This is our choice: to isolate and fortress ourselves with our personal concerns, or to step into the vulnerability of community and create a different way to live, day by day by day.

Coming into Community

Communities have several elements in common. They are held together by specific purpose, focused tasks, tangible work and tangible results. People join community because they feel needed. They experience a sense of being essential, being validated for what they contribute, being honored and sustained. Community is the extension of relationship from the personal to the collective. People give to the community and the community gives back. There is mutual exchange, mutual interaction and mutual acknowledgment.

The experience of community resonates within us. In community our social-genetic heritage is revitalized. We are having both the reality of present experience and living in accordance with our evolution. In community, the sense of "being at home" is such a powerful experience that it is often beyond rational explaination. People long for community. When we manage to wrest community from isolation, it is a meaningful and life-changing experience—even if the community is short-lived or falters. We invest heart-energy in community. We understand that it is a covenanted relationship.

When Ann moved to Duluth in 1979, she and her husband bought a little house overlooking the University of Minnesota campus where he would teach. Coming from a strong environmental background, Ann began acquainting herself with the natural beauty of this small city at the edge of wilderness, jogging and skiing through the terrain and enjoying her surroundings. It seemed a great place to raise her two children and she settled into making this place a home. She sought community.

When she needed support with child-care, she joined a baby-sitting collective. When she was concerned about how to feed her family well, she joined a food cooperative and volunteered her time. When she wanted to lay a solid academic groundwork for the children, she and her colleague, Paul, home-schooled their families together for several years. To learn about local environmental issues, she joined the Audubon Society and took her turn as chapter president and conservation chair. And when she wanted to get into the woods, to jog, to ski, to take the children on nature hikes, to restore herself in what she calls her "first place of knowing," she trotted a half-mile over to Chester Bowl, a wild ravine and hilltop which crowned the city of Duluth.

The city fathers of Duluth had had the foresight to create parks by zoning all the creek beds that ran from the ridge down the steep hills of the city to Lake Superior as no-development zones. Chester Bowl is one of these protected areas: a combination park, recreation land and wilderness. The ski jump on the highest ridge produced several of America's first Olympic medal winners in the sport. The rock outcroppings along the meadows of the ridge are some of the oldest exposed rock face on the planet—volcanic slabs one billion years old. And in the early 1980s, Chester Bowl was threatened.

A real estate developer had gotten the land through back taxes and began making a series of proposals. First he wanted to put up condos and townhouses, and when that proposal failed he tried to get rights to partition the land into lots for large single-family dwellings. Ann seated her children in a wagon—roly-poly paperweights on top of a stack of flyers—and began making her way through the neighborhood as part of the effort to "Save Chester Bowl."

What usually draws us out of isolation and into community is this kind of urgent necessity—the need to address a specific problem, concern, or challenge.

"I didn't know my neighbors, except those involved in childcare with me, but I couldn't let anyone destroy this beautiful resource without a fight," Ann says, "so I went door to door. 'Do you know what's happening?' I'd ask people...and tell them the story. Get them to sign a petition. Find out if there was something else they were willing to do.

"People would say to me, 'Here, take ten dollars, do something...how can I help?' There was tremendous community spirit generated by all this: town meetings, block parties. The group, led by the Chester Bowl Improvement Club and neighboring landowners, hired a lawyer and took the case all the way to the Supreme Court of Minnesota, contesting the developer's right to gain an easement through the park. It was a legal technicality, but that's all we needed—something to keep the land intact while we kept bringing attention to the issue and generating support."

Stories of community activism are common and inspiring. People see something happening they like and want to support it, or something is happening they don't like and they want to challenge it. Size is an essential factor in our ability to assume personal power and act. When we set about to foster change, we need to start at a level that is tangible and immediate: this household, this school, this church, this company, this block. When we address a problem, we need to have it presented in a size we can imagine handling: this creek, these children, this garbage burner, this city office, and so on.

By the time the case was settled, Ann's children were adolescent ski champions in their age group races at Chester Bowl. "When I left Duluth," Ann says, "I left with the knowledge that the special places which had sustained me—the rock I sat on to look at the stars, the trails I hiked and skied, the den of foxes I found deep in the woods—would remain for others to find and hold dear. There was one place I called Listening Point. It was magical to me. Helped me hold my life together through very significant changes. Sometimes I wonder if someone else goes there now, sits in the field of summer daisies or a snowy night, and wonders if any other human being has ever passed this way and asked the same questions of the earth and stars."

Chester Bowl was doable, and people hung in with the project year after year until their activism worked. The sense that an issue is the right size creates an empowering relationship between something that needs doing and the people who are ready and willing to do it. What created a relationship between myself as a child in Minnesota and the famine in India was the face of one other child.

Show us one child, one animal, one tree, one situation, and we are much more likely to get involved. We react irrationally to the personal—our hearts open in connection and extend into the world with empathy and understanding. And it is exactly this heart energy that is the source of true fierceness. The mind may understand yet remain immobilized, but when the heart understands, we take action. The heart connection is raw response. The mind clicks in and helps us be thoughtful in our actions, but it is the release of heart energy which fuels our journey into the world. Perhaps that is why in a society that reinforces isolation, we are so careful with the heart, so armored, so defensive. If the heart's gates open, we will let in the world. And if we let in the world, we will be compelled to interact. Love is a verb. Compassion is a verb. Community is a verb.

About the same time as the Chester Bowl development threat was happening in the early 1980s, Ann joined a community effort with an even broader purpose: to "resettle" Duluth. The city was a struggling blue-collar town with a depressed economy. The steel plant had closed, the iron ore industry was in sharp decline, the mines were worked out. People were coming into Duluth from the Iron Range further north looking for work, while residents of Duluth were looking for work in Minneapolis and St. Paul and Chicago. With a population of 100,000, Duluth was a community whose problems were still manageable in size. A call was put out to all citizens to join in dreaming a new city vision, and a cross section of community thinkers in arts, education and business began meeting to revision the town.

"The group met with great enthusiasm," Ann remembers. "The meetings were an experiment for all of us in holding council. We saw that adults could work together in a spirit of cooperation—something we forget if there's no opportunity for its expression—and we learned as we went along. We were envisioning a city comprised of strong neighborhoods, regionally-grown food, regionally-inspired and controlled industry, gentle development that respected the land.

"After a while, despite all the enthusiasm within the group, we saw that we were not communicating with the larger community, we didn't know how to carry our vision into the real world. After we got a grant to publish a book, all our effort went into defining the vision. In the book, "resettling" was defined as a call back to neighborhood, back to community, back to self-reliant cities and regions—based on harmony with the land and its resources—and back to being in control of our lives. But we didn't have a tool for bringing our passion for community into the community. We had council but no circle, no design to involve others. We ran out of energy to implement the vision. My big regret is that we didn't resettle Duluth, we just thought about it."

What Ann admits was missing were the elements that hold community together: *specific* purpose of a size the group can handle; *focused* task that is based on intention worked out by community leadership and council members; *tangible* work that is measurable, so people have a goal; and *tangible* result so that people can see their accomplishment.

Circles of Recovery and Healing—The Bridge

Since the founding of Alcoholics Anonymous in 1935, circling has been reintroduced into Western culture in dramatic ways. From the onset, AA's founders assumed that making a circle of peers was the only form of council that would really help them to abstain. Dr. Smith and Bill W., both alcoholics, had tried many time to relieve their compulsive drinking through willpower or by submitting to various promises of cure. It was only when they decided to place themselves in a circle and place Spirit, renamed Higher Power, at the center of the circle, that they were able to stop drinking. Something in them knew what to do. These two white men, one a struggling businessman, the other a small town doctor, reintroduced the circle as a form of social and spiritual power and their discovery set off immense changes in western culture. AA was the first "self-help" group, the prototype for the awakening to consciousness that was to follow several decades later.

A Twelve Step group like AA meets weekly in a circle, with the facilitator changing meeting by meeting. People introduce themselves with a first name and a statement of their condition. "Hello, my name is Jack and I'm an alcoholic." Everyone is present for a similar purpose. The meetings open with a recitation of the Twelve Steps which provide the focus of the group. One Step is discussed and meditated upon at each meeting, with people sharing their stories and talking about what that Step means to them. They listen without interrupting each other. There are strict guidelines for confidentiality, safe social structure, and support or guidance. *The Big Book* provides each group with a sense of history and format. The group has its own vocabulary, its own slogans and affirmations. Meetings close with ritual —usually the Serenity Prayer and the invitation, "Keep coming back!" It is a system that throughout its sixty years has kept a clear sense of peer leadership and peer support.

Yet, so far, the application of the circle's power has been incomplete. Circles like these have become places of solace and retreat—places we go in order to deal with our wounding. But the power of the circle has not yet been widely applied to changing the culture in areas beyond healing, recovery, and self-exploration. We have been so enculturated to the need for a leader that many circles do not really function as peer groups, they are hierarchy disguised, hierarchy curled into an innocuous ball to make itself more palatable.

There are times when we need to admit our ignorance and place ourselves in the role of student. We don't want to get in a jet with a pilot who has never been to flight school, or be examined by a doctor with no medical training. We don't want the pilot or the doctor to turn to us in the middle of flying to New York, or conducting brain surgery, and suggest we take over—as a peer. It is, however, the wise teacher who asks, in every setting where s/he is teaching: *What have I come here to learn?* And it is the true student who asks, in every setting: *What do I already have to contribute?*

When I finished writing *Life's Companion* in 1990, I had the distinct impression that I had "finished" my life to date, healed my past as much as possible. *Life's Companion* was the forum through which I shared that healing and how the spiral into spirituality had led me back into the heart of the world. The evidence of the end of my old life was everywhere around me. It was exhilarating and disorienting. I was traveling now without a road map.

In 1992, I worked for the first time on the staff of a large spiritual gathering called the "Women's Alliance Summer Camp." Around a small lake in Washington state, we took over a girl scout camp, set up an elaborate altar in the meadow behind the dining hall and called ourselves into community. Women who had public careers, who were known for their body of knowledge, their books or music, became the staff and designed a week of lectures, electives, rituals, and fun. This had been the basic structure of Women's Camp for over a decade. Many facilitators and participants returned year after year for replenishment. It's a good model, based on an acceptable and successful format, and one that many seekers are familiar with in a number of settings.

I came to this camp from the Midwest, from my life in the middle. My teaching had been the place where I stretched and challenged myself. All that summer, while Ann paddled around the lake, I struggled with my own journey. "Life as I know it is falling apart," I kept telling her when she would call in occasionally from a phone booth at the edge of wilderness, "and I don't know what's coming next. I'm as at sea as you are, without the same level of danger. Without a way to explain the chaos inside."

Before the camp, I taught in New York, in Taos, in Duluth, and attempted to put together ideas for a new book. Nothing was working—not in my professional life, my private life, not even in the circle as I knew it. As the months progressed, I could feel my panic rising. As on that day in Glastonbury, I was again at the beginning of a quest, a turning point, and I was failing it. *"What is it?"* I shouted inside myself. *"How am I supposed to change? What do you want?"*

It's hard to not sound melodramatic about these times of transition. Ann was risking her life kayaking every day. What did *I* have to say? How could I say anything? What was missing was so subtle—and what was trying to come in felt just as subtle. I did what I usually do. I put on a brave face and just kept going.

Then, under the full sun and full moon, the ten facilitators and five Alliance staff from six states and one province gathered for a staff retreat to set the vision of the camp. We wandered the rim of the lake and selected teaching sites. We sat on the dock with our feet dangling in the water and mapped out the week. We sang prayers to fill the space, laid out registration materials and put up signs. It was August again, hot again, one year after my questioning began at Omega.

Despite years of travel and teaching in circles, Women's Camp was my first experience carrying the circle out of its safe cultural backwater. Accustomed to large and small groups of journal writers where I was the only facilitator, it was awesome for me to be sitting in a circle of peers. I'd never been in council before, used a talking stick to hold the floor, or collaborated with other teachers who'd been leading wilderness treks and vision quests and rituals. Round and round the circle we went, sharing experiences from our work, getting to know each other. I didn't even know what to call what we were doing. *"Maybe this is feminist process,"* I thought, *"maybe this is what I've been reading about in books by Californian authors."* I contributed my own pieces, watched and learned. In my mind I kept asking, *"Where have I been? This has been going on for years and I've missed all this foundation to the movement. All these women know each other, and I suddenly feel like I don't know anybody!"* I got angry at Minnesota for its stolid middleness. I endured alternating waves of insecurity and confidence. This was what I'd been looking for—and I was both excited and afraid.

Saturday afternoon, the camp filled with the energy of arrival and the expectations of a hundred and fifty women. I'd made my adjustment, and assumed everyone else would arrive and adjust. Women who had taught at or attended the previous California camps also assumed that everyone would know what to do—that we'd close the gates of the compound, enter a strange and marvelous world without men or patriarchy or television or outside concerns, and community would develop by osmosis. By Saturday evening I was giddy with the sense of this new adventure.

When we held the first convocation, the staff made announcements but didn't mention the contracts of respect and confidentiality I'd been using in my circles for the last fifteen years. We were ushered into the meadow and told to put something we'd brought onto the altar, but no one explained the meaning of this large draped construction at the edge of the forest, or talked about how one might show reverence for what we were doing. I traveled along with the crowd trying to look as though I fit in, as though I understood.

The next day, issues arose about ritual. Some women were using community rituals as an opportunity for deep catharsis and would allow themselves to fall down, crying and screaming. Other women were upset by this type of release; they felt it was disrespectful of the spiritual traditions the rituals represented. Still others wondered whether or not enough safety net was being provided. I was as new to ritual as most of the others in camp and didn't know what to expect. If something happened, I thought this must be what usually happened, that only I was surprised—after all, I was from Minnesota.

The responses to these concerns—in the morning meetings, in Circle Groups, in Listening Council, in our staff circle—were stuck halfway in the old mode of hierarchy and halfway into circle. There was a structure to follow, services to provide, meals to prepare, electives to teach, rituals to organize. The staff met each day in brief council, trying to hear each other out while still running the camp. *"We're missing pieces, we're missing pieces..."* ran like a chant in my mind, *"but what?"* I had to stop trying to be wise, trying to act as though I knew what I was doing. I tried instead to look at Camp as though I knew nothing, assumed nothing. *"If I'd just landed here from Mars, what would I be able to see without assumption?"* I asked myself.

"Lack of context" was the phrase that came to mind. We were trying to put the circle into place without first setting a place for the circle to be. We didn't help people arrive. We didn't lay the ground-work so women knew what to expect. We hadn't set the tone for the community. We didn't hold full council before we held ritual. And we were all refugees, retreating from competition, violence, mistreat-ment, and other abuses of power. We had washed up on the shores of our willingness to learn. We were strangers in circle, and yet this was our homeland. We knew there was a right form here somewhere. If we kept struggling through our confusion, we would discover what was right for us to do. We knew that to sustain each other in change we had to share leadership, share resources, share questions, share knowledge. Our experience was imperfect, but we we were willing to try again and again and again.

In the intensity of this total immersion, I *got* it—the circle is more than a nice way to hold class sessions and seminars, more than the parlor game of new consciousness. In circle, we have the opportu-nity to refashion how we live together, to teach, to learn, to govern, to celebrate. In Camp, the circle appeared everywhere in our language and as an organizational form, but the requirements of actually living in circle-based community were only partially defined or understood. The immensity of our experiment stunned me. The camp was a threshold between two worlds—the one we knew and the one that might be. I crossed this threshold and said "yes" to the circle. Said yes, I will be your student. Said yes, and came home.

Nights at camp, sleeping under the moon on the upper boat deck, my mind swam with images. I dreamt of circles: women and men in the forest, in the desert, in caves, in sacred groves and tem-ples. My social-genetic heritage shifted into consciousness. I couldn't get out of the circle. I didn't want to get out of the circle. It felt as though I had walked into a group of strangers, "recognized" them, and picked up intimate conversations that seemed already in progress. I left behind the familiarity of the journey I had been on and stepped into raw creation.

In my dream *I am walking along a ragged edge of a high cliff. Behind me, in procession, is my life as I have known it. I see the child-selves, solemn-faced, sensing the importance of this ritual. The smallest one, a blond baby, toddles along holding a sandbox bucket and tiny metal shovel which clang together irregularly like an untuned bell. She hold hands with a six-year-old whose hair has darkened and who carries in her other hand a stack of red and blue books—Dick and Jane and Sally—her guides into the magic of reading. There is a nine-year-old pulling along a blue bicycle as though leading a docile beast to the altar for blessing. The fourteen-year-old presses a blank notebook to her chest, protective, unsure, cherishing this first journal, the seed of her writing falling on fertile ground.*

The family—barely comprehending—is clustered together. The brothers tolerate being here because they love their sister, despite her weird ways. They will walk to the edge with me, but won't look when I go over; they will retreat with relief to watch sports on TV, eat chips, talk about business. My father will join them. My mother is a shape-shifter, changing and dropping her former selves like used clothing along the path: the fright-ened bride, the harried young mother, the furious wife, the wild seeker at mid-life, the crone opening to her own selfhood. Her hair is still dark in her seventies and she makes a steadfast companion to her granddaughters in a way she could not for her daughters. The blood under her feet has healed.

This procession is accompanied by a heart-beat. In the distance, the tribal drummer stands on a hummock of grass, the Mother drum suspended by leather thongs on a burnished wood stand.

Boom...Boom...Boom...Boom...

She catches my eye, nods and smiles without missing a beat. Her short blond hair is wrapped in a gypsy scarf. She looks confident, as though she has attended these rituals before. Boom...Boom...Behind her I see the others of my tribe ready to circle the drum, to take their place and keep the beat. Their eyes look old to me. They know where I am going. They have been in this procession themselves. Sisters in freefall.

Friends and lovers, the men and women who have been my long-time companions, are walking en masse beside the self-of-me they knew best—in my twenties, thirties, forties, with changing styles of hair, weight, dress. I see the consistency of gesture, smile, gait. These life companions each wear a banner proclaiming their gifts to me: "She shared her virginity with me when we were twenty-one." "I helped blow open her soul at twen-ty-four." "I introduced her to her shadow side. I took the hurt." "I brought out her real sexuality." "I taught her to go the distance, to claim her fierce-ness, to think for herself." "I took her with me to death's door that she might not fear it." "I would not forgive her, and so I taught her care-full-ness." "I brought up all her shame so she could learn accountability." "I am her con-tinuity, our paths diverge then cross again." "We love each other in ways that are many lives old." "I came when I was needed and shook her loose from everything she thought was true." Their feet make a cadence that echoes the drum.

Like the point of a spear, I walk at the head of this procession. I walk with the energy of all my experience, all my relations, pushing me. I walk on a trail I have laid out in words, over and over again, teaching, writing, saying I would be willing to take this path. Saying to others, you, too, must be willing. I walk toward the drum, toward the precipice. There is no more meandering. There is no more escape—not one more errand to run, not one more load of laundry to wash and fold, not one more phone call to answer, not one more letter to type, not one more word I can write until I take the next step. Until I am willing to fall.

Standing at the very edge of the cliff I shout at god/us, "Are You sure I'm ready for this? It seems we've been moving awfully fast these past few years. I already feel as though I've been hurtling from one experience to the next. The only time I've had to assimilate is in my dreams, and those I don't even remember. How do You know I'm ready?" The updraft lifts my words away, makes me tremble. I spin around, face my old life one more time. It is burdensome, this history, but familiar. Boom...Boom...Boom...I am staring into the bright eyes of an angel. Eyes of infinity that tell me nothing and everything. Her wings ruffle in the cool breeze. A wisp of angel hair blows across her face; she does not brush it aside. "You cannot know if you are ready until after you fall," she says. "This is a leap of faith." She unfastens my clothes, unwraps the scarf I wear over my heart, pulls off my favorite sweater over my head, helps me step out of a soft cotton skirt, signals me to remove my deerskin boots. Naked, my skin snaps alive in the wind. The angel leans forward, kisses me on the lips. "Love is all that is real," she says, "good-bye." She turns my shoulders around. I face the edge. I do not jump. It is more subtle than that. I simply let go...

Boom.

EVOLUTION

We spend a great deal of time in this culture trying to abdicate our responsibility to the right leader or trying to replace our own changeable thoughts with the perfect wisdom. We raise up, venerate, and then turn our collective fury at being let down on one fallible human being, or one imperfect experience, after another. The search for the right leader is a false quest; the search for the right circle in which to assume our own leadership is a true quest.

This is the experiment offered in this book: to help us design and call and participate in circles for the purpose of mutual empowerment and spiritually-based cultural change.

We need a revolution in the West. Not a violent overthrow, but a re-evolution, a willingness to take responsibility for the course of history that is being set forth through our compliance. We need a re-evolution determined to activate broad, inclusive social change. We need to insist that our homes, schools, neighborhoods, places of work, cities, states and nations dialogue with us about the values set in place for this next millennium. As I stood in the meadow at camp, I knew the re-evolution had begun for me.

If a circle is powerful enough to help addicts stop using life-threatening chemicals, powerful enough to help abusers stop abusing, powerful enough to help guide people through therapy, powerful enough to help women and men tell each other the truth about their lives, powerful enough to call down the moon and form learning and living communities, **what else might a circle do?**

This is, I hope, the question that a vast community of people will ask.

Back in Minnesota several months after the camp, as I was beginning this book, I visited an Al-Anon meeting that convened in the basement of my church. I had attended Al-Anon to deal with my own co-dependency and it had been a very helpful circle for me. Seeking out this little group felt like touching base again. I didn't want to explain the complexity of my life to these strangers; mostly I just wanted to be there, to be held in a circle and allowed to rest in the familiar form of the meeting.

Eight or nine women were gathered. Several of the long-time members began reciting their stories about alcoholism in their families, about their own co-dependency, and about how long they had been coming to Al-Anon. Five years. Seven years. They sounded sad and spoke with a resigned tenor in their voices. I stared in amazement and they stared back. Finally I blurted out, "What are you still doing here?"

"Recovering," they said. "Trying to recover..."

I wanted to tell them that there were other circles out there, other things circles could do, that they didn't have to keep defining themselves as needy in order to have the presence of the circle in their lives. I wanted to tell them that there is more than just one circle for each person. Circles can do anything: empower our lives, change our homes, our workplaces, our government, our churches and synagogues. I wanted to tell them that anyone who had been sitting in a peer circle for six or seven years was needed in new circles, that they were "the elders" of the movement, and a place was waiting for them.

I couldn't tell them this. The vision wasn't fully realized. But the need for the evolution of the circle came boldly into my mind that evening. I thanked the group for letting me visit, and left full of hope because I believed I could take the circle forward with me.[1]

We don't have to leave the succor of the circle to take the step from healing to action. The circle will evolve with us to meet our evolving needs. We are beginning the process. We are ordinary people setting out to create our own culture. As we step into this act of creation we see where the circle is, and where it is not. And we begin to discern *where the circle could be.*

•

Delores was a widow, living in a sturdy house in the middle of twenty acres of California redwoods. The house had been on the market for two-and-a-half years, with no offers. Her friends didn't know her financial straits, and she didn't tell them. When a logging developer finally convinced her to sell, it broke her heart knowing the trees would be felled, but she needed the money. *The circle wasn't there.*

•

Cindy and Jack took the kids to New Mexico, and came back to Boston full of excitement about moving to Santa Fe and starting their lives afresh. It would require career changes for both of them, and new schools for the children. As the weeks back home progressed, the family grew ambivalent, yet whenever they looked at their vacation photos, they got excited all over again. One night, at a

---

1. There is no intention do dissuade people from attending Twelve Step groups, or using the Twelve Step Program for life-long maintenance in recovery. The intent of this anecdote is to challenge the habitual use of any group or program to stay in patterns that no longer help us grow.

potluck, they asked some friends and neighbors to help them think through all the pros and cons. *The circle was there.*

●

When no one else in the family took responsibility, Jay moved her mother to Minneapolis and placed her in a retirement complex. Her mother phoned a dozen times a day, insisted Jay drive her to shopping and appointments, and complained inconsolably over the loss of her former home. Within the year she had advancing dementia. Jay carried on her business schedule with increased stress and isolation. Her partners and colleagues listened to her, but didn't know how to offer help. *The circle wasn't there.*

●

The next year at Women's Camp, we met first in community circle to agree to contracts and guidelines for governing ourselves. Rituals were explained and set in context. Morning lectures were replaced with full councils—staff-led discussions on patterns of respect. The council was held with an open chair for community members to speak from, to join in and say their piece. The community designed its own closing ceremony. We were learning, and *the circle was there.*

●

Even though for many of us the circle is not yet fully *here,* is not yet an integrated part of our everyday living, the circle is possible. *The circle can be here in whatever form we need it.* And you and I can actively create and sustain this evolution of growing the circle in our lives.

Everything the Power of the World does is done in a circle.
The sky is round, and I have heard that the
earth is round like a ball, and so are all the stars.
The wind, in its greatest power, whirls.
Birds make their nests in circles,
for theirs is the same religion as ours.
The sun comes forth and goes down again in a circle.
The moon does the same, and both are round.
Even the seasons form a great circle in their changing,
and always come back again to where they were.
The life of a (person) is a circle from childhood to childhood,
and so it is in everything where power moves.

Black Elk
Black Elk Speaks

CHAPTER FIVE

PeerSpirit Circling

*I*magine being in a circle where we have gathered comfortably together and calmed ourselves from the rush of daily concerns. Imagine soft light, perhaps firelight or candles. Imagine silence, and attuning ourselves to communal breath. Imagine contemplation, thoughtful dialogue, probing questions. Imagine singing, chanting, drumming, dancing, laughter and high energy.

Imagine being in a circle.

Imagine being in a circle where the entire group has committed itself to problem solving rather than positioning for power. The group works together to define what the "problem" really is, and puts this challenge out for all to work on in a setting where each person is willing to assume moments of leadership.

Imagine being in a circle with a clearly defined task and agreements which keep people focused on task. When a circle meets with clear guidelines for group respect, a sense of social, emotional, and spiritual safety is set in place. Imagine not being shamed. Imagine not being blamed. Imagine being supported in the actions you take.

Imagine being in a circle.

Imagine being in a circle where men and women allow each other to finish their thoughts without interrupting; where we listen to what is being said rather than planning rebuttal. When a talking piece is used in council, the person with the piece has the floor. The rest of us listen, and trust that when it is our turn to speak, we will be able to draw forth the words we want. Now is time to pay attention to another member of the circle.

Imagine being in a circle where tension is dealt with by someone calling for a moment of silence, for a stretch break, or that people realign with the purpose of the meeting by focusing on the symbols that have been placed in the center. Imagine a process of mediation and negotiation already in place when we need it. Imagine being listened to with respect because the entire group believes that you or I may be the one who brings forward the needed wisdom for the community.

These are not historic or futuristic imaginings—such circles exist and they are growing in number. Soon, circling may be a commonplace way of doing things together. Even though we are in the middle of all our busyness and ordinariness, even though the days and weeks rush by and the list of things we never quite get to keeps growing, *we call the circle because it is the tool we need to sustain ourselves in the midst of tremendous change.*

Many of us have become "conscious" only to discover that we've increased our level of awareness without increasing our empowerment and ability to act. The circle provides a way for us to take the step from consciousness to action. We may draw deeply on the circle as a traditional form. We may combine this form with the skills and insights gleaned from the rise in human consciousness; we may apply practical, problem-solving skills and organizational models and create a new amalgam. I call this combined circle of council, consciousness and action **The PeerSpirit Circle.**

Carol and John were successful with their first PeerSpirit circle. It worked! People heard each other out, and stayed creative in their thoughts and suggestions. Before they went home that night, the group had come up with three alternatives to the strike and the proposed budget cuts, and Tom, Arlene, and Bev Ebble volunteered to communicate with the PTA, the Teacher's Union, and the School Board. They set another meeting for ten days later and left with quiet confidence.

Bev ran into trouble at once.

"Who the hell authorized you to talk about this outside the union?" the head of the strike committee asked angrily.

Bev paused a long time before answering. "You know, Joe, I've been teaching for thirty years. I still like the work and I still like the children. This alone is amazing to me. I've been through two strikes and two threats to strike. Each time, those have been tremendously difficult years. I don't look forward to this kind of a fight. I hate taking the wrath of the parents, dealing with the confusion of the children, and listening to the bitterness of the board. This meeting was the first time anyone has made a cooperative plan for reconciliation. You were invited and didn't come. So now, we've come to you—here are parents and teachers working together, do you want to pick a fight or listen to us?"

Put in those terms in front of his peers, Joe chose to listen. Actually, the strike committee thought the proposals were pretty good and joined in their support. Later, driving home, Bev found herself talking aloud in the car, "Well, I'll be....this stuff actually works."

Arlene and John went to the PTA. "We're an ad hoc group of parents and teachers," Arlene said. "We just want to help the school. Parents are an essential part of keeping this system vital. To sustain some of the extra activities we want to provide our children, we have to find out if there is volunteer support out there and organize it. People say they're too busy, but if they get asked to do something manageable and specific, we think they'll come forward."

The entire circle went to the board, along with the strike committee, the PTA officers, and a petition of support signed by three hundred parents. The teachers had signed an agreement to avert striking if the board would begin to carry out the suggestions. A new PeerSpirit circle formed made up of representatives from all these groups.

THE PEERSPIRIT CIRCLE

PeerSpirit circling empowers ordinary people. PeerSpirit circling trusts ordinary people to know how to hold ourselves in council, to take charge in making the incremental changes that make our lives better and make society a better place in which to live our lives.

There are three simple elements to PeerSpirit circling: *leadership is rotating, responsibility is shared, reliance is spiritual.*

These are not new ideas in the world. Twelve-Step and other self-help groups meet with a rotating facilitator; committees and task forces share responsibility; and from the business prayer breakfast to Bible study groups to meditation retreats, people acknowledge reliance on spirit. What makes PeerSpirit circling different is the combination of these elements. *When we combine leadership, responsibility and spirituality, we create an atmosphere of personal and collective empowerment.*

Circling is a new skill for many of us, but it is a skill we may learn and teach each other. We may apply the structure of PeerSpirit circling to the next group experience we encounter or want to create. When we shift from whatever leadership model has been in operation to the three principles, we may apply PeerSpirit circling to groups already in existence. Where do we start the next circle? We know when we find ourselves asking: *What are we attempting to handle in isolation that would benefit from community, from reminder of sacred presence, from the shared support of others?*

Two months after her school board experience Carol phoned again. "Okay, let's do lunch," she said. "I've been trying out circling at the office and..."

"At your office!" I interrupted, "At the software company?"

"Sure, why not? I have a theory about technical wizards—when they finally get the connection they arc into the metaphysical. I think the circle will work here, but I must admit, I'm having a little trouble figuring out how to talk to management."

Carol is a human resources manager in her company. A soft-spoken, soft-bodied woman with firm resolve under pastel hues of femininity. "The token people person" she calls herself. Her personal agenda is to keep interpersonal communications functioning while others are engaged in programming or sales. She likes her job, but sometimes wonders if the others quite understand her, or value what she's up to. Over lunch a few days later she filled me in. "After our success with the school crisis, I decided to bring just one aspect of circling into the office to see what would happen. I brought a candle." She smiled with a little mischief. "Simple enough, one taper in a silver candlestick. I put it on my desk and didn't say anything. Only, whenever someone came to see me with something important to say, I lit the candle at the beginning of our conversation and blew it out at the end. I think they were afraid to ask what I meant by it, but after a week or so I noticed a few people would come in and light the candle as a way of signaling they wanted my careful attention. Pretty neat, huh?"

I smiled at her inventiveness. "Pretty brave...barging right in and starting with spiritual center...Hasn't the fire code gotten you?"

"I didn't ask permission. And I guess nobody has told. Now management wants to develop a new product. It's pretty revolutionary, I guess. They want a program that can carry out all the functions of custom design and be interactive on the Internet. They're pulling a creative team together and turning them loose for six months to a year of R&D. They want to be innovative in how the whole project is carried out, and don't really know how. My boss wants me to facilitate the group. It's a risk for him because I don't have the technical expertise but in his last company he saw an R & D team destroy itself because no one was communicating. He's gun-shy. I want to introduce him to the circle. What do I do?"

"Well, you need to get really clear about what the benefits of the circle are in this situation and how you see its applications for this group. You need to create and articulate a clear intention."

Setting Intention

Intention is the statement of circle purpose. Setting intention begins by asking: *What is this circle about? Why am I calling it? What do I want?*

In a community action effort, after a woman was attacked on a neighborhood walking trail, several women put up posters stating: "This is our path! We will not lose it to one violent act or person. All fierce women and gentle men are invited to meet at the fire station this coming Saturday at 2:00 P.M. to discuss safety options, to offer escort and care of vulnerable people who want to continue enjoying this trail, and to design a ritual to reclaim and cleanse the space."

This intention statement lets people know that leadership will rotate, responsibility will be shared and spirituality will be part of the process. It clearly states the purpose and who is invited.

A church looking for a new pastor formed the customary Search Committee with co-chairs and ten members. They approached the national office and began going through resumes. After several months, they realized they had not taken enough time to carefully articulate their intent in terms of what new directions the congregation might move in, or who they wanted to call to lead this movement. As a result, tension was developing. One of the members decided to call a council. "I think we need to back up," he said, "so we can clearly frame the vision of our community and the kind of person we want to call."

This call for intention addresses the root cause of group tension without shame or blame and offers a process that can draw people into working together.

Upper management at the software company wanted the design team to work innovatively together in order to free up their thinking for this project. Carol said, "A project team really is a circle, only they aren't aware of it. It's not that much of a leap, they need the structure, a few tools, and the language to help the process run more smoothly. Stuart wants me in there to facilitate communication, but I don't want to carry all the interpersonal responsibility."

Setting intention means getting clear about what it is we want to change or accomplish. "Last time," I told Carol, "You put together a circle with spit and polish. You barely had time to write an intention paragraph and get on the phone to people. With a project of this size, you'll need to get really focused."

Carol worked and worked to articulate a clear intention statement. "I want these guys to succeed…"

"Too vague," I said.

Broad intention provides the basis for reconsideration and self-education. Carol's intention that she wants to support innovation is a broad values statement. A circle called with an expansive intent will be a good think tank and discussion group, but is not likely to take action until its intention has been narrowed in focus. There is nothing wrong with broad intentions—they tend to be highly educational. The talk will be framed by the questions: *How can we think about this? Where and how do we begin?*

"I want to keep them off my back and out of my office, so I'm not arbitrating every little competitive squabble..."

"Too negative," I said. "Intention is a vision of what we want to create, not a statement of what we want to avoid. If I ask you what you want to get out of the day, and you tell me you don't want to get run over by a truck, there's no vision there, nothing to guide you except a reminder to look before crossing the street."

"I want to use the circle to provide tools that help the project team think creatively and act cooperatively for the purpose of product development."

"Much better," I said.

Focused intention provides the basis for action. Carol's intention that she wants to provide helpful tools that allow the project team to think and act creatively suggests that a specific plan of action will develop out of the circle. Certainly people in this circle will talk about the overall context of their work, but these conversations will be held within a concrete focus that calls the group back to specific action. The talk will be framed by the questions: *Specifically, what do we want to do? How do we get started?*

Intention is the most powerful foundation to PeerSpirit circling. Clear intention is the fundamental service we provide as the caller of the circle. *Intention is the verbal transmission of the idea.* Like a stone dropped in water, intention ripples outward and lets people see what the purpose of the circle will be. Once a circle is gathered, we do not control the growth process; we take our place sharing leadership and responsibility and allowing spirit to guide the group. Clear intention insures that the people who respond to our invitation have similar expectations in mind so the circle evolves in a direction compatible with our stated purpose for calling it.

In the summer of 1993, I began looking for a circle of people who work with a spiritual perspective and who could co-mentor each other as we sustain and build our careers. I sent the following letter of intent to ten women:

> *Dear _____,*
>
> *As I near the completion of my book,* Calling the Circle, *I want to call a circle of my own. I have been thinking about this for several years. While trying to uphold my own spiritual values in a competitive and confusing environment, I long for a circle of peer women, each of whom is committed to making spiritually-based contributions to the culture. I am writing to you because your career is also already established and I sense you are doing your own breakthrough work. I also believe that you are committed to doing this from a spiritual base: you walk your talk and talk your walk.*
>
> *My vision: I want my life, work, and art to have sacred impact, to radically change our culture. I cannot do this in isolation. I know I must implement change by modeling change; I need to be around others who hold similar intent, integrity and intensity. I need a circle of peers who will sit in council with each other. I hope we may talk openly about our careers as they are and find ways to help each other fulfill our dreams while dealing with practical realities, consequences and costs. We may create accountability, trusting each other to confront and challenge as well as love and support. We may design a resource base and help keep each other on track.*
>
> *This circle is a combination of skill-matching and heart bond. I am serving as caller of this circle with the understanding that at our first meeting this responsibility will shift to include all of us. If you are interested in joining, please think about your own intentions and need for circle, places to meet, and further information you need to decide on this commitment.*

In a business setting, intention may be called a mission statement. "I know I want the circle to change my relationship with the design team," said Carol, "and for the circle to change their relationship with each other, but I can't seem to articulate how PeerSpirit circling can impact results in a way that people new to the idea will understand."

"Maybe the reason you can't answer this is that it's not just your circle...Maybe you should be talking to some of the people involved."

Talking with Others

A story explains our thoughts, feelings and actions to others. A story helps other people understand why something is important, what significance it has, what our hopes are, and what the plan of action is. A story inspires others to think, feel and act with us. Talking with people and sharing what we're thinking is good practice in clarifying intention. When we talk, we get practice transmitting the idea, and also practice responding to other people's questions, concerns, ideas and additions.

As Carol began planning her circle, she talked to a number of different people.

- People she was pretty sure would understand, be supportive, and interested.
- People who thought very differently from her. She listened to how they challenged her thinking, and practiced not getting defensive.
- Long-time colleagues who previously had seen her work develop from ideas through stages of implementation.
- New colleagues, on a hunch that they might be interested.
- Friends and family, even those she assumed were far apart in their thinking.

Her story ran like this: "I'm going to be part of a project team working on a very innovative software product. Top management wants me in there keeping the peace, but I don't want to be defined as the one who takes care of the interpersonal while the engineers and programmers do all the thinking. So I want to design a peer group circle as the basis for team management where *everyone* is committed to sharing leadership, responsibility and acquiescing to group wisdom. I think working in a peer circle will help insure that the project goes smoother and faster. It also introduces innovation into the process as well as into the outcome. What do you think?"

Every time Carol mentioned the idea, people asked another question.

- What do you mean by "a circle?" Is this just semantics?
- What are you going to do if they don't need you to keep the peace?
- What do you want this experience to provide for you?
- What do you want this experience to provide for the rest of the team?
- What do you want the team to do for each other?
- Is the circle composed only of people who are on the project? Who else might be useful?
- Why are you trying to combine human potential with a high tech project?
- Is the team still going to be part of the company, or will you go off and cloister yourselves?
- How is the team being picked? Will they know the circle is the organizational model before they sign on to the project?
- What if someone wants to work the project but doesn't want to work in the circle? Will they have a choice?
- Is it going to be all men except you? What about some diversity? What dynamics are you trying to protect? What are you open to having change?
- How will the circle contribute to a better product?
- How will a circle reduce production costs?

In Santa Fe, New Mexico, nine police surrounded and shot to death an Hispanic, armed only with a steak knife, who'd been perceived as threatening and creating a disturbance. This caused tensions to erupt and the divisions between citizens and police were brought into focus. The city council and many concerned citizens began asking questions.

- What can we do in response to this crisis?
- Is this an isolated incident or a systemic problem?
- What's the level of real and perceived racism? prejudice?
- What needs to change about our community? How?
- Who has the power to start making these changes?
- What would signal a serious response from government? From the police?

The Citizen Roundtables opened up a level of communication that had a sustained impact on the city. Citizens began to expect their government to be responsive and responsible again. They began to have hope of impacting what was happening in the community. In 1994, Debbie Jamarillo was elected mayor in a race that pitted outside development interests and community action. When our editorial circle met there the week of the election, there was much enthusiasm and hope among my friends.

After gathering *her* questions Carol asked me, "Will you come with me and talk to Stuart, the head of product development? I don't know how to explain this."

Stuart is a bright, second generation manager in this established company. His office reflects his personality. It is furnished with chrome and glass furniture, leather chairs, the latest computer hardware and photos of his wife and baby set among a row of racquetball trophies from the health club. "This product could create an important new market share for us," he said. "The concept is experimental, though it's a natural extension of what we—and a lot of other companies—currently provide. I hear hoof beats in the industry and I want us to lead the market. I'm willing to take some risks in how the team is managed as long as it fosters creativity—quick, efficient, cost-effective creativity."

"What's the nature of the team you're trying to put together and what environment do you see them in?" I asked.

"I think they need to be protected, to be kept away from the rest of the business. They need to be fascinated by the problem. They need to be just plain smart at what they do. They need to be creative risk-takers who are still responsible about budget and timeline concerns. And they need to be people who can work together and value each other's contributions."

The screensaver on his computer is shooting microdot fireworks in the corner of my eye. "Why have you pulled Carol in on planning this?" I ask.

"Because every now and then you put a team like this together and it crashes and burns. It costs a lot of money when that happens, let alone what it does to careers. There's a lot riding on this project. We need something tangible to come out the other end, and we want somebody in the inner circle who speaks plain English, who can liaison out to us."

"So, you're already thinking about a circle..." I smiled, and pulled from my briefcase a small model of a geodesic dome. "Here," I said, handing it across his desk. "What's so unique about the geodesic dome is that nothing appears to be holding it together. The strength is all carried at the joints. Each joint supports its share of the weight. Each is connected to the whole. It's very strong."

"I get your point, but how does anything get done? Who's taking the lead?"

"The *group* takes the lead, by rotating leadership," I said. *"Rotating leadership means that every person helps the circle function by assuming small increments of leadership that carry out the group's defined purpose.* The leadership model in PeerSpirit circling is like a baton that passes among group members depending upon the skills and resources available in any particular group."

What I want Stuart to understand is that in a PeerSpirit circle, leadership doesn't only occur when we talk, it occurs when we listen, when we pay attention to someone else's ideas and concerns. As people experience PeerSpirit, it becomes clear that the circle's direction is not decided by battling out who has the best idea or strongest ego; direction comes from discerning what spirit seems to be moving within the group, and how members align themselves with that momentum.

Carol leaned forward. "In this kind of circling, with the idea of rotating leadership you also get a sense of shared responsibility. It's like the joints on the dome—each person takes responsibility for how they are connected to the whole. It's very pragmatic. The structure here is group purpose: what this project team is going to do—design an innovative and successful product. That's our mission. *I* don't want responsibility for the quality of life people have while working on this team. I want the team to take responsibility for itself, with my help...and with Christina's help, as we need it. Ultimately, it's up to the team to figure out what leadership and responsibility we take on a day to day basis."

Shared responsibility means that each person pays attention to the social, emotional, and spiritual elements of the circle and works to sustain a respectful environment. "In a PeerSpirit circle," I added, "shared responsibility means that we listen to each other and have the courage to say our own truth." In a PeerSpirit circle, we share responsibility by paying attention, by noticing the subtleties of interaction, by being aware of what we and other people need in terms of support. We think before speaking, take time to consider the consequences of actions, ask for help in setting directions we know will have long-term impact. We examine our own boundaries and help each other stay focused.

"There's one more element to the circle," I told Stuart. "People need to draw on the energy in the center to keep them focused and provide support. When you look at this dome, and when you imagine that every joint is a person contributing to the whole, you can imagine that the center gets pretty charged with the way people's minds play off each other. And something more begins to happen. There's a kind of energy to the center that is more than just the sum of people's thoughts. Creativity contained within the circle develops its own energy and contributes back."

"Yeah, I know what you mean. Group think...group dynamics." He tapped his pencil along the desk rim, and paused to think. "That's the part of R & D that seems the most unpredictable to me. Group thought can be supportive or it can be a real drain. It can became so negative that it pulls people down. In this circle model, what's to prevent that?"

"What's acknowledged as being held in the center is essentially spiritual energy. Maybe you call it wisdom," I said, and held my breath.

Reliance on spirit means that each person places ultimate authority in the center and takes their place at the rim. Through simple rituals and consistent re-focusing, the center becomes a symbolic place where everyone's willingness-to-listen dwells. Center may be called by whatever name is comfortable in a particular setting. In private seminars and spiritually-based groups, I call it "sacred space." My drummer friend Barbara calls center the "heartbeat" of a group. Ann calls it "the center peace." In the business world, Carol and Stuart refer to it as "group process."

The shifts in consciousness that occur when we apply circle principles are so powerful that the rituals of centering may be very subtle and still hold much power. Placing flowers in the middle of the table, lighting a candle, or spreading out the things people need for the meeting in an attractive way impacts the expectations of those who come together. Symbolic center changes our consciousness about what we are doing in a gathering. Over time, as the work of the circle deepens and its energy becomes clearer, reliance on spirit will grow, whether or not this reliance is ever expressed in spiritual terms.

"Several years ago, teaching journal writing as a stress management tool to sixty-five hospital administrators, chaplains and nursing supervisors, I walked into a conference room with chairs all in rows," I told Stuart. "The sponsors said they thought the group would be much 'too threatened' if I rearranged the setting. I made some modifications, moved away from the lectern, spread out a subtle centerpiece of flowers, a candle, my journal and pens arranged on the sprawled contours of a scarf I'd been wearing. I didn't mention circling, just sort of held one without putting it into words. After a few hours I suggested we spend the last thirty minutes of the seminar reading from our journals. Most of these people had only been keeping journals since nine that morning. The exercises I'd led them through were designed to build writing confidence and practice being vulnerable on the page. We moved the chairs into a large ring. I placed the scarf and candle into the center and this group, half of it men in suits, read from their private pages, let their eyes brim with tears and bore witness to their stories and the stories of their colleagues. This vulnerability emerged out of a sense of safety—some spirit that is different from ordinary interaction."

"Just a minute…" Stuart said. "This is a software company. People have the right to believe anything they want, religiously, and to believe nothing at all. I don't want you two doing anything that smacks of New Age or Jesus or any of that stuff. It's not appropriate in business."

"Stuart, how would you describe the ideal conditions that will produce the product you want in the time you have?"

"Good team playing. Smart team members. No infighting…Each one doing what he or she does best…taking responsibility for the whole…people supporting group ownership of the idea, instead of letting their egos get over-involved."

"Besides making good people choices, what would have to happen for these conditions to exist?"

"Some kind of containment, a group that gets permission to set aside the usual duties and details, that faces inward around the problem to be solved, believes in itself, develops loyalty to the team, trusts how they work together."

"The circle is a container," I said, "Look at it..."

All three of us glanced at the geodesic ball, as if waiting further instructions.

"Okay, I get it. But nothing hokey, nothing religious, nothing New Age."

"Wisdom." I said, and relaxed back in my chair.

"Group process," Carol said.

"All right," Stuart said, "What'll we do next?"

"Well, you and Carol, and anyone else in the loop, need to decide who's on the team. And you need to make sure they know that the team will function a little differently than usual, that they're signing up for the whole package."

People and Process

The intention statement addressed the question: *What does someone need to know in order to decide if they are interested in responding to this invitation?* The next question is: *Who do we know that we hope will be interested?*

There is a synergy to the gathering of groups—an attraction that occurs when "the call" is clear. Sometimes we may be in charge of the whole gathering, like Carol was when she called together the school group. Sometimes we will hardly be in charge at all, as Carol is at the office. In both instances, synergy will work to the extent we are clear enough to allow it.

The dictionary defines synergy as *the interaction of elements that combine to produce a total effect that is greater than the sum of individual elements.* In calling a circle, synergy means trusting that resonance will occur between the clarity of the intention statement and the readiness of a person to participate.

If someone asks us to participate in a circle that goes directly against our beliefs, values or politics, we have an immediate reaction—no way. The challenge to our clarity arises when we need to practice discernment. Who do we trust to be in circle with us? Do we want to be in circle with them?

A circle is a form of social intimacy. There are boundaries to a circle—each member retains responsibility for private issues—but there are fewer secrets and more emotional content. Story is the basis of the circle's form of council. Story is not the same as reportage. Reportage can divorce fact from feeling. Story is based on personal experience and leads to inclusive and integrated interactions.

At one point, part of the circle which supported me in developing this book—my publisher, editor, teaching partner and I—met for four days of manuscript critique and review. We opened and closed our sessions with silent meditation. We read each chapter aloud, asked for clarification, suggested stories that might be included in places, discussed issues underlying what appeared on the page, made some drastic changes in text and direction, and reached consensus over and over again about what we thought the book most needed. They asked pointed questions. I cried sometimes—and so did the others. We got to know each other's journeys as our experiences related to the work we were doing together. Synergy occurred as we built the vision of the book. Integration occurred around the intended task. Story sustained the gathering.

Synergy also occurred in the church search committee, especially after they backed up and reappraised their task. Bruce, who called the council, introduced the basics of PeerSpirit in such a clear way that the committee turned itself into a circle. Two members left, three more joined.

And after our conversation in the office, Carol wrote an intention statement that went out under Stuart's name to ten people:

"We are organizing a project team to develop software that combines customization and Internet capabilities. If you join this team, your other responsibilities will be suspended so that you may devote full time to this enterprise. The team will manage itself as a peer group working in the service of product development. This peer group will operate as an intentional circle, using the structure of council. I've asked Carol Dillon to serve as a liaison between the team and management. If you are interested, she will explain the use of circle more fully in the application process. Please read through the attached specifications sheets to determine your interest in this project. Carol and I will begin meeting with potential team members next week."

To function in a PeerSpirit circle, people need to sustain basic psychological stability. Circle members need to be people with whom we can imagine rotating leadership, sharing responsibility and allowing spiritual energy to work in group process.

"What the hell," said Stuart, "as long as we're making this big a commitment, we might as well try to put together a team that we think can succeed in *how* it works, as well as come up with the product development we want."

Stuart and Carol made a list of people they could imagine working well together, who might find this new way of doing things intriguing, who would enjoy the circular process of research and development. They came up with twelve names and decided they wanted eight people on the team. They prioritized the order in which they talked with people so they could keep adjusting the mix.

To create a strong circle, we need to draw upon people who mix well, who bring together different skills and personality strengths. We probably already have some people in mind who seem natural for our circle, perhaps people we've talked to during the intention setting process. We need to consider honestly both the rational and intuitive reasons we want to see them in circle. We also need to include in our thinking any hesitation or ambivalence so that we can dialogue about it—in writing with ourselves, speaking with others on the calling team or with the individual person.

This process of discernment is about clear appraisal—looking critically, but not judgmentally, at the skills we need in order for that circle to carry out its intent. In a circle called for community action, people need to have interest and commitment in the cause. For my Peer Group circle, people needed to have similar careers so we could provide good cross resources and counsel each other. In a business circle, people need to have shared goals for the success of the project.

Around the conference table in the Human Resources department, it doesn't surprise us that Carol and Stuart are having frank discussions about team members, but away from a business setting we may not be accustomed to thinking about people with conscious discernment. We may want to be openly, even passively, inclusive. We may be afraid to say "no" if someone asks to join. Or we may be overly concerned with control, not open to anyone who might challenge our way of doing things.

There are times when inclusivity is exactly what the circle calls for—opening up discussion in a work setting, a community action meeting, a civic group. In Santa Fe, in response to the community/police crisi, city coucil member Debbie Jamrillo called a series of "Roundtables" to bring people together for discussion. With this type of issue, everyone needed to be invited. And there are other times, especially when the circle is specific and personal, that we need to honor our work by calling on people who can best contribute to the intent we have created. My initial invitation to a peer group circle went out to ten women I thought would work well with me and with each other.

When we have invested time and energy designing clear intent, we become the stewards of that intention. We are—for the moment—the carriers of the idea. After a while, the idea seems to take on a life of its own. It grows and changes us in the process of becoming clear. We have a relationship to the idea, which means there is *interaction*. If we have trouble making decisions about which people to call into the circle, we need to remember that the people we invite will be making similar decisions about being in circle with us. This evaluation of interest, of readiness, of choosing a good match in personalities, works both ways and sets the synergy in motion.

At the beginning of 1994, I had three people I knew would be in my circle, long term, and others with whom the sense of matching our lives was still settling. At the end of the week, Stuart and Carol had their team put together: three topnotch programmers, Bill, Chen and Mike; one interface specialist, Demetria; a marketing person, Doug; and two technical writers, Lindsay and Philip.

The circle was called.

An epiphanal community
of two or more people
expands the imagination of the culture around them.
The more organic, less structured the community is,
the more powerful the pace of change.
A group of people who are inspired
from an imagination that has been illuminated by
Nature's presence,
and has contact with the Voice of the Sacred
within each of them,
generates a great deal of power
to move through large, rigid organizational structures.

David T. Kyle
Human Robots and Holy Mechanics

CHAPTER SIX

The First Gathering

Once we were brownies or cub scouts. Once we were elected to student council. Once we sat in a church or synagogue circle. Once we served on a committee at work or school, or helped with a co-op daycare center, or headed a task-force. The vestiges of circling that have survived and been adapted into the larger culture are familiar, but PeerSpirit may be our first experience with intentional circling.

The first gathering of a PeerSpirit circle needs to put the three principles in place, and show by example and format how PeerSpirit circling is different from other forms of meeting. As people arrive and settle in they may be wondering, "Why didn't s/he just ask me to sit on a committee? Join a task-force? Implement an office directive? What is this circling concept anyway?"

It's our role as the caller of the circle, or as an experienced circle member, to help the others understand how circles are different. We need to illustrate the process of coming into circle in a clear manner so that people will know what PeerSpirit structure offers. In each new circle we have the opportunity to create an environment that supports our words —to make the circle manifest.

While Carol and her project team were setting up their first circle, I was in Taos, New Mexico, at the Mabel Dodge Luhan House calling a circle of writers. Nine women had gathered from five states for a seminar called, *The Self as the Source of the Story.*

The evening of our arrival, we ate supper together and came into first circle in the Rainbow Room, a small library off the main living room. Mabel Dodge was a wealthy New Yorker who came to Taos in 1917 and fell in love with the light, the desert, the Native-Hispanic-Anglo cultural mix and with Tony Luhan, a Pueblo Indian. They designed and built a hacienda-style great house and began attracting artists and writers. In the 1920s, Willa Cather, D. H. Lawrence, and Georgia O'Keefe were among Mabel's notable guests.

Now, Edna, Jean, Sas, Joannah, Kathy, Jane, Elizabeth, Susan, Dana and I had gathered here. This is probably the most common circle in our culture right now: a small group of middle-class women who are both comfortable and struggling, married, single, or divorced, with children partially grown. Women filled with a sometimes vague but persistent determination to make something of our lives, to understand, to be counted in the culture, to discover in ourselves what our real contribution is. We are women in our late thirties to early sixties, financially able to scrape together the money for educational travel and able to get away from the usual routines for a week. Telephone calls went out from Taos to spouses, to partners, to children, to someone at work. "I'm here, I made it safely...have a good week, I'll call you later." We sank into a kind of timelessness within the walls of the house, enjoying the quiet routines of writing at the edge of this high desert town.

SITTING IN CIRCLE

The need to literally make a circle is essential. We cannot understand the circle if we are sitting in rows being lectured at. The physical dynamic and magic of circling only comes from making a circle. Even when our minds have forgotten the power of the circle, our bodies remember; half the work of comprehension is accomplished when we find our place at the rim. The circle gives us time to notice who's here, to greet each other, say names, get comfortable. As the circle gathers, thoughts of family, work, home, and other details are still on our minds. We need to arrive. We are often coming alone, or maybe have one friend along for support. The circle begins with some ritual which draws a boundary that says: Now. Here. Come into the body of the moment.

In the Rainbow Room we sat under the massive ceiling beams and pastel-shaded *latillas,* painted by Mabel Dodge sixty years earlier. We sat in the ambiance of thousands of conversations that have occurred here among the bookcases. People were chatty or quiet, handling the newness of things in their own style. The magnificent history of the house and its literary traditions created common conversational ground.

We sat in a circle of mixed sofas, chairs and floor pillows. Jane was here from Texas because at forty-six, she told us, she was questioning everything in her life. "I've been writing for years—advertising, interviews, humorous columns, magazine articles, letters. I like research and details, and all of a sudden the inner life has overtaken me. I'm uncomfortable and doggedly determined. I spent all weekend before I came telling myself why I shouldn't, how I wouldn't fit in, didn't have enough experience. I was driving myself nuts. I feel so isolated in Houston—I had to get away." She infuses her story with humor, her red hair as vibrant as her voice, but we also hear her pain.

We invoked the circle itself, remembering the story of Dreamtime, how the circle formed the basis for human community and council. I talked by candlelight, playing my role as caller of this circle. "Once upon a time the circle was central to life in community, not something rare, exotic or faraway. Once there was a commonalty between the cultures scattered over the face of the world—the commonalty of the circle."

· The women were tired from travel, but alert to being here, both lulled and excited by the house and the new presence of each other. "In the time of First Culture," I said, "when something needed doing, everyone joined together in doing it. When the salmon were running, everyone fished. When the rice or grain needed harvesting, everyone threshed. When the lodge house needed constructing, everyone built. This week our dreams need addressing; everyone writes. Everyone reads. Everyone listens. We meet in circle, rather than in class, because the circle models the relationship we may have with our creative process, as well as with each other.

"A circle has specific purpose, focused task, tangible work and tangible results. We know why we are here. We can tell, by the structure of our contracts and commitments, what we are supposed to do. We can figure out how to fit our skills into the overall process. We can measure accomplishment. We can tell who our community is by who supports and helps us. We can see the spiritual core by how ritual is shared, how thanks are offered, how we tend each other's vulnerabilities. And the circle holds."

The room was lit with wall sconces which provided soft background lighting. In the shadowy stillness we each spoke our names and the first pieces of our stories to the group.

Edna, who arrived from Albuquerque after a three hour drive in her rental car, was small, energetic, sixty years old, a therapist turned business consultant from Illinois who spoke with passion to the group. "I'm in the generation of women who have had to come up from invisibility, who have had to learn to take risks. Maybe I want to write a book for women my age. A book of reflections and exercises. Or interviews with women who have consciously taken risks and can talk about how they got through their fears. In other words, I'm still trying to teach myself what I need to know. Mostly, I need space to think about my dreams—so I'm here."

In daylight, far away from Taos, the Project team first convened on a Saturday morning at a conference center located twenty miles outside Minneapolis. The meeting room faced into a courtyard. Light streamed in, a small pool had several lazy Koi carp floating under water lilies. Carol arrived early to arrange the room and make sure last minute details were in place. The padded, comfortable chairs were set in a circle with a sense of spaciousness. She placed a coffee table in the middle, arranged a vase of flowers, put out notebooks, pads of paper, new pens. Her now familiar candlestick was set to one end. Several paper easels were set up with markers in the tray. Over a small sound system, she put on synthesizer music. Stuart arrived.

"Gosh, it's awfully ahhhh, I don't know...casual in here...something."

Carol turned and smiled. "It's Saturday. It's not the office. Relax. The music was composed on computer. I thought it fit the moment."

"Where am I going to sit?"

"Any place you want—as long as it's in the circle."

Stuart tried out several chairs, one by the easel, one nearest the coffee service, one facing the courtyard. "I feel like Goldilocks—one chair's too soft, one's too small, too hard..."

"They're all the same, Stuart, exactly the same."

"Oh, well then, that's the problem..." he laughed, "no throne."

"Right, no throne." The door opened. "Morning Chen, Mike, Bill, you guys ride out together?"

"Of course," said Bill, "Programmers are shackled at the ankles. Didn't Stu tell you? That's how he got all three of us to commit to this."

"Boy, this better be good, or I'm outta here," said Chen.

"What, the circle?" Carol was nervous.

"No, the coffee. I'm not starting anything without gonzo coffee." Chen is twenty-four, the wizard in the company, straight from MIT. With a small build and boyish looks, he takes a lot of ribbing from the older men. He is first generation American, and sometimes works too hard at fitting in, as though his co-workers might not notice he is Chinese. Mike is thirty-five, introverted and serious. He went through college wearing beige sweaters and a row of pens in his shirt pocket. His nerdishness is vindicated now—he has found the right niche for himself and his work. Bill is corpulent, corporate, slightly rumpled and bald. At fifty, he is the oldest in the group and confident of his track record, . They're an odd team, but they've worked together before and get along.

Soon they are joined by Doug from marketing. "I drink only Pepsi, you know," he said, rummaging through his pockets for quarters, "I'm starved. Can you get some sandwiches from the kitchen, Carol? I suppose this is a non-smoking room." Even on Saturday he's arrived in a suit, as though marketing himself.

Lindsay and Philip, the writers, arrived with laptop computers tucked under their arms. Bill greeted them with immediate ribbing..."Geez, we've got six months, or are you just going to write down every brilliant thing I say?"

Lindsay blushed, "Habit, I guess." With short spiky hair and her small frame in a tunic and tights, she looked younger than her thirty years. Only her writing skills gave her confidence, her product manuals being concise and helpful.

Philip admitted, "Security blanket. I never go anywhere without this puppy." He is tall, angular, dark skinned and careful around strangers. They fell silent. Demetria was late. They waited.

Doug came back with two cans of Pepsi and the last vapors of a cigarette still clinging to his clothes. "It's seventy-five cents in the machine," he said into the room. "You got hold of the kitchen yet, Carol?"

"I'm not the go-fer," she said. "There's a phone on the wall, I'm sure someone will bring down some food if you ask." The momentary tension was broken by Demetria's entrance.

"I'm sorry...I'm sorry...This place is farther out than I thought." She set down a large woven satchel, pulled out bottled water and the remains of a rice cake she'd been eating in the car. She folds herself quickly into a chair, an engrained habit to draw attention away from her height, and shoves black corkscrew curls out of her face. "I know I've held us up, let's get going..." The others settled in and turned expectantly toward Stuart. He waved his hand and pointed to Carol.

TELLING THE STORY OF THE IDEA

At the beginning of the PeerSpirit circle, we who have called the circle, framed and held its intention, now set the tone for what is to come by how we hold these first moments of gathering. Our willingness to talk first gives people time to get comfortable and models what they might want to say in a few minutes. We set the context which helps everyone see this circle with similar expectations. This is not an expectation we impose—it is a model of storytelling, helping people understand *how* to come into this particular circle.

The dark desert night over Taos was full of stars, and in Mabel's house just one candle was burning, making pinprick reflections in the women's eyes. "I would guess," I said, "that all of us in this room are in some kind of dilemma. Something in our lives puzzles us, causes us pain and wonderment. And in response, we have the opportunity to become more creative in how we explain our lives to ourselves, and how we explain our lives within the context of the times. We are gathered here to write together. To take a piece of our lives, hold it up for scrutiny and work it into art and story. After years of journal writing, and listening to the journal writing of others, I believe that for many of us there is a personal mystery we are trying to solve. This circle evolved out of the desire to take personal material and delve into it, to address that mystery."

Through my words, I want people to feel included in the net of intention. I want to convey invitation, the chance to bring forth both their own stories and to hear a bit of my own. How I set the circle in motion, how anyone who calls the circle sets it in motion, changes according to the purpose for which the circle has been called.

Carol had to begin with practical background and a brief introduction of circle concepts. She cleared her throat, smoothing the contours of her softly draping skirt and twirling her wedding ring unconsciously. "A few months ago I had my first experience using something called PeerSpirit circling to respond to a crisis in my children's school. The teachers were about to strike, community intervention had failed, the board was stalemated, and I felt helpless. At the suggestion of my friend, Christina, who teaches PeerSpirit circling, I asked a group of parents and teachers to my house and called them into a circle. I knew we needed to break the pattern of how the different groups were relating to each other. We experimented with holding a simple kind of council: passing around a kid's ruler and letting whoever had the ruler have the floor. We worked with three principles: leadership would rotate, responsibility would be shared and we would rely on group process to provide guidance. In one evening, we talked out our differences and came up with some creative solutions."

Doug popped the lid on his second can of Pepsi. "How does that apply here? We're not in crisis. We don't have differences." Demetria shot him a withering glance which he totally missed. "We've got one thing to do—design a product. "

Stuart leaned into the line of vision. "Give it a minute, Doug. Carol and Christina explained this system well enough for me to get interested in seeing if it can positively impact how fast and how well we get the R&D done here. If it doesn't work, we'll adapt."

"That experience of the circle changed my life." Carol plunged quickly on, "I believe now that small groups of ordinary people can create constructive change and have powerful impact. We averted a teacher's strike and laid the foundations for a stronger school system. When Stuart asked me to sit with this team, I convinced him to let me introduce the circle as our structure for self-management because the circle allows us to create a team that can do the job and avoid crisis. If we're going to come up with something that revolutionizes the industry, I thought it would be helpful if we experienced a revolution in *how* this product came about."

"It'll make a good story," said Lindsay.

MAKING SACRED CENTER

Demetria dug deeply into her bag. "Are we beginning?" she asked Carol. "Is the circle called?" Carol nodded. Demetria slid forward off the chair, a book of matches in her hand. She lit the candle. "What a beautiful centerpiece you've laid out here, Carol; thank you. It's the little things that begin a meeting well. Look at this, you guys. Every binder has a name on it. Philip...Lindsay.... Mike...Bill..." She passed out the notebooks, offered each a pen.

As I talked in the Rainbow room, I began unfolding a basket from the deerskin bundle that holds it and all its small treasures. "This basket started traveling with me in Vancouver in January 1993, empty except for a few Lake Superior stones I had put in myself. It has been across the continent, east and west, north and south, gathering things to itself. It is tangible evidence of the growing circle. Everything in here carries a story—some I know, some are mysteries. Occasionally someone asks if they might take an object that's become meaningful to them, and they add it to their own basket, or altar, or writing nook."

We spread out the contents on the coffee table, reached in and fingered this or that piece of what this basket carries. We lit sage and sweet grass, passed around a shell smoldering with this incense. We held silence while each of us wafted the smoke over her body, washing off the concerns of travel, the responsibilities of families left behind, and jobs deserted for this week away.

Sometimes in new groups I sit in the center, unpacking the basket as I speak. Sometimes I light candles, or serve food or drink from the center. My favorite altars are large, sprawling affairs, several sarongs or a rug laid on the floor, candles, even in daylight, because they evoke our sustenance by fire. Neutral and natural objects—a shallow bowl of water, a small vase of flowers, rocks, shells—create a sense of inclusive spirit without reference to any specific religious tradition. The center is a nourishing place, and we need to touch, mold, contribute to and interact with it.

Opening the basket brings the center to the circle. And the center is the holder of the energy. I can let go now, for something else is present. I can take my place on the rim as a peer among peers. And in this peer spirit, there are guidelines that make the circle safe.

"Forty thousand years ago," I said softly, "when we first came into campfire, we were a species just learning social behavior. One of the first things I suspect we decided, once we got to the fire, is that we shouldn't eat each other." The women smiled when I said this. We were full from supper. "We consider ourselves more civilized now, but there are subtle ways we 'eat' each other. For the circle to work in safety, for us to be able to share leadership, responsibility, and rely on spirit, we need to understand the social net that supports us."

SETTING GROUP CONTRACTS

"Stuart, are you going to be part of this too?" asked Bill.

"No. I'm here to get you started, to talk about the project specifications, what the company expects from you, and then to turn you loose with Carol."

"No, turn us loose with each other, to learn to be a team," Demetria interjected.

"I can't be on this team, because of my other management responsibilities, but I don't want to be a complete outsider either. I came today for the opening of this circle so I could see what I'm asking of you."

Carol's attention snapped back into focus. "The first page in the notebooks," she pointed out, "is a list of group guidelines. These are the contracts under which a PeerSpirit circle functions, so we know what to expect from each other, so we know what's appropriate..."

Michael looked puzzled. "What's usually appropriate is to focus on programming. Aren't we going to get to that?"

"Yes, once we have the structure in place."

"Wait a sec," said Philip, "I'm new to this. Usually nobody calls in the writers until much later in the gig. We end up trying to explain what you all thought made perfect sense. If we weren't doing this process stuff, how would the meeting begin?"

"Last time I was in a skunk works," Mike leaned forward eagerly, "we covered the conference table with sheets of paper, put our goal at one end, our current state of information at the other, and tried to fill in the gaps. We divided into groups of two and three, went directly to the hardware. I don't even see a computer around here. And it's Saturday and I'm missing the game."

"Whoa, I've got something to say," said Stuart. "Some of you know this about me, and some of you don't. It's a story that may explain why I let Carol talk me into this. And before I tell you this, I realize I want to know if you're going to tell anyone else..." There was a murmur, a few shaking heads. "I'm looking at this page of guidelines, and now that I have something in mind I want to say, the list makes sense. So—you want to hear my story? Let's get some agreement on the ground rules. Carol?"

"All our social interactions occur with mutual expectation." Carol began. "For example, when we speak we expect people to respond. We expect people to drive on the right side of the road. We count on everyone observing social contracts. It may seem strange this morning to state our contracts straight out, but the circle works through contracted social understanding. That Stuart is waiting for the contracts before he speaks says a lot to me about how potent they are, and how much we need them."

"We've all signed non-compete clauses with the company," said Doug, "and we know better than to open our mouths outside the circle—I mean the team—so I don't get why we need contracts. I've got no intention of talking about anything other than business."

Demetria leaned forward. "Fine. I don't care if I know your story or not, but I care a whole lot if you're blabbing mine around the dining hall."

"I won't, okay? But what I don't get is why any of this is even going to come up? This is a product development team..."

"No. It's a circle. In a circle we don't go from point A to point B, we go in a circle, we go in a spiral..." She brushed back her hair from dark brows and intense eyes.

"That's not efficient," Doug counters.

"Yes it is. That's what you did previously, breaking off into those little teams, huddled over the hardware, working this angle and that, trying to get into the core of the program, seeing what you can make it do. It's not linear thinking! It's highly creative, circular, tangential. That's what I love about my work—I can get into the soul of a machine and make it interface with me—a human being."

Doug reached into his pocket, began fingering his lighter. "I gotta take a break. So tell me again, why is it that we're gonna tell each other the story of our lives as part of this *circular process?*"

"Because maybe if we know each other better we can work together better…" Demetria struggled a second, went on. "Maybe if I know your story I won't think you're rude, and you won't think I'm pushy, and we'll have enough understanding of each other to get the real work done."

"Okay," he said, "You want to understand me—fine. Just let me grab a smoke."

"After we agree to the contracts," said Carol forcefully.

1. What is said in the circle, belongs in the circle.

"Confidentiality means that we hold the business of the circle within the circle. We may talk to other close people in our lives about what we are learning here, but we don't talk about other people, or their stories, or how things are going between us. We deal with conflict within the circle. We keep confidentiality regarding the project."

2. The circle is a practice in discernment, not judgment.

"Discernment means we practice listening to each other. We don't have to be in total agreement before we allow other people's opinions and views to matter. Someone else's view doesn't have to be right or wrong, it may simply be different. The circle doesn't need to always be like-minded, but it needs to be mutually respectful."

3. Each person takes responsibility for asking the circle for the support they want and need.

"Asking for what we need allows us to avoid power struggles and personal drama as ways of getting attention. This applies to asking for technical support in the midst of task, or for some kind of interpersonal support in the midst of a meeting."

4. Each person takes responsibility for agreeing or not agreeing to participate in specific requests.

"We can support someone and not take direct part in what they need. We may choose to not support a request. We may challenge whether or not a request serves group purpose. If a request fits the task and orientation of the group, someone is likely to be willing to help carry it through. If a request doesn't fit, we need to work together to hold the intention."

5. Contracts are updatable. If something is not working, we change the contract and maintain the process.

"Contracts define how the intent of the circle is carried out. If trouble develops, the group can work together to search for a contract that will better support group process and group intention. Group process is the *way* we meet together; group intention is what the meetings are about—what we set out to do."

6. Ask before touching; practice listening without interrupting.

"We don't usually touch at all around the office, except for an occasional handshake, but in circle the boundaries change because the level of intimacy changes. We may become friends, and want to negotiate for a more relaxed atmosphere. Listening without interruption is a practice of council that's very ancient—a practice it looks like we need, and I'll introduce it in a minute."

7. When troubled, call for silence, space, song, or other ritual that re-establishes the center and reminds participants of the need for spiritual guidance.

"The way we maintain the circle is an act of shared responsibility. If one of us senses the need for time out, then we should call it. This doesn't mean we stop discussion every time there's disagreement; it means we take a break when discussion has ceased to be communicative."

Carol looked up and around. Faces were closed to her, unreadable. "We are so scared to talk about this stuff. I had no idea how great a risk this would be," she thought.

Demetria nodded at her, "I'll live with these contracts," she said.

"So, will I," said Lindsay.

"Yes, I guess..." said Philip.

"Okay. Now can I have a cigarette?" Doug stood up and broke the circle, and the group took a break.

Once contracts have been agreed to, they become the circle's miniature code of law. Spiritual acknowledgment holds the center; contracts hold the rim. At the circle's perimeter, contracts are the authority upon which each member agrees to rely. Contracts are impersonal, communal, and fair. Contracts set the parameters of conduct and focus—the safety net for group process

FEARS AND EXPECTATIONS

Carol barely made it into the bathroom before she broke into tears—the release of her own nervousness. Demetria found her there, reached out a hand, paused. Carol nodded, and the tall, intense Greek woman put her arm across Carol's shoulders, gave her a brief hug. "You're doing great," she said. "This is hard stuff. I couldn't believe it when you and Stuart said you were going to try a circle in this project. It's the reason I signed up."

"It is? Boy, I feel like everyone else is just barely tolerating it."

"They don't know what it is yet," Demetria reminded her. "It hasn't really started happening."

"Thank you for getting me back on track a couple of times this morning. You know something about this, don't you?"

"I've got circles all over my real life—it's the only way I can balance my work life."

"Like what?" They looked at each other through the reflection of the mirror.

"I have a circle of friends that's been meeting for several years to provide support about career stuff and co-mentor each other. And there's a group of women who meet every month on the full moon to celebrate and talk about women's spirituality. You should see my house—it would shock everyone here, maybe even you; it's full of circle energy."

"I'd like to see your house sometime...I don't know you very well, do I?"

"Well, you will, if this idea works. I'm sorry I lost my temper with Doug. He's going to be a real challenge for me. I get so tired of taking baby steps with men. I want them to give up their precious control mania and let us get into circle so we can start communicating, let a few walls down.... I don't know if this is going to work with him, but *I'm* sure glad to be here."

"You know so much more than I do, you should be leading this group—not me."

"No, I shouldn't...leadership rotates, responsibility is shared...we need to get back out there and help everyone start leading this group."

The first fifteen to thirty minutes of the initial meeting are often difficult for the caller because the principles haven't clicked in, contracts haven't been set, and unless people have been in circle before, no one is quite sure what to do. The more we can let go of worry and control over how this first meeting will go, the more synergy will be available to help the group coalesce, the more spiritual energy can arise and help hold the center. This doesn't mean we—as callers—withdraw energy and attention. It means we call upon that which we have asked to be present: clear intention, gathered spirit, common interest.

In the first gathering of the peer group I had called for career support, I presumed all the members were equally familiar with the structure of circling and that intention was more deeply shared. I think I relaxed too quickly and didn't hold the rim in ways that would have helped. Looking back, I wish I had read aloud the letter of intent to call us into focus. I wish I had been more thoughtful in how I set the tone as our meeting started. I wish I had had the confidence to hold the leadership a little more during the first hour.

None of us are perfect and the circle still works. We find the balance. We discover the interconnectedness in how we help each other hold the vision of what we are doing. We discover the challenges we present each other and still sort out our conditioning and abilities to hold the circle together.

The peer group went very well on the social level, but we
didn't know enough to set the underlying structures of circling in
place. We relaxed, told stories, got to know each other, and on the second day each took a turn as the focus of the council. But intention
didn't gel and our ability to articulate what we needed was scattered.
We ended the weekend with a great deal of affection for each other
and respect for our career paths, but without a clear idea of how to
actually help. The experiment continues, and the synergy is still gathering. Now I understand more about what I want, and the complexi-
ties of arranging it.

GROUP PROCESS

In Taos, less than twelve hours after convening, on a morning
when we expected to start with writing exercises, something happened that changed our agenda. Susan, the director of Mabel Dodge
House, who had set aside her usual duties and joined the group for
the week, came up to me just as we were finishing breakfast. She was
agitated, nearly in panic. Her long fingers gesturing in the air around
her said almost as much as her words. "There's been a mistake," she
said. "The women who requested private rooms for the week have
been undercharged. I know this place is expensive for many of those
who have gathered, but our business is desperately struggling. We
can't afford to not charge for these rooms. We have a bank notice due
next week…we're in crisis here…I don't know what to do."

I ushered her into her office. "Talk to me," I urged. "Tell me
what's really going on because there are already rumblings about the
fees, the confusion of what costs what, the financial stretch it is for all
of us to be here enjoying this site." In tears, Susan told me the story of
their struggle to protect the history and integrity of the house as a
place where artists and writers could gather. Standing with her in the
small back room that faced the mesa lands of the Taos Pueblo, I
thought certainly there must be some way that we as a circle of
women could address this issue.

We'd had a dusting of snow overnight and the contour of the
land stood out as I had never seen it before. Each bush and piñion
tree was silhouetted white against brown, and off in the distance a
cluster of native adobe homes, usually invisible against the backdrop
of the desert, stood solidly under the frosted mountains. Here were
the remnants of First Culture right in front of us. And here was the

strife caused by Second Culture—the struggle to maintain a piece of prime real estate in a sacred manner. As I listened to Susan, I felt the clench in my own guts: fear over what this money issue might do to the workings of the group, fear over my own money issues, my mixed sense of scarcity and generosity. This issue is so often loaded with emotion for women. How do we have enough? How do we share what we have? How do we address a problem without going into isolation? Susan had been struggling without much support as she tried to save the house. Her impulse in trying to solve the money issue was to assume a similar lack of support.

"I think it's essential we take this into council," I said. "If you just start calling women one by one to the registration desk and saying they need to pay more money, each of us will fall into whatever fear or shame or guilt this issue brings up in us. I know there are women who can't afford to be here and have come anyway. I know there are women who are comfortable enough that this is not a hardship. Our circumstances must not be allowed to divide the group. We have the chance to trust this circle. The contracts are in place. The circle is in place. Will you speak from your heart? Will you trust us?"

"Yes."

And so we reconvened.

The circle is not happening in isolation. Years ago we pretended that it did. We'd form a circle in a retreat center and talk about our personal journeys with hardly a reference to the journey of the world around us. There is no more getting away from these realities. They have come to our attention in ways we cannot avoid. In a group as small as nine, there are women, married or unmarried, who have to be responsible for their own retirement and aging; women who have survived incest and cancer, women taking great risks with their lives. We are aware of our connection to the ways women are limited in the larger culture, and the toll this places upon us. We are aware that we are still among the most "privileged" group on the planet. Our stories occur in context and the real world of our lives accompanies us into the circle. In the face of Susan's panic, we had the chance to face each other and not retreat.

USING A TALKING PIECE

One of the traditional structures of council is the gift of uninterrupted speaking time. To designate whose turn it is to speak, a talking piece is traditionally introduced as a tool for holding formal council.

I first saw a talking piece on a trip to the Pacific Northwest in the late 1980s. In a shop of Native carvings, one long cedar pole caught my eye. Carved with ornate totem animals, the pole was five feet long with a firm tip, like a cane, and at shoulder height there was a smooth, rounded section for holding. To wrap one's palm around this stick was to experience a hint of the power of council: what it means to have the floor, to hold the attention, to stand with spirit helpers—the carved images of Eagle, Raven, and Orca—in our hands. To stand with this stick is the opportunity to feel the grounding tradition that has come down to us—to call up in our minds what the earth has to say, what the body and heart know, and to pull down into our minds what spirit connects us to god/us. I have used this staff in council and its power evokes great lineage. It doesn't travel easily. It wouldn't fit in Carol's office decor.

A talking piece may be any object designated to grant the person holding it the right to speak without interruption. It needs to be something comfortable for the specific circle: a rock, feather or other natural object, a child's ruler, a gavel, a rosary, a family heirloom. The small brass figurine from the basket is what we used in Taos the morning we tested ourselves in circle.

At first, the presentation of a talking piece may seem foreign to people, especially in business or academic settings, but once the piece is in hand, it tends to have the same impact as forming the circle itself—from somewhere inside we remember what we are supposed to do next. When one person has the piece, the rest of us listen without interruption. The purpose of using a talking piece is to make sure all people are heard, or have the opportunity to be heard. The use of a talking piece reminds us to restrain our impulse to interject remarks, to interrupt someone with jokes or sympathetic commentary, or to ask questions which divert attention from the speaker's contribution.

"Before we begin talking more generally about writing this morning," I said, "we need to listen to Susan and resolve a problem that's facing the circle. We will use a talking piece for this part of the morning. Susan will speak as much as she needs to, and then we'll put the talking piece on the altar and the rest of us may take turns, holding the floor as we have comments to add. In this way of holding council, it works best if we trust ourselves first to the act of listening, to paying deep attention. Oftentimes, after such attentive listening, I don't know what I'm going to say until the piece comes into my hand, and then the thoughts that have gathered in me speak."

Susan spoke eloquently and passionately about her attachment to the vision of Mabel Dodge House as the kind of space where circles could gather. She and the owner/director, George Otero, have held on tenaciously in the face of huge personal debt, rising costs, expensive bank loans, pressure from big developers to sell and let the place be turned into a resort. The town of Taos is changing around them. "We are becoming like Santa Fe," she said. "There is a lot of money coming into town as people with independent incomes buy up land and drive up prices. But for most people in town, this is still a five-dollar-an-hour economy. The prosperity is not reality-based. I love this house...I don't know if I'm being asked to guard it, or if I'm too stubborn to let it go. I want there to be some place like this that can't be bought...that *we* can have."

The group listened carefully. "I'd been off work, on the first rest I've had in two years, and things got confused while checking you in. I'm sorry. I apologize. We don't usually do business like this. I'm angry and ashamed of all the mixed signals you've been getting. If we were more flush, I'd say this is our fault and we should take the loss, but we can't afford to do that..."

What happened next is that the circle worked. In myself I felt a range of emotions: sympathy, respect, resentment, fear, helpfulness. I rode each emotion out in silence, kept bringing my attention back to what Susan was saying. I prayed, too, very aware of a part of my mind that asked for guidance, for presence, for help in keeping us all focused on our unity rather than our isolation. My prayer was like a simple mantra running just behind my attention, being part of the attention: "Help me hold the rim, let the circle spin, be present to Spirit."

As Susan finished, I reached for the talking piece. "I don't know how the women in the private rooms feel they can respond to this, whether you have enough money to make up the difference. The reason for calling council is to see this as a group challenge, not an individual one, and to call upon the problem-solving skills and wisdom of the group. We will make this adjustment together..." And we did. Not only did the group make up the difference in the room costs, but women sat down with George and Susan throughout the week, brainstorming alternatives, discussing financial resources they or their husbands had at home...Positive energy was released. The trust level of the group was sustained, and the week proceeded.

The talking piece is a great equalizer among those who have unequal status outside the circle—those of different gender, age, racial, ethnic or economic mix. The piece assures that everyone has equal voice. I have seen the introduction of a talking piece work in groups of children as young as six, who are able to revere the designated power of the speaker and accept their role as listeners, knowing they will have their own turns. I have seen the piece restore group process in circles where tension was running high; the piece seeming to gather the energy as it passed from hand to hand, to calm down some and to awaken others to their leadership. Its use diffuses personality issues and power struggles. I have seen very shy people stand up for their right to be uninterrupted once they have the talking piece in hand. The piece becomes the arbitrator, instead of one person taking over leadership or several vying for control. If someone is disrupting group process, the piece becomes the authority, determining who speaks next.

Later that evening Edna walked with me from the dining room to our rooms in the conference building. "*Why* did you do that this morning?" she asked. "I supported you in the moment, and learned a lot—saw the risk you were taking and the good results. I guess my question is: How did you know to call us into council? How did you know it would work?" Her dark brown eyes searched my face.

"I didn't know for sure that it would work," I admitted, "but I knew that if we backed away from the power of the circle, let any one of us be isolated without any option except pay or don't pay, we would have lost the cohesiveness and trust in ourselves as a group, and probably not have been able to recover it. I say I trust the circle with my life, and here was a chance to put that belief in action. Now that we've had a communal experience of our power, our creativity all week will benefit from that grounding. So, why did you support me?"

"Because I'm curious. I wanted you to be right about the potential for the circle and I knew I could take care of myself in the middle of that issue—I'm already in a shared room. And because I had already had a meeting with you, there was a level of trust established. I think it's important to acknowledge that—even though this was our first formal meeting. When I chose to speak, it felt good to say my piece, to know the spirit in which the group would listen."

Most often, the talking piece is passed from hand to hand around the circle so that everyone has the opportunity to speak and knows when their turn is coming. If we're not ready to talk when the piece comes to us, it is perfectly acceptable to quietly hand the piece on. After a complete ring, the piece may be passed a second time or placed in the center for people to retrieve when they have something more to add. In smaller circles, or among long-standing groups, the piece may simply reside in the center and people reach for it as they are ready to contribute.

FIRST TIME AROUND THE RIM

Stuart brought a talking piece for the software group, trying to make himself and others more comfortable with a bit of frivolity. It was just the right touch—a wand made out of a floppy disk and a slide rule. He used it first to tell his own story.

"Well," he said, "this project is seen by the company as my baby—if you guys produce, we'll be heroes. If you don't, I'll be taking the rap. This makes me a little nervous, as you can imagine." He brushed his hand through thinning hair. "I think I'm a good manager, but I'm not going to be in here managing. I can't. I don't have the time and I don't think you really need me. What you need is a structure that helps you manage yourselves and builds team spirit.

"In my last company there was a team like this. I pulled people together, gave them a pep talk, and sent them on their way. I checked in weekly and they kept telling me things were fine, but the team blew up. One guy was so upset he refused to finish the project. Another guy quit and walked off with the R&D in his head, took it out of state to a competitor. We couldn't prove anything. A woman on that team had a nervous breakdown. Careers splattered. I saw a lot of pain come out of what I thought was going to be a very ordinary process.

"I'm a little haunted by this situation," Stuart's voice cracked for an instant. "Those people were my responsibility and, in ignorance, I let them down. I didn't read the distress signals and the project was hemorrhaging before I even knew it was bleeding." Stuart looked around, noticed their silent attention.

"My first thought was to stick Carol in here as my safety valve, the person designated to keep everyone communicating and to communicate with me. Much to my surprise, Carol didn't want the job and came back with this suggestion to try circle management. We've tried out enough aspects of Total Quality Managment that this didn't sound too weird. So here we are. Carol says: leadership rotates, responsibility is shared, and the group comes to rely on its own energy to generate ideas and cooperation. It sounds pretty good to me, and you've all agreed to give it a try as part of your commitment to project development."

Stuart's statement set the group dynamic spinning. The circle came alive. As the dynamic begins to functions, we cannot know everything that will happen. We may have spent months gelling the ideas that brought this group together, and now it's not our private plan anymore. Right before our eyes, the council calls itself into being. A kind of circle consciousness start to develop.

Circle consciousness is the amalgam of our personal energy with group energy. I usually experience this integration in both body and mind. My attention becomes focused and my heart center opens, filling me with a warm sensation of housing spiritual presence. In groups of three to three hundred, people begin to experience the group as having its own vibrant identity. We awaken to the circle.

Most of the time, group process will move along smoothly, will hardly be noticed because it is functioning well. Sometimes group process will fall apart. This is unavoidable, and natural. Someone will misinterpret a statement or action, or need to challenge something someone else has done or said. At these moments, the center provides our guidance for holding the energy and refinding direction.

In moments when there is a pause in the process, I frequently have an impulse to jump in and smooth out the silence or help things along. I have learned to restrain myself by reciting a little internal chant. "Hold the circle," I say silently. "Watch and hold the circle. Be here and hold the circle." Over and over I have observed that *I* do not always need to be the one to react in order for things to progress. Leadership will rotate, responsibility will be shared, Spirit is reliable.

Most of the time, I simply need to stay out of the way and let group consciousness reestablish itself. The main thing PeerSpirit circling requires is the willingness to trust ourselves and others to practice it. Circling is a verb. PeerSpirit circling is the practice of thought and action. The circle has worked for so long, for so much of human history, in such diverse configurations of human community, we do have a tradition to call upon. We may tap into our tradition, and be present with the circle.

COVENANTS OF THE CIRCLE

Contracts in a circle are made with careful thought. They are an intellectual process—agreements of the head. Covenants in a circle are made on faith. They are an intuitive process—agreements of the heart.

One Christmas I invited several nieces over for the night, a kind of slumber party with three kids and one grownup. We had just been through a ceremony with their grandmother, my mother, to acknowledge her Coming of Age as the matriarch of the family. The girls and I decided to continue the ritual. We painted our faces, laid out an altar, lit candles, passed a talking piece. It wasn't a terrifically solemn event; there was much giggly energy around the rim, but with Erin, the circle took hold in her heart. This was the beginning of "Auntie Camp," our term for her chance to sleep over at my apartment most of the weekends I was not holding circles elsewhere. Erin loved to create her own altar, displaying a sense of design and ritual. Her intensity took me by surprise. For my birthday that year, she sent me a very solemn card. The inscription read, "Dear Aunt Christina, thank you for being my Earth Tribe Sister." This is our covenant, whatever other family ties exist.

Most of us have been taught to think of covenants largely in religious terms, though a covenant is any solemn agreement used in legal and civil affiliations. We made a covenant the first time we swore to be "best friends forever." We made a covenant when we recited the Pledge of Allegiance at the beginning of the school day. We made a covenant reciting the Scout's code of honor, the 4H pledge, or the Apostle's Creed. Our family life and friendships contain many covenants, although they may not be articulated any more than the social contract has been articulated.

When any two people assess their relationship, whether it is business, personal, or circled, and agree to do certain things and not to do others, they are "covenanted" to their agreement. It doesn't matter if we have gone through this ritual intentionally or spontaneously, we know what this moment of exchange feels like. A covenant is a little surprise in the mind, a kind of wake-up call that something is being exchanged. If we haven't consciously prepared for it, we'd better wake up, take notice, and decide how we want to participate. Though we may not use this terminology in daily speech, covenants are an ordinary aspect of our lives.

In Taos, the covenant was not articulated but it was directly experienced. We shall not let each other down. We will help each woman here deal with the reality of her life and what she brings into story. We were confident, even as strangers just coming into circle, that pain could be safely shared and acknowledged, at the same time writing was offered for support and critique.

The heart has its own relationship to people, events, experiences and circles which the mind may or may not understand, or even be aware of. Children are sometimes more open in letting the rest of us know what their covenants are, but all relationships that have heart energy have covenant.

If we don't acknowledge heart energy, or use covenantal language, we may ignore the presence of a covenant, but that doesn't remove the covenant; it only drives it into the unconscious. In both business and personal realms, people remain committed to extremely difficult relationships and situations because the covenant is still intact for them; people leave what appear to be easy or stable situations because the covenant has been broken, or heart energy dissipated.

A PeerSpirit circle, with its sacred center and a rim bound with intention and contract, is, by nature, a covenanted arrangement. This means people have a heart dimension involved in what we expect from ourselves, from others, and from the experience itself. This is true even when the circle is established in settings where covenants have not been acknowledged.

In a circle, we make a personal covenant that states what we expect from ourselves: *"This is what I am counting on from myself..."* We make a social covenant that states what we expect to offer each other: *"This is what you may count on from me..."* And we make a spiritual covenant with the center: *"This is how I will seek and follow guidance..."*

My basic covenant with the circle is: *"I dedicate* myself to holding this circle and helping it accomplish its task. *I take responsibility* for myself, to work in this group with integrity, to clear up issues as they arise. *I offer* my skills and ability to think on my feet. *I retain* my insecurities and competitiveness, and will take care of personal issues which do not pertain to the purpose of this group. I am a grown person and you may count on me to stay a grownup throughout this circle. *I will listen* to you, and I will listen for guidance."

In a circle where people are willing to express their convenants, the center acts as the basket to contain this released heart energy. Heart energy is called forth by the safety created through contracts, and by the centering created by holding the rim. Heart energy is called forth by claiming a meaningful task. These are the conditions in which the human heart thrives: safety, centering, and shared purpose. So we shouldn't be surprised when we feel gratitude, relief and celebration at finally being in a place where the heart's conditions are met. Heart energy needs to be part of a PeerSpirit circle, and it *will* be present, whether or not it is acknowledged.

Heart energy was present as the group listened to Stuart's story and perceived his vulnerability. In this setting, no one was likely to react with the level of intimacy that the group in Taos generated, but that doesn't mean it's not part of the circle. When Mike and Doug and Bill let themselves realize that Stuart was counting on them to both put together the project and manage the process, if they agreed to take on the whole task, they made a covenant.

CLOSING THE CIRCLE WITH RESPECT

When we open the circle with respect, with ritual, and in a few hours imbue it with communal energy, good intention, excitement, nervousness, and heartfelt sharing, it is important to close the circle with some ritual which signals that the meeting is over.

In Taos, at the end of a session, Dana blew out the candle. Elizabeth read a poem. Kathy put on music. In the conference center, Carol blew out her candle, grateful that Demetria had remembered to light it.

A fairly high degree of attention is required to hold the rim while circling. We are more alert than usual. One reason for opening and closing the circle with ritual is to signal each other when this level of attention is required, and when we may relax, have a cup of tea, or chitchat on our way out the door.

Circle business needs to happen while the circle is open, while people are expecting to have their attentiveness called upon, not during transition times. It feels good to close a circle, to signify that the experience has been successfully completed. In circles where the sacred has been acknowledged, the closing will also acknowledge the sacred. Usually, closing a circle that has only met for a few hours requires only a simple and short acknowledgment. Even the standard phrase, "meeting adjourned," is a way of closing circle. At the end of a long seminar or ongoing group where the circle energy has deepened, the closing needs to reflect the intimacy that has developed.

At the end of our five-day writing retreat in Taos, we had been reading until late in the evening and were both tired and reluctant to let the circle go. We stood in the living room of Mabel's house with a fire spitting piñon knots in the fireplace, arms around each other's shoulders. Focusing on one woman at a time, we called out the attributes we had come to appreciate—"compassionate listener...risk taker...coming into wisdom...brave...good writer..." What made these praises magic was the energy that surrounded the message and the acknowledgment that combined the heart, mind and body.

Whether we are ending a first meeting or completing a cycle, it is good to take time to close, to set into place the experiences which have occurred. We can be sad that something is over, and celebrate that it was done so well. We can be excited that something is beginning, and energized by what the circle has stirred in us.

We tell you this: we are doing the impossible.
We are teaching ourselves to be human.
When we are finished, the strands which connect us
will be unbreakable;
already we are stronger than we have ever been.
The fibers which we weave on our insides will be so tight
nothing will be able to pass through them.

We tell you this: when we are finished,
we will be a proud people.
We are making ready,
as we send ourselves out separately across the dying continent.
Holding on to shells, stones, feathers, amulets,
we are taking on their properties.

Thus we move: silently, separately;
our name is buried in various sacred spots all over the land.
We are waiting until it is safe to claim it.
Though we move silently, separately,
can you hear our joint voices singing,
singing our women's songs in ever widening circles?

Listen.
We are making ready.

Martha Courtot
Tribe

CHAPTER SEVEN

Sustaining the PeerSpirit Circle

I do a lot of flying in my work with circles, and always ask for a window seat. The miracle of hurtling through the mile-high sky at five-hundred-plus miles per hour never quite leaves me, that I can wake in New Mexico and hug good-bye to a group that's about to scatter thousands of miles and go to bed reading stories to Erin in Minnesota. What I notice, looking down on this marvelous planet en route, is that there are no straight lines in nature. Rivers meander through crevices following some mysterious path that only water knows. Mountains and hills spike up out of the flatlands, and the circle is everywhere. Not perfect circles drawn with a compass, but loose, loopy edges to lakes and fields and forests. Forms that have carved their own place in the landscape, combining stability and fluidity, while the round globes of the sun and moon, the cycles of day and night, and the four seasons revolve over all.

A human circle also has natural shape and cycle. A circle is an organism of living energy. Its progress is loose, loopy, following mysterious paths. To sustain the circle, we need to combine flow and structure in the same ways nature does.

A river flows—most of the time—in the path it has laid out for itself, whether meandering through a cow pasture or surging through the Grand Canyon. Our lives in the circle also have their times of easy meandering, periods of surging forcefulness, and occasional floods. What allows us to raft along in the life of the circle are the structures we set in place as we embark, and that we maintain meeting by meeting.

THE CIRCLE LOGBOOK

When the project team reconvened after their weekend retreat, they had set much structure in place. Some aspects of their structure were generic to circling, some had been hashed out in the first meeting, some had happened naturally in the synergy of the group. Certain structures were provided by the business setting and project orientation of this particular circle. They had a shared and articulated intention. They had defined goals that serve as their covenants. They had the beginning of rituals for opening and closing, and a basic familiarity with each other and with group dynamics.

At the second meeting, Philip walked in with a present for the group. "I thought we did a great job getting clear on our intention," he said during check-in. They weren't using the talking wand yet, just sitting in a circle of comfortable chairs with a coffee table in the space between them. The candle was burning, and Lindsay had shyly brought in a small vase with flowers. "We ironed out some of the process and defined the project's actual work and time line. So I took the liberty of taking the stuff Carol gave us and notes from the meeting and putting it all together in a bigger notebook." He dug a bundle out of his briefcase, "If I may offer Exhibit A—The Project Team Logbook."

He flipped open a standard three-ring binder divided by index tabs, leaned forward to lay it out on the coffee table. "Tab A: Group Guidelines and other Foundations. In here I put what Carol provided—contracts and a copy of *Guidelines to PeerSpirit Circling*.

Tab B: Teammates—bio pages on each one of us. My page has a photo of me and my dog, Samson, my home address, and every phone, fax and pager number I could think of—any way I thought you might need to get hold of me. Samson, of course, has a separate line. I have a page formatted for each of you and hope you'll take a few minutes to add all your own information, and donate a photo or something to personalize the info." The group nodded at him.

"Tab C: Minutes of our meetings. Lindsay and I slipped into scribe mode over the weekend. It was a good way for me to get comfortable, but I don't want to be the one doing it all the time. However, I do think it's necessary—a sort of flow chart of our progress, private tracking, just for us.

Tab D: Action items—who's working on what, with whom, what the timelines are, etc.

Tab E: Outcomes—a place to chart the completed tasks that lead up to fulfilling our project intention and put hard copies of charts and other stuff from the project management software we are using. I don't know about you, but tackling something this long and complicated, I need to see the steps and have some way of checking them off."

"And celebrating!" said Chen. "I think we ought to come up with some definite blowout points along the way—a night bowling, pizza and beer at the video arcade..."

"Hey, Chen, some of us are almost old enough to be your father," reminded Bill.

"Okay, how about miniature golf?" The group laughed.

"Obviously Tab F," said Philip, "needs to be designated for Celebrations and Silliness. Tab G is open, but I suppose we'll have to generate some kind of official paperwork."

"I like it," said Demetria "that we have some tangible place to house our progress. Thank you."

Even in this business setting, rituals are developing—from the center space to plans for playing together to the maintenance of the logbook. The real life of any circle is what happens as it continues to meet and enters into the work that it has been called together to do.

TIME AND COMMITMENT

In the Tenfold™ seminars that Ann and I co-founded, we introduce women to a three-day life-sorting process which helps participants define and present the next goal they want to set for themselves. At the end of the seminar, Tenfold becomes a contractual circle. Having taught basic PeerSpirit and council-holding skills, Ann and I step back and Tenfold evolves into a peer circle. Its first order of business is for each woman to decide whether or not she wants to continue meeting and, if the answer is yes, for how long.

In a Tenfold setting, members contract for six months to a year of support, with the intention of recontracting or releasing the group at the end of that time. In the Project Team, time frame is set by the nature of the work and the business structure which supports it.

Circles need intermediate exit points. Even circles that hope to go on forever, like intentional communities, intimate partnerships, or a writing circle of committed friends, need times when the contract is carefully reconsidered and all people concerned are invited to recommit or to leave with the blessings of the group. When we acknowledge the circle's impermanence, we are provided with an opportunity for cherishing each other and our time together. A specified time contract creates immediacy in the circle—a sense that we need to get things done because this isn't going to last forever.

MAKING THE CIRCLE A FAMILIAR PLACE

What holds a circle together is a sense of being a distinct group. People bond to a shared purpose, to each other, and to similar values or respect for diversity of values. Much bonding and group identity within a circle occur through familiar ritual and routine. In the early meetings of a circle, we put these structures in place so they may serve as the bedrock upon which we stand when challenges to group unity occur.

There are twelve women in this Tenfold circle,[2] ranging in age from early thirties to late fifties. Some members work in the city, some live in the surrounding small towns. They drive within a twenty mile radius to attend evening meetings that occur every three weeks. At the last meeting, when Rachel volunteered to host the next group, she folded up the altar from Cathy's living room floor and took it and the logbook home with her. A week before the meeting, she activated the phone tree to remind people of this date: six o'clock potluck, seven o'clock circle. Everyone is here. Everyone is usually here because the circle is important to them, a priority in their lives. This is their sixth Tenfold meeting. Routines and rituals are both established and evolving.

2. In the interests of privacy, the following story is an amalgam of Tenfold experiences from several groups, but the process of sustaining the circle is authentically presented.

When members arrive at Rachel's house bearing casseroles and salads and trays of brownies, they hug and chat and help set out supper. This is informal time; women talk about pets or children or local news, suggest books and movies to each other, and generally catch up. They are friendly, but not necessarily "friends" in the complete sense of the word; they don't expect others in the circle to track the totality of their lives and are selective in what they ask the others to hold with them. They wait to share the deeper issues on their minds until the circle is gathered, when they know they have the full attention of the group.

A Tenfold circle opens and closes with ritual that honors center. In the living room, away from this early part of the evening, Rachel has already laid out the basics of their altar. This Tenfold has its own basket with its unique collection of small treasures representing each one in the circle. It is dusk when the circle convenes. Rachel starts a tape of soft music playing, and lights a stick of incense. The women filter into the room and settle down in silence. Each pulls out a candle from her purse and sets it in front of her place. Each pulls out a small notebook. There is a tape recorder set up as part of the altar, and one large pillar candle. Rachel sits by the altar and removes a ball of red yarn from the basket. She passes it out to the rim, and the women unroll it hand to hand, laying the outline of a circle on the carpeting. They sit within the circle of their own creation, within rituals of their own designing.

Rachel lights the center candle. "I have a quote I want to read tonight from *The Feminine Face of God*. This is from a dream Sherry Ruth Anderson had that gave her permission to write the book. Since we are women taking up our own tasks and responsibility in this circle, I thought it would be appropriate. In the dream, Sherry is dancing with the prophets and patriarchs of Judaism, who pass on to her the spiritual responsibility for her life. They tell her she is taking up her service to the planet. *'And you are not the only one,'* they say. *'Many, many women are coming forward now to lead the way…. You will be teachers for each other. You will come together in circles and speak your truth to each other. The time has come for women to accept their spiritual responsibility for our planet.*

'Will you help us?' I ask the assembled patriarchs.

'We are your brothers,' they answer, and with that the entire room is flooded with an energy of indescribable kindness. I am absolutely confi-

*dent in this moment that they are our brothers. I feel their love without any
question. They say then, 'We have initiated you and we give you our whole-
hearted blessings. But we no longer know the way. Our ways do not work
anymore. You women must find a new way.'"* 3

There are thoughtful nods among the group and the women
fall silent for a few minutes. Then Rachel lights her personal candle,
slides to her place at the rim of the circle, and lights the candle of the
woman next to her. They light each other's tapers, one by one. They
pass their talking piece and check in. Now that the circle is gathered,
each woman knows that the others are listening with great attention.

The intent of a Tenfold circle is to support each woman in her
defined task, so check-in has to do with their progress. Margie says,
"My intent is to find work that satisfies my values. I have to do something more valuable with my time than sell lingerie in the mall. These
past three weeks I have interviewed two women business owners,
and contacted a magazine called *Business Ethics* to see what's happening out there. I've started my own logbook to find out everything I
can about how people create meaningful work. I call my logbook,
Women Who Do What They Really Want. I'll show it to you later during
council time. I'm going to need support so that I don't get involved in
this as a crafts project, and lose focus on what I'm really doing—trying to find a new way of life!" She passes the talking piece on.

Trudi says, "Let me see…this month has been so hectic. The
baby's been colicky, and I've been cranky. I think we cycle off each
other. My mother-in-law insists on coming over to help, and it's not a
help. I feel as though I've spent the month trying to redirect her energy rather than find my own. I need help from some of you who have
been mothering longer about what reasonable expectations are for
this time in my life, and how to set goals that I have some chance of
meeting."

Check-in, in this circle, takes about forty-five minutes. It lets
everyone know what agenda items are likely to come forward and
helps them design the central portion of the evening so that they
respond to the concerns. As part of their ritual, after check-in the
women break into dyads, scatter around the house in nooks and cran-
nies and take turns speaking monologues. Each woman has twenty
minutes of uninterrupted time to speak her mind to her listening

3. Sherry Ruth Anderson and Patricia Hopkins, *The Feminine Face of God* (New York: Bantam
Books, 1991).

partner. If she falls silent, fine; her partner is simply present and does not prompt, interfere or interpret. At the sound of Rachel's kitchen timer they switch and the second woman talks. They have done this at every meeting starting with the seminar weekend; it builds interconnection within the group.

In this Tenfold setting, women practice the three major forms of meeting. They open and close with *council*, using the talking piece in ways that allow for uninterrupted statements. They break into the informality of *discussion*, especially when a member has presented the progress of her defined goal and asked for group feedback. They often record these sessions, playing back the information to use as guidance in the time between meetings. And sometimes they fall spontaneously or purposefully into *meditation*—like the night Gail spoke of finding a lump and being diagnosed with breast cancer.

"I'm so scared," she whispered. "I'm only thirty-eight...this isn't supposed to be happening to me. I want to remain thoughtful, to hold onto my own power, not to suddenly let doctors make all the decisions without asking my deepest self what is the right course of action. I mean, I want to take the circle, and learn how to hold it inside myself—to apply PeerSpirit to the course of medical treatment. I'm going to need your help and support..." She was crying softly.

Cathy leaned forward, "Would you like some backing?" she asked. Gail nodded. Without breaking the attention of the circle, Cathy slipped behind Gail, her arms and legs making a basket, and Gail relaxed against her and continued speaking. "One out of seven women is way too many of us. I hope I live through this, and I hope I find circles of women who can help me, who are already smart and savvy and angry and fierce..." Coming into the circle, this was a concern that needed to be held first beyond words. When Gail was finished speaking, Cathy called for five minutes of silence and meditation. The women dropped into heartspace together, many of them gently holding their hands over their own hearts, emptying themselves of their own immediate reactions so that they could listen to the source from the center and offer back some piece of wisdom or energy.

The group intention is changed as the individual goals of the women change. A Tenfold circle is adaptable, and yet focused. Issues will arise over this event. They will choose to support Gail, and also support her in finding other circles of women who can walk through this with her. There will be some tough and tender calls about how to spend their time and energy together, how to maintain balance so that each woman in the circle continues to get her needs met. They will learn a lot about leadership, response-ability and reliance.

We live the circle moment by moment. We lay the structures in place at the beginning and keep reinforcing them in moments of ease so that they are there, available, part of our automatic response and skill, when we most need them, when we face the interpersonal challenges of circling.

CREATIVE RESPONSES TO DIFFICULTIES

Everyone in a circle is in a learning curve. We bring our various backgrounds, previous experiences, our vulnerabilities and blind sides, our confusion about what the principles mean and whether or not they really work, and enter the moment. And in the moment, we are from time to time out of balance—aggressive when it would be wiser to sit back and trust group synergy; passive when it would help if we'd lean forward and speak our truth.

When the circle is out of balance, we need to become *more* willing to be there, not less. The safety and structure we need is contained in the circle's practices and principles—if we follow them. *To the extent that everyone in a circle is capable and willing to rotate leadership, share responsibility, and rely on Spirit—the circle works.* No one has ever told me their circle is faltering because of the principles.

It wasn't a great surprise when Demetria and Doug got into conflict. The surprise was how they handled it.

Though tension had been accumulating for some time, there was a moment when it blew open. Demetria was making a point, talking piece in hand, and Doug cut her off, "I get it, Dee...let's stop talking about whether or not we can make the program work and get back on the machine."

"Dammit, Doug...I know you're impatient. I know you're frustrated with where we're stuck in R & D, but don't take it out on the circle, and especially, don't take it out on me—you've cut me off every time I've had the floor for the past week."

"No, I haven't!"

"You just did it again!" She thrust the talking wand toward him across the space of the circle. "The purpose of this thing is to give me the chance to finish my thoughts without having to worry about interruption...Lately I've come to *expect* interruption from you."

"You're just touchy."

"Stop!" said Mike. "If we're going to use the form, let's use the form. Either respect the stick, or put it down!" Demetria paused for a moment.

"I want to put it down," she said. "All of it—the wand, the anger, the way you and I go at each other, Doug." She took a deep breath. "I have a point I want to make here and I need to know if you're ready to listen. For my part, I want you to know I won't attack—and I want the same reassurance from you."

There are really only two kinds of conflict: conflicts with people who will step forward and work with us to resolve the issue, and conflicts with people who escalate the problem by doing everything possible to avoid resolving the issue. The actual issue is far less significant than the attitude toward problem-solving.

This is the moment when both Doug and Demetria have to decide what their attitude is toward conflict resolution within the team, and toward each other. This is the moment when the rest of the circle is called to pay attention to the underlying issue of frustration that they are all carrying to some degree. *What is the frustration really about?*

In a very real way, Demetria and Doug are symbols of the frustration loose in the middle of the project itself. Chen can look energized, Bill can look relaxed, Philip can remain detached, because Doug and Demetria are carrying the charge of their frustration for them. As such polarization develops and comes to a head, the rest of the circle needs to support those who have brought it forward. They need to redefine the issue in ways that release polarization and redirect the energy toward healthy creative tension and momentum.

"I need a break," says Doug, "and then I'm willing to spend five minutes on this. No more. I'm not interested in getting into some kind of big feeling session with you or anyone else...but for five minutes, I'll do everything I can. I'll listen. And I'll speak."

"If we're both willing to solve the problem, five minutes ought to be enough."

Maybe this or that circle isn't going to be the cozy home base we thought it would be. Does that mean it isn't functioning, or does that mean we need to look realistically at its intent and purpose? Maybe this or that circle is getting too personal, too close to the bone for our comfort. Do we wish it would just handle business and not ask us to speak or act from the heart?

When the project team regathers after break, Mike moves his chair over next to Doug's. "I don't want you to get the feeling that you're being cornered," he says. "So if it's okay with you, I'd like to sit next to you, to watch what's going to happen here from nearly the same angle." Doug looks surprised, but nods.

Demetria asks Carol for backing, and Carol sits next to her with her arm across the back of the chair, her palm resting gently between Demetria's shoulder blades.

Bill sits in the point halfway between them, Lindsay is across the circle from him. There is a sense of four points being held with attention around the perimeter of the group.

Every circle has its more and less dominant personalities. Every circle has people who are more and less aware of their behavior, or the impact of their behavior on the circle. Every circle has a matrix of affinities: people we respond to and resonate with more quickly, easily, or deeply than others. These affinities change over time and change all the time. Sometimes we feel closer or more distanced from one person or another.

Bill assumes leadership, "I'm going to hold the rim. Lindsay's going to help me. We're going to act like referees in a boxing match—though that isn't the image I want to convey. You guys aren't in opposite corners, you're both on our project team. One team. Doug, if you get hot under the collar, I'm going to say one word to you—'halt.' That's your signal to stop talking and think about what you're saying. If Demetria gets hot under the collar, Lindsay will do the same." She nods. "If five minutes doesn't do it, then I'm going to ask us to consider the next option. Each of you gets to make a statement and the other responds. Back and forth until it's clear what *you* need to do differently and what we need to do differently. Who wants to start?"

"I do," says Doug. "Ummm, I'm not comfortable with what everybody calls group process. I like to take charge. What makes my day is to get things done. To make a list and check off real items. It's a kind of sport with me—how much can I do? I'm on this team 'cause I love the idea of this new product. I want us to beat the competition to the marketplace. I want something I can be proud of. I want a feather in my career cap. When the brainstorming is rolling along, I love how we work together. But when we seem to be meandering, getting nit-picky, it drives me nuts. I just want get up and running again. So that's where I'm at."

"I know you like momentum, Doug," Demetria begins with a sigh, "so do I. I don't think you know this about me, but I used to ride bicycle marathons on weekends, and can still get out and do 30, 40 miles a day. I know about speed, about the exhilaration of getting uphill on my own strength and coasting down. I also like competition, to come in first. I don't have any differences with your goals. But what happens when I'm the focus of your impatience is that I wind up waiting for you to interrupt me instead of thinking out what will get us back on track. So I'm not giving my best thought to the project because it's divided between our goal and the way we're getting there. Does that make sense?"

"Yeah...But I'm just impatient. It's not about you. Why are you taking it personally?"

"Because your impatience seems to be expressed more openly when I'm talking. You don't always verbally interrupt me, but you look at your watch, flip through papers, your body language has you half in and halfway out the door. It may be just a chemistry thing between us, and I don't care if we ever spend time getting to the root of it—that's not the kind of colleagues we are. But what you're doing distracts me to the point where I'm not being the best member of this circle I could be. I'm being pulled away from making my best contributions."

"So, what do you want me to do?"

"When I'm the one holding the circle's attention, however that happens, I think you need to be more conscious of your impatience than you are when Mike or Chen are holding the circle's attention. They don't seem to bug you the way I do. If a little flag went up in your mind that said—*hold still, listen, support this woman and we'll be moving along faster*—that's all I need.

"Mind if I write that down?"

"Nope. Whatever works."

"Hold still. Listen. Support Demetria. She's a speed demon too, if I don't undermine her momentum. Got it."

Bill interjected, "Five minutes are up. Anything else?"

"Yeah," said Demetria. "This is great. Doug and I, well, we both probably feel really okay right now…and that's a little unnerving. Because this kind of project is frustrating. No way around it. So if we relax, somebody else is likely to get less relaxed. I want to put that out where we can think about it together, and to let you know I'm available for backing or bike racing if anybody in this circle needs to let off steam." And the circle went back to work.

The ability to create PeerSpirit is based on communicating without shame or blame, pulling out of polarity and seeing the underlying issues. We are building a new skill, exercising a different kind of energy and patience. If we aren't going to call for someone or something else to come in and act as the authority to fix our circle when it's not working to our satisfaction, then we are going to call on ourselves. We are going to trust that we—*all* of us in the circle—are willing to preserve the integrity of what we have created, to see our process through to completion.

When Carol met Bill in the parking lot after the meeting, she said. "Thank you. You were great in there this afternoon. I have to say, I was surprised. Where did you learn to do all that?"

"I don't know. I could see this big mess coming and I didn't want a fight anymore than Doug did—or Demetria either. But I couldn't figure out how to side-step it…"

"But how you handled it was genius…"

"Maybe wisdom works. Maybe it does come forward when we need it. It did for me last weekend…My son, BJ, got suspended from college for cheating on a chemistry exam. He didn't want to come home, of course, so he hid out at some friend's place, got picked up for underage DWI. Last Friday night, 10:00 PM, the cops call me and tell me to drive down to Iowa to get him.

"I was so scared for my boy. All the way down, I was huffing and puffing just to keep from crying in the car. When I saw him, I got into rage and practically hit the kid. Paid his bond, signed a bunch of papers, and started driving home in stony silence. About two in the morning my whole relationship with my own dad kept flashing before my eyes. I was desperate to break the pattern.

"So I pulled off the road to a resort in the woods, woke up the owners and rented a cabin, called my wife and said we wouldn't be home for awhile, and BJ and I held council. I mean, I called out the stops—told BJ everything I'd ever thought about my dad and what I thought went wrong between us, and gave him the chance to say the same about me. We passed a talking stick back and forth between us until that sucker was hot. No interrupting, no justifications. Then I drove BJ back to school, helped him get reinstated, and got back to town midnight Sunday.

"I figure if the circle can do that for BJ and me, Doug and Demetria were a piece of cake. Have a good evening—see you tomorrow." He walked to his car leaving Carol standing in amazement.

The greatest trust is built when we go through the bumpy, scary, risky and vulnerable aspects of circling. We don't know what we're made of until a circle has faced a problem, resolved a conflict, gotten several members through a crisis. Actual conflict resolution, unpracticed as it is, may be nerve racking as we develop confidence and learn to say our truth, but after a while, the empowerment is positively exhilarating.

Pre-conflict bonding is sweet, but not as potent as post-conflict bonding. The circle that has lost its innocence and come through crisis with respect for each other and the process is a circle to be reckoned with!

PROTECTING OURSELVES AND THE CIRCLE

There may come a time in a circle when we realize that we must take strong, spirit-centered action to protect ourselves, the task we have chosen, or the integrity of the circle itself.

Years ago, when I first attended a small Al-Anon group near my house, I began finding my way in the Twelve Step structure. Six weeks into my involvement, a long-time member of the group who'd been away on vacation returned to the circle. I'll call him "Tom." Everybody seemed to know Tom and welcomed him back, cordially, but not effusively. In this meeting, after the presenter had talked about the Step for the evening, people began going around the circle making comments. I noticed—in a brief flash of intuition which I then ignored—"Gee, people are staying on the surface. This Step must really present a challenge...."

This is trouble signal #1: *Safety has left the circle and people stop being vulnerable.* People try to avoid emotional risk or exposure. Even though the form of sharing may remain intact and people sound like they're saying something significant, they aren't really revealing anything. In this type of verbal camouflage, things appear the same but don't feel the same. It's like being in a grief group and talking about our gerbil's death instead of our mother's. We're all acquainted with this. When I catch myself using this technique, I call it "throw the dog a bone..."

When it was his turn, Tom spoke about the Step and expressed firm opinions about several unrelated topics—politics, women's issues, the specifics don't matter. He presented a verbal challenge: someone respond to this. Since he was a stranger to me, I had no reason to fear or accommodate him, and when it was my turn I assumed I could comment on his thoughts and engage him in friendly dialogue. WHAM! I got verbally slammed down so fast and hard I didn't know what had happened for a minute.

This is signal #2: *Anyone crossing the transaction or challenging the situation is immediately intimidated.* The show of force is excessive—much greater than is appropriate or even necessary. Its purpose is simply to exhibit power.

I am not talking about being interrupted. I am not talking about someone whose natural personality is a little overbearing. I am talking about *the intent to control,* to control completely. I am talking about *the intent to create fear,* to establish dominance. People react to this kind of intimidation in different ways: denial, passivity, rationalization, bargaining, and anything they can think of to smooth over the surface.

This is signal #3: *No one is being themselves anymore; everyone has gone into placating behavior.* I was suddenly as busy as everyone else making nano-second decisions about how to get this fellow out of my face.

The energy feels life-threatening because it is so much more forceful than is socially expected, as though we have reached out to touch something we assumed was safe and it suddenly turns on us. Our instinctive reaction is to duck for cover in whatever ways we can, to check ourselves out. Am I hurt? Bleeding anywhere except from the psyche? At this moment, the circle is shattered. The interconnections that bind us together are gone. Everyone is isolated in their adaptive behavior and withdrawal, incapable of unifying to make a thoughtful response or take any kind of action.

This is signal #4: *People retreat from everyone in the circle, not only from the one carrying the negative charge.* People go into spontaneous shock and fear. Up until that moment, to each of us, circle energy had been reliable. Suddenly it's gone. It's as though we were sitting on a chair that dematerialized out from under us, dropping us onto the hard, cold floor.

This ever-present threat gets skirted around by compliant group members while one person controls the circle like a puppeteer. In circles which are dominated by the threat of explosion, incomplete confrontations twist and turn in the unspoken energies of group process and create disorder in their wake.

This is signal #5: *The circle feels charged with underlying energies which cannot be explained by what's occurring on the social level.* We are always waiting for the other shoe to drop, and may not even know why. The night Tom jumped down my throat, I felt abandoned as every one else in the circle scuttled for cover and left me alone to see if I would take him on. They had known what was coming, had been skidding around on the social surface waiting to see what would happen to me.

This sudden sense of being abandoned is signal #6: *The negative energy is looking for its positive pole, and the group is looking for a lightning rod.* We may feel drawn toward confrontation by this energetic attraction, even though on a rational level confrontation is the last thing we want. We may feel compelled to dissipate the energy or watch another person in the circle suddenly click into the magnetism. When someone dangerous enters the circle, *other* people get weird and begin doing strange things that draw attention away from the person who is really holding the negative charge.

That night, I looked around and decided, "Nope, this is not a circle where I'm going to take my stand. I don't know these people very well, they don't know me, and this guy has been here a long time. Vacation's over and they are reconfiguring into how they behave when Tom's in attendance. I think I'll go find myself another group...." I never went back to say goodbye; I couldn't have explained my real reasons for leaving.

I can think of half a dozen moments in recent years, besides this example, when I have been present at such a shattering. I can think of a dozen more moments when the shattering was residing within a group, waiting to happen. If the explosion is implied but has not yet happened, we find ourselves immersed in constantly changing adaptive behaviors. This is the real mind-bender. Everyone is in their unconscious material and no one is able to report accurately why they are behaving the way they are, or what is happening in the circle. If we do not feel that we can be empowered, that we can live the three principles in this setting, this is a circle in trouble and we need to decide what we're going to do.

If someone is intent on destroying peer spirit within a circle, either the circle will disband, or the majority of members will work together to ask that person to leave. Instances where this is necessary are rare, but extremely unsettling. I have been in circles which have regathered after successfully freeing themselves of a highly disruptive member and have continued with deeper bonding and productivity as a result of their learning. I have left circles which could not deal with disruption and gone on to find safe space.

It is essential to remember that the sacred is still present and available for us to call upon, the contracts and guidelines are still binding, the covenants are still holding. When asking someone to leave, the contracts act as a code of ethics and behavior which determine everyone's participation in the circle. If someone is not able to contribute to the circle within the parameters of the contracts and covenants of the group, they are not maintaining circle purpose. To address the need for someone to leave based on contracts allows circle members to avoid personality struggles.

BECOMING PEERSPIRIT

There are probably thousands of circles currently meeting which are ready to adopt PeerSpirit guidelines and principles. In fact, many of these circles have already been using PeerSpirit skills, whether or not they have articulated them in the same language.

There are also thousands of circles which have been meeting with facilitation and now face the possibility of becoming peer-based groups. This is a transition which requires readiness, thought, and discussion. For therapy or counseling groups, for religious or spiritual study or academic classes, the transition from facilitated guidance to peer leadership may not be possible or appropriate. In other situations, a circle may develop the resilience and confidence to switch to peer leadership.

Demetria was facing this in her women's spirituality group. "Our rituals are well established and comfortable," she said, "a blend of earth-cherishing traditions as we ourselves are a blend of women." Spirituality groups are one of the most popular forms of circling emerging in western culture as women, men, or women and men together gather to celebrate some kind of renewal. They are intuitively taking the circle beyond psychology, business, recovery and self-help.

But Demetria felt troubled. "I wanted this group so badly. When I started it, I sort of insisted it come into being and hold together, then I mothered it through its growing pains. Though we call ourselves a peer circle, I feel the other women rely on me in ways I don't see the Project Team doing. Now that I'm clearer about peer spirit, I'm not as comfortable with my role in the Moon Circle as I used to be. I've been overly responsible and the circle hasn't had to assume peer leadership. The imbalance is subtle, is going to be hard to explain. Now that I want to change, I don't know if the circle is ready for me to change."

In the summer of 1991, I taught writing to a group that simply wouldn't stop meeting. The class, originally held at Split Rock Arts Program in Duluth, reconvened in late October. We housed ourselves in a retreat center, everybody read, and group commitment solidified. We voted to meet again the following spring. And so it went along, meeting about every six months with me finding the space, organizing meal prep and facilitating critique. The group paid for my time and leadership, but as I got busier and traveled more often, there came a time when I needed to move on. I suggested they consider what kinds of responsibility they were willing to take for holding this circle themselves—without my calling it.

When a group is ready to make the transition from facilitation to peer leadership, the facilitator needs to get out of the way and let the circle evolve or disband. Facilitation may be formal, as my role was, where I remained the defined writing teacher, or informal, such as Demetria's role as the reliable organizer.

It took two meetings for the Split Rock writing group to make the transition. First, I wrote a bridging letter reminding people of this change in structure. The letter suggested that we intentionally create a circle at the beginning and the end of the weekend, that we acknowledge and hold sacred space, that we use a talking stick form of council, that we open, read, and close with form and ritual.

In late May, people drove in from three states to meet at Jan's house in the Minnesota northwoods. She had done all the site arranging—including sending her husband on a fishing trip for the weekend—gotten a talking stick and was acting as the caller. I brought my basket and we created a sacred center. With their accumulated experience, sense of community, and a few simple circle structures in place, the group easily took over and began to run itself. They rotated the talking stick while responding to each other's work: the shyer ones now emboldened and the more talkative ones waiting their turns. They used consensus to set future dates and direction. My job was over.

The Split Rock writing group was extremely fortunate. It lived through a period with only its original contracts in place for structure and a loosely-defined intention to share their writings. Several people left, one person returned. In almost every ongoing group, there will be some people who drop away for their own reasons. The circle may want to check out what's happening, to invite return if that seems appropriate and then to respect a person's withdrawal.

What the Split Rock group has now is a solid core of individuals who befriend each other and care for each other's written words, and who are committed enough to set aside two weekends a year and drive for hours to the next location. They have their own basket/altar. They have a logbook of collected writings and mailings that go out after each meeting. And they have a tremendous sense of having come into their own power, of having moved from a traditional student/teacher model to a PeerSpirit circle.

In Demetria's group the issue is more ambiguous because she has not been acknowledged as leader, she has simply stepped in and acted as a leader in ways that undermined the development of peer leadership. Such imbalance is not intentional in many circles—it just happens. At some point there is a vacuum in how leadership is emerging, or how people understand sharing responsibility and patterns get set. Somebody wants to make sure something happens, so they do it themselves. Pretty soon others are letting them do it, and the imbalance is set in place.

We are all busy people. If one person volunteers to do all the calling or meeting arrangements, we are most likely relieved, not threatened. To rebalance a group where patterns have been set, we simply need to start doing those things which we have been letting someone else do. And the supportive blessing of PeerSpirit is that this structure allows us to rebalance without blaming or shaming anyone in the circle. Instead of saying, "I don't want Miriam to do the phoning anymore..." or "I don't like how Harry is handling X," we may refer to the three principles and call for the reemergence of rotating leadership and shared responsibility.

Demetria, for all her nervousness, found it fairly easy to shift out of her leadership role, as long as she didn't get into self-recrimination or anger. "It's come to my attention," she said one night in circle, with a bashful grin, "that I've been doing a lot of managing of this circle, and I don't need to do this anymore. I'd like to pull back my willingness to carry some of the details, and see who else would like to help. Not just one person picking up what I was doing, but several of us, working together."

Sharon laughed, "We've been wondering when you were going to get tired of being the Moon mother. Sure we'll take over...you just have to practice relaxing."

KNOWING WHEN AND HOW TO LET A CIRCLE GO

Sometimes it's easy to know when a circle is ending. If the task has been focused, it's accomplishment releases the group. The Project Team will have no trouble knowing when the project is over, though it may have trouble acknowledging grief and celebration in a business setting. In a group with a highly focused task, either the circle renegotiates to take on some new task, or we let the circle dissolve and reconfigure in some other way in our lives. But when the focus is ongoing—like my writing group, the Split Rock group, the Moon circle, the peer group, it's harder to tell what's ending, when it's ending, and how it needs to end.

Something is ending when its energy dwindles. This is true about living things, and true in the life cycle of the circle. When a circle is highly-functioning, it is charged with energy; it elicits participation, loyalty, priority. When a circle accomplishes its goal, it reaches a high point of energy, excitement, fulfillment. And then that energy falls away, either quickly or slowly. At this point, the circle may take up a new task, or it enters the phase of letting itself go. Sometimes we put off this point because it seems disloyal, no one else is bringing it up, or we don't want to enter our own grief. But if we suddenly stop regarding a circle as a priority, if we make up excuses for not attending, if the attendance is falling off meeting by meeting, if people seem aimless and the center isn't holding, it's time to bring up the issue of letting go.

For one decade in Minnesota, I was part of a writer's group that was central in my life. We developed close friendships. In the days when we all lived near each other and were working on extensive projects, we met every four or five weeks, read to each other and supported the solitary nature of creative process. Over the years many things changed—one member moved out of town, two others began traveling or living elsewhere for significant chunks of the year. We stayed in each other's lives, even when our only group meeting became an annual retreat for the four remaining members. We never called ourselves a circle, never formalized our contracts and covenants. There were times this all worked out synchronistically and times when expectations were not clearly articulated. I love these women and wish we had had the circle's structure more clearly in mind as the basis among us.

I think of us when I think about letting go. Our lack of clarity was typical of many small circles. We didn't know how to tell each other the circle was finished. We didn't know how to help our friendships survive and admit the circle was over. What we missed was the chance to grieve, and also to celebrate. We missed the chance to tell each other how important the circle had been, to look each other in the eyes and drop into heart space. Perhaps this was too scary. We hadn't been intentional, the synergy just worked. Perhaps we didn't want to jinx our connection after all these years by talking about it.

Letting go is a time when being comfortable with ritual helps. Ritual provides a framework for expressing closure and a container for emotions. Through the symbolism inherent in ritual, we infuse ordinary actions with spiritual presence and honor the mystery of the circle. In PeerSpirit circling, ritual is part of the weave that helps us sustain the circle meeting by meeting, so using ritual to create closure will not seem strange. And since there have been exit-points and discussion about commitment along the way, the idea of leaving is not taboo. Leave-taking doesn't need to be elaborate or dramatic, but simply acknowledged so that everyone knows when the circle is over.

Even in a business or academic setting some form of closure is extremely helpful. We need to be reminded of the boundaries again, that there is a difference between being in circle and ordinary levels of attention. We need to let go of our expectations of each other that have grown up in the intimacy of the circle, and resume a more casual social connection. One simple ritual is to go around the rim and invite each person to recite: *Here's what I take with me from this circle...Here's what I leave behind for the center to hold....*Circles often design a ritual or ceremony for ending. The more significant and bonded the circle has become, the more this ritual of ending is needed.

Circle work necessitates that we move in and out of many circles. We need to be intensely present in the life of whatever circle we sit in, and we need to be able to release ourselves from that energy, and move on. The only way we can do this is to open our hearts, minds, and bodies to the experience of the moment, knowing full well that we will grieve, knowing full well that we have reason to celebrate. We are able to say, with honor, "I have loved this. I have fully participated. I have given and received all I could. Now I release it."

There is a Navajo prayer which ends with the phrase, "It is finished in beauty." This is my prayer for the circles I'm in: that we may finish in beauty, finish with a sense of fullness over what we have shared, and how we have grown to love and respect each other in the process. We may love the circle, and leave it knowing there is another circle coming.

Great ideas, it has been said, come into the world as gently as doves.
Perhaps then, if we listen attentively, we can hear,
amid the uproar of empires and nations,
a faint flutter of wings, the gentle stirring of life and hope.
Some will say that this hope lies in a nation;
others, in a (person).
I believe, rather,
that it is awakened and nourished by millions of solitary individuals
whose deeds and works every day
negate frontiers and the crudest implications of history.

Albert Camus

CHAPTER EIGHT

Citizen of the Circle

When I was sixteen, President Kennedy appeared on television one day in October and announced that he was thinking about ending the world. Well, that's not what he said, but that was the risk he was taking. He had laid down an ultimatum to Nikita Kruschev, then President of the Soviet Union: Kruschev would withdraw his missile bases and armaments from Cuba or the United States was prepared to go to war—nuclear war. I remember coming home from high school and watching this man who was my hero decide on my behalf whether or not this was a good gamble. My friends and I, all of us raised on the black and white heroics of World War II movies, were surrounded by high drama. Boys and girls met by their lockers, talked about evacuation routes and whether we'd have time to reunite with our families. If we were going into our own version of *Lord of the Flies,* we wanted to be among friends. We made lists of who could be on our bus out of life as we'd known it. Some of my friends' parents were gloating over the bomb shelters they had constructed; others were filling their basements with canned goods and bottled water. People put blankets in their car trunks and talked about driving west into the Minnesota countryside where they planned to seek out second cousins who still lived on farms in Annandale or Wilmar and see if they could bunk together for a while.

I took a small metal filing box and put in it my journal, a copy of the recent newspapers, a few family photographs, a copy of LIFE magazine, *National Geographic*, and *The Diary of Anne Frank*, and buried the box under a marked tree out in the woods.

Kruschev backed down. Kennedy was a hero. We lived. I dug up the box, hid my adolescent embarrassment, found a date for the Sadie Hawkins Day dance and wrote editorials for the Wayzata High School newspaper.

That tree is gone now, and so are the woods. This early refuge of mine is covered by a townhouse development—pavement and small saplings and rows of gray framed buildings, numbered so you can find your way into the right cubicle. I went out there not long ago, walked around in the fragments of my history. And when I came out of the gully where my woods had stood, I had unburied something that had been waiting for me all these years: outrage that *any-one* could believe s/he had the right to decide for me on such destruction.

RECLAIMING OUR CITIZENSHIP

Looking back at this time, our world view seemed simple and clear: there were good guys and bad guys and we knew who we were. Our way of life was unquestionably the shining example for the modern world. But the seeds of our current dilemma were already planted. Collectively we relaxed in surety and security, until new words that were not so clear and simple began penetrating our ease: civil rights, race relations, ecology, pollution, military-industrial complex, counterculture.

Many of us have not been active citizens in a very long time. It is hard to overcome our lethargy. It is hard to overcome our isolation, to clear our minds from bombardment. We are pounded at by the intrusion of media and marketing. Sometimes, even when the radio and television are off, when I am sitting alone in my apartment and the night is as quiet as life in the city provides, it seems I can still feel the vibrations of the day past and the day coming, a sense that my culture is never at rest. Never quite restful. The "news" is rolling relentlessly on, and I don't really know how to respond. What a predicament we find ourselves in.

Most of the time we don't miss our citizenship because we are told that we have it. The word is used commonly, without requirement. The President appears on television and addresses us as "fellow (sic) citizens"—anyone tuned in is included. There is no mention of the need to participate, to think with our leaders about the issues of the age. The word citizen has become honorific, but the concept of citizenship still comes with implied duties, rights and privileges. Citizenship is an activity.

Citizenship in the circle calls us into the round where life is occurring, live, not on stage. The circle shocks us into presence, into paying attention.

We cannot sleep through a circle gathering, too much is going on. The atmosphere is charged with interaction; people are *doing* something and they expect our participation. They want our opinion. They expect our reaction, our input, our willingness to share in tasks and responsibilities. The vibrancy of the circle is like jumping into cold water: we come up sputtering. We come up awake. This is the circle. This isn't a TV show. This isn't a movie. The people around us are real. We are real. There are contracts and covenants at work. The rituals of council are occuring around us. There is dynamic intention. Someone is passing us the talking piece. They want to know what *we* think, what *our* ideas are, how *we* would like to contribute. This creative attention—the pressure to know our own minds, to contribute our thoughts and talents to the circle—is the core act of citizenship.

In the circle, citizen participation is focused around specific and interlinked tasks, issues, concerns and programs. The circle remains active and people are involved until the problem has been effectively addressed and task is accomplished. Then, participating citizens celebrate the accomplishment, replenish themselves, and prepare to address the next task. The power belongs to the act of participation. There are no political "bosses," authority rests in the process. Leadership rotates, responsibility is shared, and even though politics is considered a particularly secular setting with the separation of church and state, our reliance is still on Spirit—not on religion or dogmatism—just spirit, an openness to the idea that there is a presence within the group which is not ego-based.

In the Women and the Planet seminars Ann and I co-lead, one of the exercises during lunch is to sit with a partner, draw an imagined three foot perimeter around our space, and begin noting and discussing the environmental, political, economic, social, gender, class, and racial issues within this perimeter.

- •What food are we eating?
     Where did it grow?
     How was it raised and harvested? By whom?
     What were the growing conditions of the soil?
     Were chemicals and pesticides used on it? How do we
         know?
     How has it been transported and preserved and pre
         pared?
     What are the living conditions of the people who have
         brought us this food?
- •What clothes are we wearing? Where is the fabric from?
- •Where did this table come from?
- •How was this building constructed?
- •Whose land was this? What has happened to the indigenous
     people of this land?
- •What impact does our being here have on the land?

The questions are endless, and the exercise causes us to realize how little we know about the structures used to hold our lifestyle system in place. How little we know of the world.

In the circle, the organizational structure of citizenship is molecular: a circle of specific task is connected to another circle with similar task, and these two circles connect to another and another. I remember drawing this model, not in political science courses, not in history, but in chemistry: H_2O, $NaCL$, CO_2, H_2O_2—each molecule carefully constructed, the combining elements consisting of a circle connected with rods. A molecule is a stable form, strong and enduring, bound by energy. This is exactly how I would describe my experience of the circle.

Stability in combination is important. When we swallow a mouthful of cool, clear H_2O, we are not in danger that it is going to come apart. If a molecule is a stable enough structure to support the base elements of the universe, perhaps it is a stable enough structure to support the reorganization of our societies to better fit in the universe. Connection by connection, circle by circle.

To bring the circle into our culture allows us to combine the strengths of two great forms, not to overthrow the hierarchy, but to introduce circle consciousness into its midst and see how the molecules interact. This is another form of chemistry, a great experiment of citizenship that brings us into social relationship so that we may think more clearly, see what is going on, and discover what we want to do about it.

CITIZENS OF THE CIRCLE

There is a story about a frog in boiling water that has become a metaphor for the crisis we are in at the turning of this millennium. The story goes that if you heat up a beaker of water until it is quite hot and then throw a frog into it, the frog will register the heat and jump out. If you put a frog in cool water and slowly, slowly turn up the heat, the frog keeps attempting to adjust, and by the time it should be leaping to freedom in alarm, it is too lethargic and damaged to do so.[4]

If the circle were in place and in use in our society, our lives would be very different. In the circle, we would experience empowerment as a regular part of daily life. The challenge of circle citizenship is to put the circle in place, to introduce and practice Third Culture because we choose to do so, rather than waiting for crisis to force us to change models.

In big black letters on the metal cylinder of the fire extinguisher in my kitchen it says: "Read and review operational instructions on a periodic basis." The manufacturers know that if I come around the corner and find the wastebasket smoldering, it's not a good time to read the small print. The same is true for the circle. When we come around the corner of the twenty-first century and find ourselves in a natural disaster, a political crisis, an exploding community—it's not a good time to practice calling the first circle. We need skills in place and confidence in the circle's stamina and stability.

It's hard to think conceptually in times of crisis, though we may be very good at coming up with immediate coping responses. If the circle is to be included as a coping response, we need to practice

---

4. As they say on the television commercials, "Do not try this experiment at home." Frogs, one of the planet's most adaptable and various creatures, found on great areas of the globe, are mysteriously dwindling in number. Scientists cannot explain this phenomenon, though they link it to the global pollution problems.

it, develop skills and confidence, so that when we find ourselves in crisis we can call the circle and participate in councils which help resolve the problem.

It's pretty painful to consider the state the world is in. We understand that the path we are on leads to destruction. The water is heating up. I believe there are great numbers of us who are searching for ways to interact, to intercept, to impact the processes of destruction, and to redirect ourselves into sustainable life.

We want to help. We want to learn how to do something besides watching the world deteriorate on television. We are ready to practice effective citizenship. We remember how to pull together, how to work in circular fashion—neighbor to neighbor. The impulse to reach out is alive behind our lethargy. There is a level of crisis and challenge that brings out the best in most of us. It feels good to get involved when we have the support and protection we need to take action.

Where did it begin, this impulse to flee into our fear, our isolation? To fight each other, to tear away at whatever the other one has, to see each other as a threat instead of as "like kind?" Fight or flight is a polarity. It creates an us/them in the world, a light/darkness, victim/persecutor, winner/loser.

Polarity cannot live in the circle. Us/them becomes simply "us." In cleaving to the power of the circle, we cannot be pulled out, singled out. We are only really vulnerable when we are alone. When we believe in our aloneness. The Third Culture presents us with a third option beyond fight or flight: hang together, talk things through, step forward, regroup, stand united. The circle cannot be destroyed.

At the Mabel Dodge House in Taos, the staff had asked a patron to leave for his disruptive behavior. The man became so agitated and angry that he trashed his quarters in the building and broke the key in the lock. While George tried to climb in the window to gain access to the room and assess the damage, the man came through the lobby. I saw Susan follow him into the dark courtyard. "Don't go out there alone," I said. "What if he becomes violent?" And I went with her. Stood with her. Soon Joannah realized what was happening and came out too. We took the brunt of his verbal rage and got his license plate number, but we needed several more people to stand and hold the rim so he wouldn't feel it was safe to attack. We needed time to stand in circle, to see if he would calm down. We needed one among us to approach his young silent wife and say simply, "You don't have to live this way...come into the circle."

It takes many repetitions to understand the potential of a circle in moments like this. Once we experience the depth of vulnerability that our aloneness creates, we may prepare to offer each other the protection a circle affords. We may practice our fire drills. If we don't go into the polarity, if we don't contract into fear, if we have enough people around us, the circle is available. What if so many people had experience in PeerSpirit circles that any one of us could stand up in a crowd and call for a circle and people would come, knowing what to do? People would make sacred center, sit down in council, and rise up with intention. Some days I think this is our only hope....

The following stories are real examples of circular, molecular citizenship — of what our hope already looks like in schools, corporations, neighborhoods, governments, and social action groups.

Tribes: The Circle at School

In 1978, parent and educator Jeanne Gibbs, concerned about the impact of high mobility on so many of California's school-age children, designed a program for classroom use called "Tribes."[5] In the classroom, a tribe is a group of five or six children who work together throughout the day for the entire school year. They are seated in circles. The tribal circle becomes their home within the larger circle of the class. The purpose of the tribe is to support each child in developing relatedness, respect and responsibility. Tribe groups foster a high achievement level and a productive learning environment as they are based on long-term relationship, support and self-esteem. Teachers stay out of the circle except when they are absolutely needed to redirect study efforts or coach conflict resolution skills. Tribes function with four basic contracts:

- Attentive listening
- No put-downs
- Right to pass
- Confidentiality

5. Jeanne Gibbs, *Tribes: A Process for Social Development and Cooperative Learning* (Santa Rosa, CA: Center Source Publications, 1987). Copies may be ordered from the publisher at: 305 Tesconi Circle, Santa Rosa, CA 95401.

Gibbs's educational philosophy is practical and sound. In her book, *Tribes*, she describes the tribal community created through the use of her system:

>   Imagine for a moment that you have been invited to visit a tribal classroom. Arriving just before class begins, you are greeted by the teacher. As the children enter the classroom you notice that the voices and movement are different from many other classrooms... there is no pushing and shoving. You hear no "put-downs." The teacher raises her hand, and one by one as children notice her gesture they stop talking and raise their hands until the entire class is quiet. The teacher greets the class warmly and introduces you. There is a murmur of excitement about the presence of a stranger, but the teacher continues. "How is everyone feeling this morning? Let's all gather in our community circle." The class rearranges itself, sitting in a large circle. Two students urge you also to sit on a small chair in the circle. "To build our community inclusion this morning, I suggest that we go around the circle and say something good that may have happened for each of us lately. Be brief so everybody has a turn. Let's listen attentively to each other and remember you have the "right to pass" if you do not care to share this morning. One by one the children begin to speak:
>
>   "My dad played catch with me last night for a real long time."
>
>   "Colin is coming to my house after school today."
>
>   "Our tribe invented a great new game."
>
>   "My puppy isn't sick anymore."
>
>   "I brought some bamboo today for our tribe's project."
>
>   A few said they would like to "pass"... no one pressured them to participate. Everyone was listening attentively. The teacher nodded or made statements of affirmation; she often thanked people for sharing. Panic! It was your turn. You felt warm inside... and said, "I'm just so glad to be here. I feel a part of your community already."[6]

---

6. Ibid., p. 35.

Using group development theory, Gibbs believes that people must first feel included in the circle before the circle can function. Once inclusion has been established, each member is ready to test their ability to influence the circle. They are ready to take initiative, make suggestions, offer ideas, design and contribute to goals. As a result of their success working together, these young people develop respect and affection for each other. Students in Tribes have their contributions and feelings acknowledged throughout the process: they feel safe, they feel loyal, they feel loved and loving. In thousands of classrooms, the tribal community is preparing children to become adult citizens of the circle.

From her small, sunny office in Sausalito, California, Jeanne Gibbs' educational circles reach out across the continent. Excited teachers have become trained facilitators and introduced school systems to the program. Jeanne herself is a gentle, approachable sixty-year-old whose greatest satisfaction still comes from direct interaction with the children. On the day we met, a group of fifth graders had just been holding council with her. The group was visiting from a nearby school where the early elementary grades all used Tribes. These children had spent four years in circles of learning and empowerment. Entering fifth grade, they found themselves in classrooms working with teachers who didn't use Tribes. They came to visit Jeanne to talk over their view of her program, and to brainstorm. Twenty brightly-dressed children in the wonderful multi-cultural hues of a California classroom, and white-haired Jeanne sitting with them, eating pizza and passing the talking stick while they showed their teachers the power of the circle and advocated fervently for their right to stay in tribes.

Jo's Theater: The circle in the Arts

My friend, Jo Spiller, a producer and actress working in community theater, decided to produce a play called "Juvie"[7] about juvenile delinquents. The piece consists mostly of monologues delivered as each young character faces the court and sentencing. In Bryan, Texas, Spiller had a cast of Caucasian teenagers, none of whom had ever been in any kind of real trouble with the law or anyone else. They wanted the experience of acting, but their articulation of these

7. Author Jerome McDonough.

characters was stilted and unconvincing. Spiller called the warden at the county women's prison and arranged for a volunteer group of inmates to coach the students. She put them all in a circle and dove into the process. Later she wrote me a letter sharing the story:

> I brought fifteen teenagers and four prison inmates together for this circle. The kids came from middle-class America; the women came from jail. The empty space in the center was filled with things that were invisible: energy, memory, pain, empathy, truth. Together, in this small tucked-away town in Texas, we were producing a play about teens awaiting trial in a juvenile detention center. After an hour of gut-level sharing from the inmates and tentative questioning from the teens, I could feel something beginning to happen. A litany of silent questions raced through my mind: Are the conditions right? Do people feel safe? Are they shifting their judgments of themselves and each other? Are they feeling more related? Less separate?
>
> I had to trust the process. I had to trust my own small experience of the circle and believe in the magic it offered. I was feeling high risk. Looking at the center I proclaimed, "the circle is closed." And then added, "I wonder what it's like to be in a gang?" I looked at one of the inmates, then pointed to one of the kids. "Her character is named June and she's a gang leader. Would you play that you are a rival member and talk to her?"
>
> The dark-skinned prisoner lowered her head as she stood, unfolding her long, slim body. An ugly leer came over her mouth. With one hand on her hip, she fired words across the circle toward "June"—mean words, harsh words, violent words. Teenaged Sarah recoiled in her chair. The rim of the circle shimmered from the blows. A few of the kids started to cry, then Tommy's voice rose out of the shock, "Come on, Sarah, be June. You know what it's like. You know HER. She can't talk to you that way." His words were urgent, it would be his turn next to find character. Then another boy joined in. "You're June now. Come on girl. You're tough. You're the leader.... you've been to jail. Don't let her say that!"

Inmate #428 stood defiantly in front of her chair, arms folded and began to laugh, a hard, sadistic laugh. "You little punk," she told June, "You're nobody. You don't have it together!"

Without further coaching Sarah pulled off her glasses and went into character. The frozen teenager became a street-wise young woman. She stood up and shot back, "You talk to me that way, I swear I'll cut you from ear to ear, now you got that straight? Get out of my face you earth-eating little chicken and sit down and shut the hell up!" The inmate started to speak, but June cut her off, "You shut up NOW, or I'll personally make sure your every day on earth is living hell. Sit down!"

The black woman sat down, sucking on her teeth and shaking her head. When she lowered her face, I saw that she was smiling. "Good, good," I said. Sarah began to cry, to apologize. Her acting partner strode to the center of the circle, took the youngster in her arms and both of them wept.

A shy fifteen-year-old said, "You all aren't like anything I expected. I mean, you're just people, like us."

Inmate #428 stepped forward and took the girl's hands. "Thank you," she said, "My name is Janice." There were sighs of relief. We worked for three hours. No one knew how to say thank you or goodbye. We met again throughout production.

This show received the highest praises of any production in years. One reviewer said it ought to be required viewing by every citizen in Brazos County. Jo Spiller was hired to go into the prison and help the women produce a play telling their real stories. She is working in the circle.

Redesigning IDS: The circle in corporations

In the early 1990s, the financial planning arm of American Express, a large corporation then known as IDS, called together a group of thirty-one employees from all strata of the organization and gave them the task of redesigning the company. Their charge was to create a company that lived the mission statement: "To help people meet their financial objectives thoughtfully and prudently through financial planning." The group was to design for four outcomes:

1. to create 100% customer satisfaction
2. to reduce turnover among financial planners
3. to be highly respected in the financial services industry
4. to continue to be profitable.

Beyond that, the Design Team, as it was called, had carte blanche power. How this new company should look, what its management structures needed to be, how living the mission statement would change the ways people spent time at work, were all within the scope of their attention. A former college classmate, Charlaine Tolkien, was a member of this team. I called her from time to time to see how it was developing. It was developing into a circle.

At first, we didn't know how to make the meetings effective. Out of a company with 1300 people, thirty-one seemed a small percentage, but it was really too big to work effectively as a group. Yet we wanted to stay together. We were meeting in rows, raising our hands to speak. Cliques and sub-groups were beginning to form and it was affecting the trust on the team. You could tell there was a growing unwillingness to be vulnerable, to say what we thought, and this was conflicting with the pressure of accountability.

A consultant came in and worked with us. She suggested we divide into teams, though the accountability for every team's work would remain the responsibility of the whole group. She rearranged the room too, took the tables away and put the group into a circle: nothing between us, all of us facing each other. This one thing—the simple rearrangement of our seating space—broke open the dynamics of the group and let us really begin to function. People began to talk about feelings and vision.

"The biggest breakthrough in the group," she said, "was that every possible piece of information was shared in the team equally. And we used this information to empower ourselves. We all saw it all, so we could come to our planning meetings with equal vision. And when the vision was equal, the strata of job we came from within the organization mattered less and less. We had equal accountability for the success of the project. No one would come out of that team able to say, 'Well, that's not my piece...' Understanding our mutual accountability created entirely different behavior toward our commitment, our ownership of the work, our willingness to stand behind our recommendations. If one person felt unable to support a recommendation, it couldn't go forward until consensus was reached.

I learned that people are willing to take great risk, as long as we are empowered to do so, and have been given the tools and information to create sustainable change. We presented this plan to the company in February 1993. Within months, hundreds of people were involved in understanding the design and taking charge of how to implement it throughout the company. Project '94 is the big visible change, but the momentum throughout the company continues to create more and more team effort.

What happened to me is that having an experience where I was totally accountable to myself, my team, my work has made the idea of having a 'boss' irrelevant. I see how the hierarchical way we usually manage companies serves to limit people's potential, rather than giving them the energy to put into the work itself. I'm a misfit now. I don't know how to behave in a hierarchical structure and I'm waiting for the design to get implemented to be able to work in the environment we created on paper. I talk to others on the team and they are all questioning too. Where do we fit? Now what do we do? I've temporarily solved my problem by co-leading one of the development teams that's come out of the presentation of the design. I know I'll spend the rest of my working life in a team concept rather than a hierarchical box.

Cedar Lake Park: Citizens and local government

In 1989, three citizens who lived at the western edge of Minneapolis began contacting their neighbors, concerned about a 120 acre parcel of land that the city had up for sale and which was favored, by politicians, for development. This edge of the city had long-established homes, lawns shaded with mature trees, and one of the city's lakes provided a neighborhood focal point. There was much about the nature of the area the residents wanted to preserve. The three approached the Park Board about turning the land into a greenway that would lead from the suburbs into the city, but there was little initial interest.

This citizen group grew from a committee of three to an active, watchful coalition of 2,500 neighbors. It became an effective community action organization calling itself "Save Cedar Lake Park." It raised one-third of the needed 1.6 million dollars to buy and preserve the land, and successfully lobbied the state legislature for the remaining two-thirds of the funds. In conversations with Al Singer, research planner for the Minneapolis Park Board, he noted the difference between this and other groups he'd worked with over the years.

This project was different from the onset because citizens initiated it, instead of getting involved after the fact. When the land was purchased, a citizen advisory board was formed that consisted of fifty-four members and fifty-four alternates. People on the board were asked to make a commitment to attend at least two-thirds of all meetings, and they have honored that commitment. In the thirty-three meetings that were held between July 1992 and August 1993, a time of intense planning and decision-making, only one vote has been called (at the insistence of one of the members: and that vote was 1 to 53). All other decisions have been made by consensus.

This is a unique partnership between park board, public works and citizenry—groups which are typically at odds with each other. To work with this large a group, this committed a group, and with the consensus process, takes more time and is a bit more cumbersome, but worth it. It made us focus on areas of agreement instead of disagreement and every dimension became a learning experience. I've learned that if people are given the opportunity they can make wonderfully profound decisions.

The first step was to create a document that put forward a "statement of philosophy," what it was that we, as a group, were committed to protecting about this land, what we wanted to create in the way of public access, our principles of design, and objectives for long-term use. This little piece of land now has a one hundred-year plan attached to whatever is done on its behalf. The 120 acres will be preserved as a park with a 4.3 mile biking/hiking trail. We will plant trees and restore indigenous shrubs and grasses that will outlast the lifetime of everyone on the board. We wanted to construct this natural environment with state-of-the-art understanding of what we were doing, so we asked various environmental landscaping companies to send in designs. To make the decision process more manageable and still keep it open to citizen participation, we created The Cedar Lake Partnership consisting of two members from the park board, two from Save Cedar Lake Park and two from the Department of Public Works. We received twenty-three proposals from across the country. The large group reviewed them, as did the partnership group. The board chose four semi-finalists, the partnership chose five—four of these choices were duplicates, and we ended up selecting the same one without debate. I think this indicates how well people understand the vision and how closely we are working to carry it out.

I think a new trust level on the part of citizens toward government has evolved out of this, and I know there's a new trust level in government toward citizens. We've created a 'we.' We've made good use of people's time and energy and largely avoided burnout. This will truly be a citizen park. Citizens will be involved in all dimensions of planning, management, and care-taking—even in providing security and supervision. This has become a model for other projects in Minneapolis and is being studied by other cities and citizen groups.

Clayoquot Sound: Citizens in Environmental Action

The trees in Minneapolis are lucky; there are trees in other parts of the globe not as fortunate. Hilary Mackey and Shelly Wine are part of a collective resisting the logging of old growth temperate rainforest at Clayoquot Sound—the last great stand of rainforest located on Vancouver Island, Canada's west coast island gem which once offered its inhabitants ninety-one pristine water sheds. In the early 1990s, the government gave permission to multi-national logging firms to take five of the remaining six watersheds.

There has been a consistent group, The Friends of Clayoquot Sound (FOCS), working to defend this land since 1978. After this recent permit, FOCS went into immediate blocking action, for if the permits are carried out there won't be a piece of unlogged terrain large enough to sustain the biosphere required to support this forest.

Black Hole, a devastated clear cut, houses a residential circle of tents. With much support from people like Hilary and Shelly, who come over from the mainland, and several thousand campers who travel through the camp annually, FOCS is committed to keeping its presence felt and attention focused on the crisis. Hilary and Shelly reported on Clayoquot Sound during the week I met them at Women's Camp. They are young, intense, and committed to sharing what the experience is teaching them.

Every morning and evening at the camp, the group meets in circle to take care of the daily business of living together. Thousands of people may come through this camp in a summer; usually the circle is twenty to a hundred people who have come to register their presence, to receive training in nonviolence and peace-keeping, to learn to stop conflict between differing groups. People come because they want to be in dialogue with logging families, natives, and townspeople.

Our personal attitudes have changed since getting involved. We see that the loggers are being used by the large companies, the government, the financial backers—just as we are. The media is constantly trying to play us against each other, to keep us from dealing with the issues behind the drama on the site, but one of the things we're learning in FOCS is to keep up the pressure on many levels. We live with the trees. We blockade the logging roads. We write letters. We sit in committees with the provincial government. We hold the line. Demonstrate. Are willing to be arrested.

"The day I was arrested," says Hilary, "was a blockade of all women and children. The women blocked the road while the men sat on the side and drummed their support.

We'd been doing theme days in the summer of '93, a day for artists to blockade, for doctors, for business people. The media tries to present us as a group of aging hippies, but what impresses me about this movement is the range of folks involved. There were lots of silver-haired women in my group, and believe me, in Canada, a hundred people lining up to get arrested is a big deal.

Most of the men acknowledge their debt to feminism in how FOCS is organized. If someone begins making sexist remarks, or behaving in a hierarchical way, the group responds to help change their attitudes and re-establish the working environment we want. Women have a collaborative style of leadership in FOCS; it's almost as though space opens up and women understand how to step in and lead in the kind of environment the circle provides."

There's a coordinating circle at the camp which operates as the governing council," says Shelly. "Sometimes it's hard to be patient with a consensus model in this setting, when everyone has equal right to speak and contribute, whether they've been here all summer or are just stopping overnight. But the model is an important part of what we're doing. We keep experimenting with how to do things differently than they have been done—like Hilary does free body work on people after they've been arrested.

We're creating a video on women and resistance out of our experience. We want to take what we, and the group as a whole, are learning and see how we can apply it to something even bigger than Clayoquot Sound. Activism puts a strain on our relationship sometimes. It changes how we are together, and what energy we have to give to different things in our lives. But long-term, we see it all being to our benefit as two human beings, as women who want to make a difference.

In that strange way that science has of proving what we have already intuitively understood, microsomes have been discovered at the terminal end of a tree's root system which apparently act as a sending and receiving center for the tree. When a tree is in distress, these fibrous clusters send out a signal which can be measured and recorded as an electrical impulse. With the right instrument, or receptive intention, we may stand in a grove of trees and feel ourselves held within the circle of their communication.

The citizenship we assume, by assuming our place within the web of life, will be more miraculous than any of us can yet believe.

IRRELEVANCE AND REVELATION

Something amazing happened in the autumn of 1989. I went on vacation for two weeks and the world changed. While I wandered around the fringes of civilization, island-hopping in British Columbia and the Pacific Northwest, the government of what was then East Germany slid out of control and ceased to exist. When I got back home and restarted the daily newspaper and caught up with a stack of mail, the configuration of the world which had been held in place since 1946, the year I was born, had shattered. Our understanding of the world as split into two great camps, with showdowns between the 'Kennedys' in the white hats and the 'Kruschevs' in the black hats, was gone.

Now, without the monolithic threat of communism and nuclear annihilation, we are faced with the challenge of dealing with the nihilistic and destructive forces within our own society, our own world view, our own ways of living on—and using up—the planet. We see this drama with its chaos, pain and hope, and realize how deeply societies are in flux. The world is changing. Fast. Constantly. Relentlessly. We are living in the heart of history. The millennium is turning, and things are falling apart and coming together.

What fascinates me most about the world scheme is *how* the governments of the eastern block countries fell—without revolution mostly. **The prevailing social order, especially the prevailing order of government, simply became irrelevant.** The people went around the structures that were no longer working for them. And the old guard was so entrenched and immovable that when the energy of the populations rose up, they simply couldn't move to respond. They were stuck in place, like the Berlin Wall, and the people were fluid, energized, quick on their feet, active.

Irrelevance is a very important theme to think about in current cultures of the world. Irrelevance abounds. Irrelevance is hidden in all our social structures, and we have a hard time noticing it because the social structure is the lens through which we see the world. We have to find a way to drop the lens and see the possibilities that exist beyond our cultural training.

I believe this ability to go around what is stuck in place, to realize we are human beings quick of foot and mind, is the only kind of revolution that will work in the twenty-first century. A revolution that replaces social order rather than replacing one hierarchical power with another. We—you and I and three or four people at a time—may realize what is irrelevant and learn how to step around it and go on. We may learn to disbelieve that everything which looks like a wall is really a wall. We may decide that everything which looks impenetrable or immovable or time-honored and tradition-bound, is not worth maintaining.

Years ago, I had a recurring dream: I was confronted with a heavy door that would not open. In variations of this dream, I tried a number of ways to get through this doorway. I pounded on it, jimmied the lock, tried to kick it in, pleaded and cried and gave up and raged. Finally, one night when I dreamed of the door, instead of seeing it up close, filling the frame of my mind, I saw it from far back. From this perspective I noticed that the door was not attached to anything. There was no wall; the door hung eerily in space. I didn't have to open it; I simply had to go around it.

The door is the patriarchy. Oppressed peoples pound and hammer and plead and despair and search for sources of power, and wonder why they aren't allowed through to the other side and who the doorkeepers really are. We have been trained to see the door as the only reality there is, trained to see the door as set in a great wall that keeps some people out and lets other people in. We have been trained to think the door is the only way into the kingdom. But if we pull back far enough, we notice that there is a wider reality to which the door is not attached. This reality is real people. This reality is spiritual. This reality is the circle.

Every now and then I wake up on an ordinary morning and it occurs to me that none of our problems are insurmountable and that I have been sleepwalking again through my life. In twenty years we could create immense changes in the issues that face us. We could institute global food distribution, cease using chemicals that destroy the ozone, reforest and replant and re-utilize the available arable lands. We could find cures for cancer and AIDS and devise a formula to neutralize nuclear waste. We could make building blocks out of the

contents of landfills and house the homeless. We could raise a generation of children with values and hope and a nonviolent attitude
toward the world. Only we do not rise up as citizens and mobilize
toward authentic problem solving. We have been thoroughly convinced that the problems facing us are so complex and unresolvable
that there is very little the ordinary citizen can do about them. We
have been schooled to forgive governments and institutions their
ineptitude in responding effectively. Every now and then I wake up
with enough clarity to think about the predicament we are in, to wonder how we got here and what I can do about it.

I am one person. I have ten fingers. Ten toes. Two hands. I
count in small numbers. I come from two parents, four siblings, who
now have spouses, six children, three dogs, three cats. I own a few
things—two chairs, one couch, one bicycle, one car, two computers. I
am one person. Soon there will be six billion persons sharing this
planet with me. I cannot count this high. How may fingers and toes is
that? How many parents and children? If there are six billion people,
how many chairs do we need? How many bicycles? Does everyone
get a dog or a cat? Does everyone get one meal a day? Do they get
educated? What for, what about? The newspaper says that 10,000
people got killed in an earthquake, or 200,000 were washed away by
a tidal wave. There are parts of the world where war and economic
disruption exist to such a degree I cannot imagine daily life under
these conditions. Are these people getting up in the morning and trying to keep their lives normal? What is normal? Do they send their
children off to school? Is there a school? Do they go to work? What
work? How do they make money? How do they supply themselves
with food and clothing and shelter? Don't they have to pay the rent
or mortgage? Don't they have to pay taxes? I cannot imagine. But the
Third Culture, and to some extent the future of the world, depends
on what I will imagine. What you and I, sitting in our living rooms
with a cup of tea reading this book, are willing to imagine.

Six billion people, or six billion in debt, are not numbers I can
handle. When problems, issues, and social needs are presented in big
numbers [numb-ers], it numbs us out so that we believe there is nothing we can do. Experts are required to figure this out, and no one is
expert enough. As long as we are overwhelmed, we don't believe in
ourselves as persons of power.

I am one person. You are one person. That makes two of us. Two of us, with a candle in the middle and the right attitude, make a circle.

This is what endures: a heartbeat.
This is what endures: a place, a circle,
a gathering to which I belong,
which would not be this gathering without me,
without each of us,
without all the infinite,
minute causes that come to body here.
There is always reason enough.
This is what endures.

This is what endures
even though I neglect it, devalue it, dismiss it, fear it,
what I steel/harden/shell myself against
to prove I can live without.

This is what endures—
joy and ecstasy
and daring to drink it in.
This is not to be resisted.
This is what endures—
to be found.
And if it's out there
I can bring it in,
and if it's inside
I can damn well let it out.
This is what endures
and will endure.

Helen Douglas

CHAPTER NINE

Creating Third Culture

I come from the middle—but I have moved to the edge. As I write the last pages of this book, I live in Washington state, on an island in Puget Sound. The continent backs up behind me with a great push of energy, nearly sending me into the sea. But not quite. I hold the tension. I have accepted the angel's kiss from my dream and let go, endured the freefall, and this is where I've landed.

Willow the Corgi and I sit on the deck. She is watching for chipmunks which like to dash under the bird feeder and snatch fallen sunflower seeds. They get away with this theft, but Willow's guardian presence makes it more interesting for them all. It's not that she is protecting the Rufous-sided Towhees and House Finches which are the feeder's regular visitors—she likes the seeds herself. I am watching the eagles glide silently on the updraft of the cliff which brings an abrupt end to my yard. Across Puget Sound, the Victorian town of Port Townsend splays itself against the hills and down to the water's edge. At night its lights twinkle against the blackness. By day, the smoke from the pulp mill spreads its low plume over the tip of the Olympic Peninsula. Ships go by. Tugs hauling barges, cargo ships carrying goods in and out of Seattle and Tacoma, gray military vessels with spiny antennae, the black Darth Vadar hulls of submarines, and long bodied oil tankers with their protective tugboats herding them to the refineries—Oh please god/us, safely, without mishap—and out again through the fragile waters of the Sound. Behind all this, the grand peaks of the Olympic Mountains rise snow-capped and glorious after the winter. It is spring. And I am making my way carefully into new place.

I always knew I was coming here—to the ocean, to this passionate Pacific shore, to the edge. In a children's book of Bible verses I had forty years ago, there was a picture of a slim girl standing at the edge of the sea with an inscription from Psalm 139:

> *If I take the wings of the morning,*
> *and dwell in the uttermost parts of the sea,*
> *Even there thy hand shall lead me,*
> *and thy right hand shall hold me.*

I spent hours staring at that drawing, until the sea and the girl and the longing to be led and held dwelled within me. The girl's body faced the ocean, not back at the reader. I knew her face was my own, and I knew I belonged to Great Water.

Afternoons, Willow and I walk the beach. Sometimes we find a boulder at the tide-line, swirling half in sea, half on land and scramble up to stand at the edge of the world. With sea spray in our faces and the push/pull of tides at our feet, we watch the afternoon sun make its descent, and I bow before it. I have arrived in the painting, in the imprinting that the child carried all these years as she turned into the woman, as she said to me over and over, "Come on, Christina, let's go home."

I was wise about the puppy. When Sabine called in August and said they would breed their Corgi if I was serious about a pup, we looked at my calendar, at hers, and laughed at the foolishness of adding this complication to our lives. Then, of course, we set out to do it. I wanted to travel with one living being who could see the world's utter newness and help me see it too. Maybe it's not fair to expect company in freefall, but dogs are like that—they'll go with us anywhere.

It took me twenty years of dreaming, planning, false starts, wrong places, yearning vacations and returns to the farmlands to get here. I came back from Europe in the mid-1970s with plans to move west, but the partner I had planned to move with died and I had to put my life together again. One thing led to another and another and I stayed in Minneapolis, needing its familiarity to help me make my way. Needing the lessons of the middle, the clarity of my own voice rising out of lowland hills and wheat-fields. I entered another partnership, a rich loving that lasted sixteen years and remains in changed form. Family and friends grew up around me like a sheltering bracket of fruit-bearing bushes. Erin was born. I wrote corporate training manuals, speeches for executives, marketing videos. I wrote books and taught seminars, and kept my finances strung together in bits and pieces. Life occurred, typical and atypical, busy, straining to maintain itself, to make its way, to find true path. Until I grew bold enough to leave, to withstand the grief of separations, to set out and find again.

MARKING TIME

In many ways my island is a microcosm of the world, presented in such a size that I can hope to understand the whole by interacting with the piece. When I call folks in the east, they remind me that Manhattan is also an island, and suggest that perhaps this better represents the world. They are right in many ways, but I have chosen my island in a size and complexity that I am able to understand. The south end of the island is reached by ferry, a twenty minute ride from the mainland, an hour's drive north of the city. Friends call each other and say, "I'm going to the other side, is there anything you need?" "The other side" is the mainland, the mainstream, the mall, the Boeing factory, the freeway, the cultural life of the city, the airport.

This is not paradise—but it is the place I have been called to stand. The place I choose to take my stand. We are a spread-eagle community of over twelve thousand people ranging from new consciousness types, middle-aged hippies, and small town democrats to fundamentalist Christians, conservative retirees and military personnel. There are loggers and environmentalists, clear cuts and old growth forest, and tension about what direction the island's growth will take. More and more stretches look shockingly suburban, with new houses and winding lanes that afford everyone a wink at the view. There are many For Sale signs by homes and stands of woods. Water is a major inhibitor, despite how much of it falls from the sky.

Several areas have imposed a construction moratorium due to water shortage. Making a living has always been hard here, and that has protected the place from destruction. The only reason I can be here is that I fly out to teach.

In 1963, Puget Sound was one of the most polluted bodies of water on the continent, contaminanted by run-off from the paper mills and other industries. And they have brought it back, although the fishing industry still struggles and the oyster beds are sometimes spotty with red-tides. Up the beach a ways a man found an eagle walking on the sand, too lead-poisoned to remember how to fly. During its recovery a call went out in the local press asking people to donate doorstep mice that their cats brought in.

On an island, we become aware of the interconnectedness and consequences of everything we do. On an island we are reminded that everything that didn't grow here has been carted on—by boat and truck—and must be carted off, or used up, or recycled, or disposed of with respect, or else we foul the place we have sought out because it was unfouled. Many people arrive here in shock from the devastation and violence of the places they come from. If they decide they must "own" a piece of this peace, they often go about staking their claims in ways that destroy what they have come to claim.

My cousins, who have lived on the island for years, talk about wanting to put up a decompression chamber at the ferry dock, to pull people aside, help them slow down, get acclimated, re-educated and provided with basic good sense for island living. Actually this would be a very good idea—The Humphreys B & D, Bed & Decompression.

Talking to two carpenters who are putting up a pretentious, angular house on the corner of my little road, we mourn the clear cutting of the lot. "Yeah," say the young men, "They come in here with an architect and say take down the trees...so we do. And then they find out the land is only perked for a two-bedroom home. They have to throw away the plans and start over, only now, they have a square of mud to deal with."

On an island, it's harder to hide our mistakes, the toll is too immediately obvious. I am sitting on the deck writing when I hear a chain saw start up somewhere down the woods, and in the next few minutes nine huge trees go down. I hear their swishing through the undergrowth and the thud as they hit. I cannot see them, but the ground beneath me shakes, and the news is telegraphed up island in the roots. I ask myself, if those had been nine shots ringing out, and nine people in final scream, would I still sit here writing? What would I do?

This is the great challenge here in my new place. I am opening the door to a new life in community, to a new landscape, to a deeper understanding of why I have come—*to figure out what I am going to do.*

We are living in the time of the Phoenix, that mythical bird which plunges into the flames, lets itself burn, and rises again from the ashes. There are no easy lives. We are living in the crucible of history in crisis. Every day the stability and status quo we pull over ourselves and our loved ones like a blanket, becomes more frayed. The Phoenix is coming for us, the burning down, the deep change.

We are approaching the millennium. Starting with information that began surfacing in the 1970s in popular culture books like *Future Shock, The Aquarian Conspiracy,* and *Megatrends,* in fundamentalist predictions of Apocalypse and The Rapture, in new consciousness events like The Harmonic Convergence, it's hard not to feel some kind of pull to understand this shift.

We have been living the past forty years in what is called, in some esoteric traditions, "Mark Time." In that theory, life on earth is divided into great mythic ages of evolution and development. Mark Time is a window of time that occurs at the changing of these planetary ages. The Piscean Age, the age of the fish now ending, was heralded by the birth of the historical Jesus. The Age of Aquarius, heralded by we don't yet know what, begins in the year 2001. In the meantime, in Mark Time, fate is an open door that swings either way—into enlightenment or retreat—and sets the tone with which we enter the new age. An early teacher of mine, Dr. John Brantner, called this "the hinge of history." One of the characteristics of the hinge of history is that the impact of individual action is heightened and the pressure to claim and fulfill our destinies is intensified.

What we do matters. This is always true in the personal sphere but, combined with the technology of a global information and communication system, combined with the ravages and hope of science, combined with the best and worst potential of ourselves as a species, our personal actions take on a sense of weightiness and expectation. The more we rediscover and decode the messages left for us from previous civilizations, the clearer the message becomes. This is the end and the beginning of the world, and we will—every single one of us—make decisions which swing the door of fate.

The Mayans, the First Culture civilization of Mexico, devised a complex astrological and mathematical calculation of time and left a great calendar chiseled in stone on their temple walls. They set the end of history as December 21, 2012. The Mayans themselves are long gone—conquered, slaughtered, decimated by disease, the remainder assimilated into the colonization and industrialization of Mexico—but their calendar remains: December 21, 2012. My mother, if she lives anywhere close to the age of her mother, will be a spry ninety-two year old. I will be sixty-six. Erin will be twenty-nine. Who knows what the world will be like?

When we have stripped life down, or it has stripped us down, we are given the opportunity to rebuild ourselves and our environment with all the consciousness we can muster. So, newly arrived on one small island, I ask myself: *What is Third Culture? And how do I instill it in my life here?*

LIVING IN CONTEXT

In the winter of my life I packed up boxes, sorting what I would bring with me. In a writing class the previous fall, someone asked, "What would it be like to leave Minnesota naked?" This served as an amazing question. For the third time in two years, I handled everything I own—every spoon, every book, every piece of clothing, every item in my closets and cupboards, and *decided* whether it stayed or went along and how I would dispose of it, pass it on, give it away. We are responsible for what we accumulate. We are responsible for what we do with all our stuff. And, we are responsible for the love and relationships we accumulate, the choices we make about the ways we let go, say goodbye, or invite continued connection.

Minnesota. Winter. Long, cold, record breaking. Willow arrived. I moved out of my apartment at Solstice. All my things were in storage—a seven by ten foot bin in which the couch was upended, chairs overturned on each other, desk buried, mattress flopped against one end, boxes stacked eight feet high, my bicycle riding the top of the heap like Queen of the Mountain. My puppy and I moved into my brother's house. I wrote, rewrote, flew out to teach, returned to the cold. I was stripped down until all that was left was the context of my life, its bareness exposed like the places in the yard where the wind had blown the grass bald and frozen.

Context is the social, political, cultural and spiritual force that shapes the life of a person. A person who lives in society, lives within society's context—whether we live comfortably in the middle of this collective force or straining at the edge. We need to be seen and understood. To be ignored is worse than being misunderstood. If we are ostracized, at least there is recognition that we are part of the whole, even as the outsider. In every society there are seekers whose role is to push the border of experience and explanation and whose thoughts and actions expand the cultural context. Ideas and social forms pass through a culture, coming first from the edge and, as they are accepted, moving to center and becoming the "norm." Eventually they pass on, become outdated and fall out of use.

Making major changes in the middle of our lives isn't easy. In the dark-paneled study off the family room downstairs at Carl and Colleen's, I moved into the middle of America with my portable computer, a box of files, and puppy training supplies. Day by day, I held to the pressures of writing, cut another cord, said goodbye to another friend. Anyone calling my old home number got referred to a voice mailbox which was vague about my whereabouts, saying I'd be checking in for messages. My heart was breaking and open. Sometimes the grief was so heavy, all I could manage was connection to this one child, this small dog. Erin was watching, and Colleen, and Carl. I was the big sister, the aunt, the outrider, the one who would go and see.

At the interactive edge between the self and society, context is constantly shifting, absorbing new information, ideas, and technology, making room for new experiences which have proven possible. *Context is the collective atmosphere inside which something is seen and understood.* Before a human went to the moon, the context for accepting that expanded reality was laid in place by scientists proclaiming it was possible, by political leaders bringing the "conquest of space" into their speeches, by science fiction novels and movies, and by the development of technology—short rocket flights and monkeys whirling overhead to ticker-tape parades for astronauts. And one day in July 1969, when Neil Armstrong was hopping around in slow motion and moon dust, we were prepared to absorb this reality.

Context is amazingly important. In recent years my mother has said to me, "I remember waking up in the 1950s. You were a little girl. I had three children under the age of six. We didn't have much money. Whatever your father and I had, it was hardly a marriage. I looked into the faces of both families, looked from horizon to horizon, and could see no one who would know what I was talking about, no one who would be there with me if I stayed awake…and I was not strong enough. I went back to sleep." She tells this story with breaking emotion. She is in her seventies now, a woman whose timing is off by one generation: a member of a generation of women who will not have the options their daughters and granddaughters have, but who will have something—because the context has arrived for their awakening, and it is not too late.

Pushing the context is how a culture changes, both in expansion and reaction against expansion. As groups of minorities, women, gays/lesbians and others have struggled for rights in society, each group has pushed out the contextual edge, insisting that the culture make room. When Martin Luther King said, "Nothing can stop an idea whose time has come," he understood the power of contextual opening—and the need to seize the moment. The cultural acceptance of civil rights may be stalled and reacted against, but it cannot be wiped away because the context now includes it. The visionary's dream has become part of collective consciousness. It is there, part of the bedrock.

NOW is a moment when the circle is coming into the cultural context and we may place the power of the circle into the bedrock of the culture. We could not have had this conversation about circling without the help of context. Context creates the understood "we" who have traveled these pages together. Context holds us in readiness to consider new ideas and brings us into circle. The collective mind has expanded to make room for the idea of circling, and while this openness exists we may move forward quickly. Riding context is like riding the surf. We are swept up and moved by forces which we have not called ourselves, but which set the pace and support us on the journey. Context is a very important aspect of what we do now, what we do next, for we need cultural context to carry the circle forward and help us lay the groundwork for Third Culture.

Ann and her children are also resettling on the island in a house six miles away. They face east into a view of the Cascades, overlooking good kayaking water. Ann is a morning person and it's good the sunrises come to her. We are combining our seminar businesses and teaching under a new name: PeerSpirit. Much of our work is centered in the west, and this combination of land and sea and the people who are drawn here deeply sustain our energies. I begin to see myself situated in a neighborhood that extends from Denver to Santa Fe to Santa Cruz to Portland and north to Victoria and Vancouver—all one range of spiritual territory, enclaves of people who share context. And so we come to this tiny place, working to impact the culture in the largest sense possible.

In March, driving a U-Haul during the week of the move, Ann and I stopped at the rest stop near the Washington border to make ceremony in a small grove of trees. It was a Friday afternoon and we were following the sun through changeable weather, watching storms on the horizon sweep toward the Interstate, envelope us in rain and hail and move on. The sunset was brilliant under black clouds and rainbows sprouted to the southeast, a double arc that seemed to extend all the way back, back, back to Minnesota, and all the way forward to the Pacific coast. We had driven under this bridge, happy and stunned. We pulled the car over in order to cross this line with intention. I had the tobacco pouch, and we each carried symbols of what we were leaving behind. We walked among trees. Willow was rooting in the tall, dry grasses. Ann's children were still in Duluth, coming home from their last day of school, and would fly out a week later.

New context is created by *how* we carry on our daily lives. If I want to live in a culture that validates the circle, then Ann and I better sit in council when we are crossing the border. If I want to live in a culture that honors the sacred in every day, then I better get out of the car and show my respect. So we prayed, two middle-aged women in wool sweaters, that our days would be filled with sacred presence, with new community, with peace and confidence in our choice of new place. We poured a libation upon the ground, left our trinkets under the roots of a tree for the chipmunks to find and the ravens to carry into their spring nests. We called two friends in California and shouted exuberantly into their answering machine, "We're here!"

But of course, it takes a while to get anywhere. Especially, it takes a while to create Third Culture.

I am unpacking in my rented house. The first books out of the boxes are those which provide the context for this book—they represent the space in the culture that allows the circle to re-emerge. It has taken all of us twenty years to get here, to discover in ourselves a frame of mind open enough to become encircled again. Every word counts. Every action helps.

Next I unpack the altar, spread out the basket and its contents on a corner shelf beneath windows where the sun and rain reflects on all that has been gathered in the journey here. And day by day, I lay out a circle of stones carted up from the beach to the entrance of the house. I cannot come in or go out without stepping through the circle.

In April, a month after arriving, I invite to dinner some of the people who have helped me make this move. My cousins Bill and Donna; Sally and Bob, who hosted us during house-hunting expeditions; Laurie, who I met at Women's Camp, and her partner, Ilgvar; my mother, Ann, and myself. We have supper, enjoy the view, chat in twos and threes as the pace of the evening meanders comfortably along. And then after dessert I ask if people are willing to sit in council. "I've just made a tremendous passage," I tell them. "And part of this passage is that I'm finishing a book on the circle. So I thought we might hold circle for a few minutes as a way of marking these passages in my life." I bring a rattle from the spread altar, introduce the idea of a talking piece and suggest for our topic that we share with each other something about changes in our lives.

These are mostly people I don't yet know well, though our connections seem solid and comfortable. I want to thank them in a way that conveys the spirit of my gratitude, and helps us glimpse who we might be to each other. Inviting sacred center into the evening seems a good choice.

Sally came to the first circle in Taos, returned here and called Donna and other women from their church into writing circle. Over and over she says, "I would not be able to recognize my life from then to now, only the externals have remained the same…inside I feel like I've turned into a new person."

I imagine that Bob has watched this change with both support and apprehension. It is the first time we've met and earlier in the evening he greets me, "Ah, the phantom is real!" There is a smile on his face, and we shake hands warmly, but as we dim the lights and bring candles to the center space among the circled chairs, I do not know how the men will react or what they are thinking.

Watching my cousin Bill hold the circle, I remember us as children. When I was seven and he was twelve, he played his violin for me on a visit to Missoula, Montana. When I was thirteen and he was eighteen, I had a crush on him and he sweetly took me on my first date. I see that "Baldwin" stamp to his features, which Carl and I also carry. I watch his square hands holding the talking piece and remember Grandpa's hands, and our father's. We belong to a lineage that has good, solid values and traditions coded within it— and which we must now go beyond if we are to respond creatively to the challenges facing us, and the next generation of Baldwins.

What we say in this heart council is private, the context of our comments not important to repeat. The importance is that this happened. When enough people in a culture have similar experiences, and live through the struggle to integrate and explain them, the context expands. My first island circle is comprised of people who are, in their worldly roles, an artist, a child psychologist, a teacher, a geological engineer, an office manager, a former school board member, a piano teacher, a naturalist, a writer. The circle includes family, friends and bare acquaintances. The circle includes people at home in this form and people new to this form. And so I see—the middle is at the edge, and the edge includes the middle.

This particular Saturday night, this dinner party, is an interlude we take together in the force-fields of our lives. I say that the island is a microcosm that reflects the macrocosm, but this is only partly true. We are in much better shape here than the macrocosm.

CULTURAL CURRICULUM

In the early 1990s I designed a curriculum for workshops that raised the question: *What would a culture look like that valued peer leadership, consciousness, the natural world and relationship to Spirit?* The course was designed so that students first determined and articulated the values that activate this culture. A syllabus of books on comparative religion, anthropology, social issues, and bio-diversity provided a common frame of reference.

After reading these materials, participants sat in council to discuss, define and write value statements which would provide the foundation for cultural institutions and interrelationships. What an amazing exercise—starting the world over. Not from scratch, but by seeing ourselves in context at the end of the twentieth century and taking the space to ask: within these current conditions, within our body of knowledge, what values provide the basis for changing the world into a more humane place?

Guess what...we know. Ordinary people, provided with a situation where contemplation on these questions is encouraged, can articulate the foundations that need to be in place. We draw upon our wisdom and discover that it's there.

The council met with consensus as the basis of decision-making. No statement could become a cultural value until it had been thought about, carefully phrased, and worked through the consensus process. The full council had to agree to the values they would adopt.

In a library, a church basement, a company cafeteria, people arrived a few minutes early to pull the rowed chairs into a circle, to create the right space in which to think together. To each session they brought small treasures that represented their search; they created a center space lit with candles and decorated with natural objects and symbolic representations of the values they held dear. The council was open to everyone; if new people entered the council, more space was made for circle seating. People acted as observers as well as joining the circle. Observers sat along the outer rim, holding the edges of attention, looking up needed references, taking notes.

The most interesting groups were ones with the most diversity. A twelve-year-old and an eighty-year-old make good companions in such council, and people of various racial groups and different backgrounds and from all walks of life bring rich perspective to the question of values and how they function. Once the foundation of value statements was in place, people divided into design teams to construct the culture. We looked at different social structures:

- religion, spirituality, and ritual
- business and agriculture
- architecture and community design
- music, art and literature
- entertainment and media

- kinship and friendship
- charity and civic organizations
- health care
- government
- legal and penal systems.

Each group carried the value statements with them and designed these social structures based on the work of the council. The design teams met in circles and hashed through problem after problem until each team presented its vision back to the whole council. A rich and comprehensive view of the world developed.

The culminating experiment of these workshops is to go out and live for one day as though we are living in this new culture, to keep track of what happens, write about it, and share our experiences.

•

Ron and Janet start their day by waking without the alarm clock. They tell each other a dream they recall. They touch, spooning bodies against each other, being still a few minutes, petting each other's heartspace. As they rise, they look into each other's eyes—even thirty seconds seems timeless in this silence. They look for each other, for a sense of how they each are. They anchor themselves in the solidarity of their relationship before going off to their workaday worlds.

•

Sonia clears off a shelf in the kitchen over the table. Replaces the napkin holder and salt and pepper shakers with a pottery bowl of rosewater, a candle, photos of other family members far away, a small book of daily meditations. Alone in her kitchen, she lights a candle and reads the devotion of the day. She takes the rosewater and dabs a drop on her forehead, her throat. The smell is subtle and sweet. She sits very quietly with herself, then writes out her intention for the day, creating a manageable list of things to do and articulating the attitude she will hold in the midst of all these activities.

•

Margaret decides to break out of the suburbs and expand her sense of the world. She calls a local shelter and asks, "What do you need that I might do today?" They tell her that one of the volunteers who usually cooks lunch is out sick. "I'll be there," she says. By the end of the day she is signed up on the regular schedule and has a copy of their "wish list"—needed supplies that she can find among the excess of her own life and among her circle of friends.

•

At work, Harry is floor crew supervisor, overseeing a crew of a half-dozen people on fork-lifts who load and unload semi-trucks full of merchandise. It's a kind of industrial ballet. At 8:30, everybody starts the day by gathering in the lunchroom. Harry serves coffee and soft-drinks. The day's orders are spread out on a long table. Harry explains what he sees needing to get done before the end of the shift. Instead of assigning people tasks, he asks them to divide the workload. They discuss where the possible bottlenecks are and create a strategy to cope with the changes that occur in the day. They are a team.

•

Renata talks a local nursery into donating end of the season stock, and she loads up a pick-up truck with urban forest saplings, drives into a devastated neighborhood and enlists a group of children in helping her plant trees. They get permission before digging, and a commitment out of those who dwell nearby to keep the young trees watered. She makes new acquaintances and they begin to talk about what else this neighborhood needs, and how they might band together to provide it.

•

At day-care, Dale wants to play with the Lego blocks. Two other children are already busy with them. "Go away," they tell them. He sits down next to them.

"In my family, we share," he says.

"I'm not your family."

"Yes, you are. I knowed you since I was a baby. And today, we're going to share." He doesn't move. He doesn't grab. Pretty soon the other boy has handed him some of the blocks.

•

At the end of their day, Ron and Janet put the children to bed and meet in the living room. They take the phone off the hook. They make quiet space together, creating an ambiance that fits their mood. First one and then the other speaks a half hour of monologue. There is no interrupting. There is no rebuttal: this is check-in time on what's happening in their individual lives. The second hour they negotiate for whatever they want: listening to music, playing cards, making cookies, making love.

To live for one day in a world where leadership, consciousness, the natural world and Spirit really matter is to live in Third Culture. Even though this culture does not yet fully exist, the exercise proves that we are capable of thinking about and creating the kind of world we want to live in—a world which combines circle consciousness and the modern age. Our role as citizens of the circle is to carry the seeds of Third Culture into our daily lives, persistently, and however we can.

THIRD CULTURE

Third Culture is not a country we visit, or a formula already devised. The circle is not a product. Not an industry. The circle's requirements are intangible. Co-leadership, shared responsibility, reliance on Spirit are not things we buy; they are gifts we bring, skills we acquire through practice.

You and I will choose what Third Culture is. We will set the context. We will decide what Third Culture looks like and how it acts toward its citizens. One circle after another circle, as we take back increments of self-determination over our lives and destinies, we make choices to assume leadership, to share responsibility, to trust the nature of Spirit in the world.

Our culture as we've know it is approaching cataclysm. Second Culture is devouring itself. We do not know what kind of ending this will be. In a social context which stresses material reality over anything else, we see "ending" as a form of failure, loss, death. But we are more marvelous creatures than we have been led to believe, and so the end of the age offers us more marvelous possibility than we have dared to hope.

Assuming leadership, responsibility, and trust creates tremendous changes in each human being, in each of our environments, in our experience of Spirit. This is re-evolutionary thought. As we become accustomed to assuming leadership, how we designate and empower cultural leaders will dramatically shift. As we practice sharing responsibility, how we view and respond to social issues will dramatically shift. As we trust Spirit, how we practice religion will dramatically shift. Third Culture will emerge from all these shifts in relationship.

Third Culture is interpersonal. When we change how we interpret and interact with the circumstances and people right around us, we create Third Culture. Want to be in Third Culture? Then let us begin by radically changing how we interact. Don't blame me; talk with me. Don't sue me; negotiate with me. Don't withdraw from me; step toward me. Don't shun me; embrace me. Don't let our differences blind you to our commonalty. Don't assume; ask. Who knows what risks we will take if we are asked, if the task is explained clearly, if our contribution is valued, if we count on each other. Even the smallest child responds to the challenge when s/he is relied upon. Even the lowliest member of society has something of value to offer the whole.

Culture has always been created by taking new social risk. It has always been scary to step out of our isolated journeys into the circle of firelight, to show up in the company of strangers, to stand there and ask for entrance, or to offer it. Our hearts race with adrenaline: will we have the courage to see each other? Will we have the courage to see the world? The risks we have the opportunity to take in the twenty-first century are based on the risks human beings took forty, fifty, sixty thousand years ago in First Culture. We are not different from our ancestors. They are still here, coded inside us.

We are animals, encoded with instinctual drives toward self-preservation and protection. Coming into contact we posture and position ourselves, encircle the young and vulnerable, go submissive, or raise our hackles and look for threat. These instincts are not wrong. They are not bad. They have simply grown enormously out of balance, manipulated by the mind until we view our survival as a right of conquest instead of as an act of cooperation.

We are beings imbued with spirit, drawn intuitively into reverence and respect. Our desire to be in awe of life is as instinctual and deep as our desire to survive. Coming into contact we tell our stories, and listen to the stories of others. We are inspired by the raw experience each life embodies. We cherish what we carry and often volunteer to help each other carry the load of life a little further. We are moved by acts of gallantry, courage, compassion, selflessness, the ability to persevere.

We may trust these instincts. We may tap a wisdom inside ourselves that bridges from First Culture to Third Culture. We may extract and integrate the best of Second Culture. We may embody the amalgam and become the change we are trying to make.

COUNCIL

Several months after settling on the island, Ann's daughter, Sally, phoned me one summer evening. Her eleven-year-old voice was breathy and solemn. "Mom wants you to come over," she said, "She's down on the dock. She's crying."

When I arrived, Ann was still in tears. We sat in the long evening dusk and I backed her while she had her feelings and gathered her thoughts. "I feel lost," she said. "Brian was so sullen at dinner. Sally was snippy. Stress is cumulative and I just lost it. Lost confidence in what I'm trying to do with my life, in what adjustments I'm expecting the children to make. My heart doesn't feel connected to our dream. It's too hard. It's too much."

I sat with her silently, not at all sure how to offer comfort. I wasn't in very good shape myself. For weeks we had been trading back and forth our moments of clarity and panic. When I fell apart, she held. When she fell apart, I held. My heart seemed to be functioning in only two modes—wide open, or slammed shut. The pace of change had finally slowed down just enough for us to realize our exhaustion. It's hard to hold onto vision when that vision leads us to make drastic changes in our real lives. Finally, words gathered inside me. "Our stress builds up because we take our dream seriously," I suggested. "We're insisting that it become reality. Now. Day by day. So we are living through a learning curve—learning how to carry what we believe into action. We're not perfect at it. Sometimes we're not even very good at it. But we are doing it. What was Brian upset about?"

"He says he hates it here. That he misses his old school and friends in Duluth."

I shifted my buttocks on the worn planks of the dock. "Sounds reasonable. He's fourteen. You knew this would be hardest on him."

She turned her tear streaked face toward me in the evening light. "I just threw down my napkin and walked out. That's exactly what I tell him he can't do when he's mad. Sally came after me and kept asking 'What's wrong? What can I do?' When I couldn't stop crying I asked her to call you. She lit out of here, so relieved—"

"Relieved to do something helpful, to have another grownup to call, to help out this grownup she loves who's in trouble. She called us into council, so you and I could get re-centered, calm down, go on."

"Right now I don't know how to go on," Ann replied. "I don't know how to re-enter the house and restart…"

"In council. Let's talk. All four of us talk."

A few minutes later we sat in the living room, Sally slouching in an overstuffed chair, a sheet of long black hair shading her face, Brian, with his arms wrapped sturdily around his torso, backwards cap covering his mod haircut. Ann sat on the other end of the couch. I sat on the other chair, and Willow panted hopefully at Brian's feet. We lit a candle set on the coffee table, and used a round beach stone as the talking piece. Ann started. "I know this is a hard time for you kids. It's a hard time for me too. We're making big changes in our lives. I know that you're not sure why this had to happen, but I believe this is the right place for us, and the right decision to be here together. I believe we will grow as a family, and that all our lives will be enriched. We all have a lot of feelings when there's this much change going on. It's all right for you to have your feelings, but you cannot just take them out on me." She put the stone back in center.

Sally reached for it next. "I know I've been moody. Sometimes I don't know I'm mad—that I'm mad at you, Mom. It's hard to say, 'I'm sorry' when my feelings are all mixed up." She hands the stone toward Brian who shakes his head—no. He doesn't speak.

There are steps to this kind of heart council, a process in which each person may say what they feel, what they think is happening, what they want to see changed in the situation, how they intend to take care of themselves whether the situation changes or not. We are raw this evening, doing the best we can. There is no facilitator and the connection anyone of us feels to Spirit is private and tenuous. The small taper candle burns, and that's all the ritual we've got. There are long pauses that are neither meditative or comfortable, but we stay in council. We each hold the rim. No one leaves the circle. We keep talking, pausing, waiting for clarity. Brian is quiet, his energy seething, but I feel his presence steady in the midst of his emotions.

After another pause Ann says, "Brian, I want you to say something here too. I need to hear from you."

He glares at her, returns his gaze to center and I reach for the stone. "He's right, Ann. He has the right to wait for readiness, to remain silent. You can't manage his participation. There are consequences to not talking, but he may choose whether or not to add his voice to council and shouldn't be coerced."

We sit in silence again briefly, then Brian reaches for the talking piece. He is absolutely clear. "First, I'm not a 'kid.' A kid is a child under ten. I am a maturing young adult who knows how to hold council, and I don't ever want to be referred to as a kid again. Second, just going into high school is a terrible time for me to have to make this adjustment. Sometimes I hate what's happened to my life. But I'm all right. I don't need to be fussed over, I need to be heard. Third, you keep bugging me and Sally about having friends over, and I don't want to invite someone over because you want me to. I'm enjoying what I'm doing, reading and resting up before the summer gets busy."

Ann turns the stone over and over in her hand. "You're right—you're not a kid. I'll work to make that change in my mind and words. Will you keep talking to me about some way we can help each other be angry or afraid without being mean to each other?" Both children nod.

I take the stone. "You know, if we can get underneath our anger, I think we will find our grief. Grief about all this change, about being far away from the things we counted on as familiar. Your mom and I, we pulled ourselves out of a dream—a dream that things could go on as we once expected them to when we were young. Our choices are pulling you out of a dream, too. Out of a dream that it's possible for things to stay the same. You don't have to see the world the same way we see it, or have the same dreams, but we need to keep talking so we can help each other really live our lives."

I am speaking as much to myself as I am to them. I am speaking to the child I once was. I am speaking to the path of my life I let go of. I am speaking to show she who becomes afraid and slams closed the doors of my heart. My words are only the tip of reflection, a few moments of peeling back the veil. I acknowledge again my submission to Spirit. I don't know what piece of my words speaks to them: I am listening to the pieces that speak to me. At least we have reached a point of relief between us. That is all we can do this evening—and it is enough. We finish council, blow out the candle and adjourn to the dining table for several hands of Skipbo. We are living in Third Culture. We are two generations in this experiment together, learning as we go. Ann and I head into another week of business details and writing, and the foundation is solid underneath us again—as solid as it can be for any of us making our way through Mark Time.

All I know is that none of us can travel further by ourselves. Alone, our hearts become stony and guarded. Alone, we become frightened. Alone, each of us can only stand and watch the next tree go down, watch the child fold over in hunger or pain, watch the woman be raped, watch the man die inside, and whatever intervention we make is not enough. But, when we are traveling in the company of many, then we are a great body that can effect change. Then, the circle is called.

And something is called forth within us by the circle. We find strength and renewal. We can be life's faithful pilgrims again, able to touch source, to touch stone, to be grounded in Spirit. We have come to this place in time to receive a gift, and to know how to offer that gift back to the world. We have come to this point in history to fulfill a purpose which we may not fully understand. We prepare the place inside us which will receive, which will give. We go inside and make center, make altared space. Make ready. Clean the cobwebs, light the oil lamps, set the sacred objects into their niches. Hold the place so that the circle may come. Hold the place so that the circle may lead.

Endpiece

THE PEOPLE
    Formed a circle round the Fire,
        each showing an attentive face
           to every other person.
AND THEY SPOKE
    each waiting quietly
        till the other had finished,
           as they had learned to do,
        a circle of silent listening
           framing the wisdom each contained
        until the wisdom of all was spoken,
           contained at last
             by the Circle of the People…
Thinking now
    of the quiet circle of listening hearts,
        they were filled with understanding
           of the value of their way.

AND A FIRM RESOLVE SWEPT THROUGH THEM.
THEY DECIDED
To be a People
    who would perpetuate and refine
        this manner of ordered council
           which they had achieved.

So that the children's children's children
  might benefit from greater understanding.

And their paths through joy or sorrow
  might be eased
    by the soft sounds of wisdom's voice.

For they saw the People
  like a Great River—
    spreading out upon the land,
    spreading out across the waters,
    dividing down a thousand thousand paths
      not yet seen.

AND A SENSE OF TOMORROW
    ENTERED THEIR HEARTS
        AND NEVER AGAIN LEFT THEM.

SUCH WISDOM IS OUR GIFT
    FROM THOSE WHO WENT BEFORE.
MAY WE OFFER EQUAL MEASURE
    TO THOSE WHO FOLLOW US.

Paula Underwood, *The Walking People*

RESOURCES

The following sections of this book contain additional material useful to those who wish to apply PeerSpirit circling in their lives.

The largest section is *Guide to PeerSpirit Circling*. These pages explicate the support, structure and guidelines imbedded in story and example in chapters five, six and seven. This additional guide is intended to serve as a quick and thorough reference for calling your own circle.

The Guide to PeerSpirit Circling is also produced as a separate booklet so that circles may order copies in bulk for use among their members. An order form has been placed in this book. If it's missing, inquire for further information or order booklet copies directly from PeerSpirit, P.O. Box 550, Langley, WA 98260, USA.

GUIDE TO PEERSPIRIT CIRCLING

A PeerSpirit circle is a council held together by consensual authority. Council is not just another discussion group; it's a called circle, a conscious act of coming together.

THE THREE PRINCIPLES

PeerSpirit circling is based on three principles:

1. Rotating leadership. Every person helps the circle function by assuming small increments of leadership. In PeerSpirit circling, leadership shifts moment by moment and task by task. Rotating leadership trusts that the resources to accomplish the circle's purpose exist within the group.

2. Shared responsibility. Each person pays attention to what needs doing or saying next, and is willing to do their share. In PeerSpirit circling, responsibility also shifts moment by moment and task by task. Shared responsibility is based on the trust that someone will come forward to provide whatever the circle needs: helping each other take action, calling for silence, or offering the next meeting space.

3. Reliance on Spiritual. Each person places ultimate reliance in the center and takes their place at the rim. Through simple ritual and consistent refocusing, the center, literally and symbolically, becomes *sacred space*—a place where everyone's willingness-to-listen dwells.

CALLING THE CIRCLE

The four steps of calling a circle are stages of preparation that occur before the first actual gathering of people.

1. Set intention. Intention provides the basic foundation for calling a circle. Setting intention means getting clear about what needs to be changed or accomplished, what seems to be missing that you are trying to find, what you are trying to fulfill for yourself. To clarify the intention for this circle, use whatever focusing skills are most helpful to you.

Begin a *Background Book*—a three-ring notebook that allows you to create divided sections for inserting newspaper and magazine articles, notes from telephone and personal conversations, copied pages from other sources, and blank pages for writing, sorting and editing ideas. The Background Book serves as a collection point for all the pieces of information, ideas, questions, and suggestions that relate to your quest for clarity.

Write a simple statement of intent. The simpler the statement, the easier it will be for people to decide whether or not this circle fits their needs, directions, goals and aspirations.

2. Talk to people. *Share your thoughts.* Talking about an idea is good practice. Two helpful things happen when you talk: story and question. A story explains your thoughts, feelings and actions to others. It helps others understand why something is important, what significance it has, what your hopes are, and what the plan of action is. A story inspires others to think, feel, and act with you.

- Talk with people who will understand, support, and be interested in what you say.
- Talk with people who think differently than you. When they challenge your thinking, practice not getting defensive.
- Talk with long-time friends who know you well and have seen you work an idea through stages of implementation.

- Talk with new people in your life; follow your hunch that they might be interested.
- Talk with your family, even if you and your partner or children or parents are far apart in your thinking.
- Try out your thoughts on friendly strangers sitting next to you on a bus, plane, or waiting in the grocery line. Who knows what valuable contribution they may make?

When people listen to a story, they raise questions which help you sort through your assumptions. In the Background Book, keep track of their questions and use them like homework assignments—to research and clarify your intention.

3. Envision the circle. Story and question lead to vision. The more you refine your intent, talk with others and respond to questioning, the clearer the vision becomes of the circle you want to call.

Imagine being in a circle that is carrying out the intention you have defined. Ask yourself these questions:
- What intention is this circle based upon?
- Who is there?
- What is the size of the circle, the number of people?
- What diversity do I seek: gender, age, ethnic, racial, religious, economic?
- Why am I seeking or limiting diversity?
- What shared understandings do people need to have?
- What kinds of clarity do I want members of the circle, including myself, to be able to contribute?
- What do I provide for other members?
- What do *they* provide for me?
- What would circle meetings be like? Frequency? Length? Location?

4. Call the first meeting. Invite people to this first meeting by writing out your intention in one or two paragraphs. *What does a person need to know in order to decide if s/he is interested in responding to this call?* Go through several stages of editing this statement until it reflects your intention. Even if you are going to invite people verbally, by talking on the phone or meeting with them, a short written paragraph is a good way to clarify your statement. People may want to see something written so they can consider the invitation.

The next question is: *Who do I know that I hope will be interested in responding?* While you have been setting intention, talking to people and creating your vision, who has come to mind as a potential contributing member for this circle? Who has expressed interest? Think about the attributes you hope they will bring. Make a list of these people. Work through your list. Pay attention to the synergy of personality mix. Choose carefully. Choose people with whom you think you can carry out the intention of this particular circle.

THE FIRST GATHERING OF A NEW CIRCLE

1. Preparations. *Arrange the seating in a circle.* It is essential to literally form a circle. Even when minds have forgotten the power of the circle, bodies remember. When people find their place at the rim of a circle, half the work of explanation is already done. Sitting in a circle allows time to notice who's there, to greet each other, say names, get comfortable and settle in—to gather, in a deepened sense of that word.

Make a sacred center. Have something tangible in the center of the circle to focus the energy of the group. Attention is always held within the perimeter of the circle. Attention focuses at the edge when people are talking and focuses at the center when there is silence or the need to remember guidance.

- The center is collective energy; it belongs to the group, like the open space of a village square.
- The center is the symbolic repository for the gifts each person brings to the circle.
- Placing objects in the middle of the circle reminds everyone that collective energy is real. Don't step on them if they're laid out on the floor; don't shove debris into the space if the objects are laid out on a table.
- Respect center. You may contribute to it, and take from it. You will, in the course of the circle, share responsibility for collective energy many times and in many ways.

2. Open the circle. Use some form of ritual to begin the circle. Silence, lighting a candle, reading a quote, a song, something to call forth the reflective attention of the group.

3. Tell your story. *How did this idea come to you and why have you asked this particular group to gather?* Your willingness to talk first gives other people time to get comfortable and models what kinds of things you might want them to say in a few minutes. You are setting context—the frame which shapes how people see an event.

If you have been sitting at the center of the circle while talking about the center, it is important now to move back to the rim, to be part of the group in a very egalitarian way. Be organized in your thoughts; it's okay to have written notes or guidelines. If you tend to be long-winded, follow your outline and then be quiet. Answer the questions:

- What idea or need started me thinking about all this?
- Why did I respond to this idea or need by calling a circle?
- What does circling mean to me?
- What is my understanding about the principles of rotating leadership, shared responsibility, and willingness to listen to Spirit?
- Why did I chose these people to sit in the circle with me or what did I hope they would bring?
- What do I intend to offer the circle in exchange?

4. Introduce the talking piece. If you sense that you have talked long enough and that others are ready to speak, introduce the idea of a *talking piece. The purpose of using a talking piece is to guarantee that people are heard or have the opportunity to be heard.* A talking piece may be any object which is designated to grant the person holding it the right to speak. When one person has the piece, *others listen without interruption or commentary.* The use of a talking piece controls the impulse to pick up on what people are saying, to interrupt with jokes or sympathetic remarks, or to ask diverting questions.

The practice of using a symbol of power that passes from hand to hand has been used in councils from earliest times. The talking piece is a great equalizer among those who differ in age, race, gender or status. The piece assures that everyone at the rim has an equal voice.

Most often, the talking piece is passed from hand to hand around the circle so that everyone knows when their turn is coming. If someone is not ready to talk when the piece comes by, it is perfectly acceptable to pass and hand the piece on. After a complete ring, the piece may be passed again or placed in the center for people to retrieve if they have something to add. In smaller circles or among long-standing groups, the piece may simply reside in the center and people reach for it when they are ready to contribute. Trust the process. Don't carry on when you have nothing to say, and don't be afraid to take your turn when you have a contribution to make.

Not every conversation needs to be held with the talking piece, but it is an excellent way to heighten attention and slow down interactions so that circle members really listen to each other.

5. Set clear group contracts. Contracts, or guidelines, provide the social safety net for group process. *As spiritual acknowledgment holds the center, contracts hold the rim.* At the circle's perimeter, contracts are the authority to which each member agrees to acquiesce. Contracts are impersonal, communal, and fair. Contracts set the parameters of conduct and focus—the mutual understanding inside which the circle functions. In a circle, where people spend significant time and energy and practice new ways of being together, contracts need to be articulated so that everyone has a similar understanding of appropriate behavior.

Generic group contracts:

(1) What is said in the circle, belongs in the circle. Confidentiality allows people to speak their minds knowing that they will not be gossiped about. Confidentiality allows people to take verbal risks, to experiment with ideas, to keep changing their minds as their understanding grows.

(2) The circle is a practice in discernment, not judgment. Discernment is the ability to listen, sort, and speak without having to be "right" or in total agreement with other people's opinions and views. Someone else's view doesn't have to be right or wrong, it may simply be different.

(3) Each person takes responsibility for asking the circle for the support they want and need. Asking for what you need next allows you to stay at the rim, and avoids power struggles and personal drama as ways of getting attention.

(4) Each person takes responsibility for agreeing or not agreeing to participate in specific requests. You can support someone and not take direct part in what they need. If the request is appropriate to the task and orientation of the group, someone in the circle will have both the willingness and resources to carry it out. If a request doesn't fit task and orientation, there will be a lack of interest. It is also possible to *not* support a request or even challenge whether or not it serves

group purpose. In discussing how to expend resources of time and energy, intention is maintained.

(5) *Contracts are updatable. If something is not working, change the contract and maintain the process.* Contracts define how the intent of the circle is carried out. If trouble develops, the group can work together to search for a contract that will better support group process and group intention.

(6) *Ask before touching; practice hearing without interrupting.* The circle reinforces the belief that each person is intact in their own boundaries. You bring what you have learned individually and offer it to the community of the circle. In that offering, you are still intact in your autonomy, discretion and diversity.

(7) *When troubled, call for silence, space, song, or another ritual that re-establishes the center and reminds participants of the need for spiritual guidance.* PeerSpirit circling is a new form of gathering, a co-creative process. Everyone is learning how to practice skills that have not been developed in hierarchy. Growth is uneven. If all group members are committed to the circle's success, then the bumps of uneven growth will be held within that commitment and the process may continue.

There may be additional specific contracts that apply to your group, either now or in later sessions. Be prepared to write this list and additions, to have copies available for the group, and to bring contracts up for review after the circle has met for a while and people know more about how they want the process to work.

6. The first time round the rim. The first time around the rim is a *check-in*—a chance for everyone to introduce themselves, react to what has been said, and share their own stories about what brings them to the circle. The use of the talking piece greatly helps this process.

One by one, as people take the talking piece and make their first statements, they release their personal energy and excitement into the circle's center, into group process. As the caller of the circle, this is a crucial moment for you. This is the moment when all your preparation pays off—the moment when the principle of rotating leadership and shared responsibility must replace your natural sense of possession over the intent you set in motion.

7. State covenants. Contracts in a circle are made with careful thought. They are an intellectual process, the agreements of the head. *Covenants in a circle are made on faith. They are an intuitive process, the agreements of the heart.* When any two people assess their relationship—business, personal, or circled—and agree to do or not do certain things, they are "covenanted" to their agreement whether they have gone through this ritual intentionally or spontaneously,

A PeerSpirit circle, with a sacred center and a rim bound with intention and contract, is, by nature, a covenanted arrangement. This means people have a heart dimension involved in what they expect from themselves, from others, and from the experience itself: *"This is what I am counting on from myself...This is what you may count on from me...This is how I will seek and follow guidance..."*

A typical covenant is: "I *dedicate* myself to holding this circle and helping it accomplish its task. I *take responsibility* for myself in the process, to work in this group with integrity, to clear up issues as they arise. I *offer* my skills and ability to think on my feet. I *retain* my insecurities and competitiveness and will take care of personal issues which do not pertain to the purpose of this group. I am a grown person and you may count on me to stay a grownup throughout this circle. I *will listen* to you, and I will listen for guidance."

By the end of the first or beginning of the second meeting, it is helpful for members to state their covenants with the circle. Members may want time to think about their covenants, to write them down and bring a statement to the next gathering.

8. Keep track of commitments. You already have a Background Book—a notebook full of your intention building and preparation—and this, or another notebook, can become the Circle Logbook.

The *Circle Logbook* contains the circle's contracts, covenants, group and individual commitments, task statements, practicalities of meeting arrangements, accountability, and accounting. In the Logbook, members maintain a record of what is actually going on in the circle and use it to revive memory and review who agreed to do what. The Logbook holds the circle's history. You may include formal sections to track the ongoing work of the circle and informal sections to keep track of the fun—photographs, anecdotes, running jokes as well as running wisdom.

Keeping the Logbook is part of sharing leadership. The convener for the next meeting will probably carry the Logbook and bring it to the next session. Some circles make a ceremonial box or basket which holds the altar objects, the logbook, and other paraphernalia that symbolizes their particular circle. Whoever has the basket calls the next meeting of the circle. The convener takes responsibility for offering or setting up space, arranging time, bringing circle materials, and making sure everyone knows the arrangements. The convener usually changes meeting by meeting so that this duty is shared among circle members.

9. Group process. Most of the time, group process will hardly be noticed because it is functioning well. Group process gets noticed when it is falling apart. Social discomfort and occasional confusion are unavoidable and natural. In the usual course of conversation, someone will misinterpret a statement or action, or need to challenge someone else's statement or action. Two members may be at odds with each other about something outside the group. Silence may carry tension instead of calm.

When there is a pause in the process, you may have an impulse to jump in and smooth out the silence or help things along. Let go of control by remembering simply to "hold the circle." Allow a small vacuum of energy to exist so there is space for the next person to lead, take responsibility, or call attention to Spirit. Use the center for guidance in holding the energy and refinding direction.

Common questions about group process:
•What do I do when someone tries to take over the direction or dominates verbally?
•What if someone is holding the talking piece and venting emotions—like anger—and I think they're being abusive?
•What if someone shames me?
•What if the caller of the circle never lets it become our circle?
•What if someone joins the circle who doesn't have the same skills or sensitivities?

The way to deal with these issues is simple: rotate leadership, share responsibility, rely on Spirit for guidance. If everyone in the circle is able to do this, the circle can recover from momentary confusion. How group process reknits itself after a crisis or challenge is determined by the contracts which are already in place or added along the way.

10. Close the circle with respect. You have opened the circle with respect, with ritual, and have imbued it with much communal energy, good intention, excitement, nervousness, and heartfelt sharing. *It is important to close with a ritual which signals that the circle meeting is over*—blowing out the candle holding hands, or offering a quote, song, or other suggestion. Even the standard phrase, "meeting adjourned" is a way of closing circle.

Attention is required to hold the rim while circling. One purpose of opening and closing the circle with ritual is to signal when this level of attention is required and when it is okay to relax. Before and after circle there is time to have a cup of tea or chat, but while circle is open people need to be highly attentive. A circle that has only met for a few hours usually requires only a simple, short acknowledgment. At the end of a long seminar or ongoing group, where circle energy has deepened, the closing needs to reflect the intimacy that has developed.

SUSTAINING THE PEERSPIRIT CIRCLE

Sustaining the circle requires that the three principles be lived, moment by moment. The most reliable way to insure that the principles function is to call them into the circle. Recite them so they are fresh in everyone's mind. Try reciting the three principles as affirmations:

> •I am willing to rotate leadership.
> •I am willing to share responsibility.
> •I am willing to rely on Spirit.

Circling has structure, orderliness, balance, commitment, and natural cycles. To sustain a circle for more than a few meetings, the group needs to adapt and follow certain structures.

1. Building continuity. Part of the mind likes structure and understands how to use continuity, repetition, and ritual to free up creativity. *Continuity* answers the questions: *When will the meeting officially begin? What's on the agenda for the evening (or for the life cycle of the circle)? When does the meeting officially end?*

One of the first collective duties of the circle is to design its continuity. Choose the framing devices which will be used to organize circle activities. In most circles, continuity building consists of the following elements:

> •*Opening rituals*—ringing a bell, lighting a candle, laying a circle of ribbon out on the floor or tabletop, invocations, meditations, silence, or shared movements.
> •*A meeting pattern*—checking in, establishing agenda, following agenda, deciding on tasks and actions, volunteering to host the next meeting, checking in with each other again.
> •*Preserving group history*—reading from and adding to the Logbook, arranging things in the center/altar, taping conversations that set group course or taking photographs of major events, occurrences, and rites of passage.

• *Closing rituals*—songs, prayers, silence, blowing out
    the candle.

2. Setting time and agenda. Circles gather because someone
says, "Let's meet here, on this day, at this time, until this time, for the
purpose of..."

It's very helpful to know how much time the circle will
require for the actual meeting time, for the amount of commitment
that may occur between meetings, and for the length of time the circle
is contracting to meet. The nature and clarity of the group's intention
will set much of the timing.

Time creates tension—the need to get things done. Correct
timing means that tasks can be accomplished in the amount of time
agreed to. The circle may contract to convene for a specific period of
time OR to accomplish goals/provide support. These two ways do
not work well in combination. Adding goal time to clock time creates
a phenomenon called, "hurry up time."

Time limits are essential. People need to know how long a
commitment they are making. They need to know that if the circle
evolves in a direction that doesn't fit their needs or interests, there
will be a graceful way for them to exit.

Circles need intermediate exit points. Even circles that hope to
go on forever, like intentional communities or a writing circle of committed friends, need time to reconsider the contracts, air problems or
tensions, and have members recommit or to leave with the blessings
of the group. When we acknowledge the group's impermanence, we
are provided with an opportunity to cherish each other and our time
together.

*Agenda is the program or schedule the circle expects to accomplish
or experience in each particular gathering.* In order to set agenda when
business is conducted in circular fashion, have each person write
down what items they are bringing up for consideration and estimate
the amount of time each needs. When the agenda item comes up, the
initiator acts as the item's sponsor, articulates it, and facilitates discussion or council.

3. Choosing a form of meeting. There are basically three forms of meeting:

Discussion is the most common informal manner of meeting together—picking up on what one another is saying, reacting, interacting, brainstorming, disagreeing, persuading, interjecting new ideas, thoughts, opinions. The energy of open discussion stimulates the free flow of ideas. It can also overwhelm those who aren't comfortable leaping into the verbal fray. There are times when discussion is essential to group process and times when process is aided by the form of council for a calmer pacing and more completion.

Council is a more formal pattern of group meeting. Using a talking piece, the authority to speak is passed from person to person. One person at a time has the floor and the others listen attentively. The purpose of council is to gather information from the whole group, show respect for each person's presence, hear collective wisdom, and create consensus. Council may be used as a form of *witnessing*, in which each person speaks without reference to what has been said by others. Or council may be used as a forum which builds thoughtfully on each other's statements.

Meditation is not usually considered a form of meeting, but it is an essential element in a circle where ultimate reliance is spiritual. Call it prayer, supplication, silence, centering inward, holding the rim, or taking time-out. Meditation is the use of soul presence in the middle of meeting, the act of tuning in to that mystery which is in the center of the circle and in the center of each individual.

Some form of calling and maintaining centeredness belongs in the continuity of PeerSpirit circling—silence, song, reflection, prayer, invocation, chimes or prayer bells, the *shofar* or conch shell. The form of meditative summons doesn't matter. What matters is that within this circle every member practices touching the Higher Self, practices touching the Sacred and being touched in return, practices being open to mystery and wisdom.

One way of structuring meditation is to ask for a volunteer to be *the guardian of the group energy.* This person stays aware of how the energy is flowing. Discussion may become heated; the facilitator may be struggling to respond to questions; someone may be holding the talking piece unaware that they have lost group attention; someone may share something the group needs to sit with respectfully. At these moments, the guardian calls for silence, ushers the group into meditation, holds the space for a few minutes, and then releases the silence back into the pattern of meeting.

4. Rotating leadership. A commitment to hold the rim is a commitment to claim individual leadership. A PeerSpirit circle is not a leaderless group, it is an *all leader* group; the leadership passes like a baton among group members. Group facilitation does not disappear, but facilitation shifts from a model of permanent leadership to a model of changing and inclusive leadership.

At the beginning of a circle meeting someone may ask, "Do we have a guardian? Do we have a facilitator? Who's opening?" In a circle of ten, there may be 1) a *caller* who is hosting the circle, serving drinks and snacks, 2) a *convener* who holds the basket and is looking for an invocation to read to the group, 3) the *scribe* carrying the Logbook who reads notes from the previous meeting, 4 and 5) *researchers* looking in the Logbook to find items they want to bring forward, 6) the volunteer *guardian,* 7 and 8) the *keepers* of the agenda items, 9) the *timer* who calls for everyone to gather, and 10) the *procrastinator* who's still in the bathroom. The circle will work, play, and meditate. Everyone will share tasks, hold the group's attention and release it. There will be no need for a "boss."

5. Restating intention. Holding to intention provides the momentum for a circle's gathering and helps prevent it from stalling out in rambling discourse or from being diverted by part of the agenda. It's helpful if every meeting begins with a restatement and affirmation of intent—a reminder of what the circle has gathered to do.

6. Creative responses to difficulties. The ability to create peer community is based on communication and compromise. PeerSpirit requires a different kind of energy, a different kind of patience. There is no leader to fix your circle when it's not working. Trust that *everyone* in this circle is willing to work in order to preserve the integrity of what has been created.

When people are anxious, or the circle is in difficulty, it is helpful to reframe the problem—don't focus on individual behavior; look at overall process. Ask questions:

• Does this circle have a clearly-negotiated and agreed-upon intent?

- What is it? Do we remember? Are we reciting and keeping it in mind?
- What are the group contracts and guidelines? Do we need to add or subtract a guideline?
- If these structures are being used, how come the circle is out of balance? Are people going passive and not assuming leadership?
- Do we trust that we will be supported if we assume leadership and address concerns and issues as they arise?
- Is responsibility being shared?
- Are we using guardianship in our meetings? Council?
- Do we desert someone who is offering a challenge or being challenged? Do we hold the rim? Do we back each other so we have the support to respond to challenges?
- Do we call for silence? Meditate together? Breathe our energy back into our bodies, back into the center of the circle? Ask for guidance?
- Are we framing circle process in spiritual or egotistical terms?
- What rituals might we call upon for sustenance?

If you are disturbed by what's happening in circle, *hold council with yourself:* write in a journal, take out a pad of paper and spend an hour discharging your thoughts. Just dump your rantings or worries out on the page so you can read them and think things through. What are your assumptions? Is your fear or anger disproportionate to the actual occurrence? Are your present emotions related to past events? Ask yourself 20 questions or list 20 assumptions you're making. Honor this internal sorting. The predicament often has 90% to do with you and 10% to do with anyone else. If you decide to ask for help from another circle member, respect confidentiality and don't gossip. Set up contracts for the conversation, be straightforward, be clear that you are not trying to gang up on someone, that you are in need of understanding your own process.

Everyone who is active in a circle is emotionally, intellectually, and spiritually challenged. Everyone is triggered into a learning process and sometimes feels their reactions to ordinary events and inter-actions are out of control. People in a circle have often spent years becoming more self-aware, and sometimes self-awareness seems to compound the problem. Perhaps you feel hypersensitive instead of hyperskilled. Everyone goes through times of feeling calm and relaxed about the circle, excited and confident, scared and vulnerable, angry at group process and irritated by most everyone present, deeply moved by the circle's healing and aware of being in the pres-ence of the Sacred. It's a circle; it moves.

Issues will arise. Period. You can count on it. Real trust comes from going through the bumpy, scary, risky and vulnerable aspects of circling. You don't know what you are made of until you and your circle have faced a problem, resolved a conflict, gotten several mem-bers through a crisis. The circle that has lost its innocence and come through crisis with respect for each other and the process is a circle to be reckoned with!

7. Consensus. *Consensus is a process in which all participants have to come to agreement before a decision goes forward or action is taken.* Consensus is applied when a group wants or needs to take collective responsibility for actions. In a peer group, there needs to be a sense that everyone is stepping forward together and supports what the cir-cle is about to do. It doesn't require that everyone have the same degree of enthusiasm for each action or decision. Consensus provides a stable, unifying base. Once consensus is reached, the circle has the authority to speak as "we."

In the middle of a meeting, consensus can be called for on each agenda item or after discussion and council have been heard and it's time to come to agreement on action or intention. One way to signal consensus is to institute a thumb process. Thumb up—"I'm for it. I'm ready to support and do it." Thumb down—"I'm against it. I don't think this is the right way for us to go." Thumb sideways—"I have a question that needs addressing or a comment I need to add before I can decide." Thumbs indicate where the process of reaching consensus is at, and are not votes.

Consensus is also applicable when the circle calls on spiritual guidance. There needs to be, in a peer group, the sense that everyone has submitted to the same process of decision making and that each has been moved to come to a similar decision. Since one of the three principles is "reliance is spiritual," consensus is the outcome of meditation, silence, and the deep petition of the group asking for Spirit's guidance.

8. Spiritual practice. To come out of an ego-driven system like hierarchy and into a spirit-called system like the circle, it helps to think of circling as a form of spiritual practice. Spiritual practice is an action which requires acute personal consciousness as well as a relationship with Spirit.

Spiritual practices are all based on the increasing ability to respond from the soul-self rather than from the ego-self. In the circle, this means listening, just listening, without preparing a rebuttal or contribution. It means having compassion for circle members instead of noting the ways you are better than, worse than or different from the others. Spiritual practice means observing with curiosity and detachment rather than defensiveness. Detachment is not the same as withdrawal. Detachment requires neutrality, an openness to hearing what others have to contribute without letting the ego jump in and narrow the options prematurely. The more you practice detached curiosity in moments when the circle is calm, the more you will be able to practice detached curiosity at moments of confusion or crisis.

KEEPING THE BALANCE

Circling is an extremely complex social form, very delicate and sturdy at the same time. There is so much going on in the moment: attention, the senses, intuition, intellect, soul, and heart are called for. Remember this when circling: you will fall down and will need to get up again. You will need to rebalance the circle and mend the connections, protect yourself, learn your lessons, trust again, open the heart and mind again. Again. Again. And again.

There may come a time in a circle when strong, spirit-centered action is needed to protect yourself, to carry out the task you have chosen or to maintain the integrity of the circle itself. You may have to deal with someone who wants control, who tries to establish dominance, who creates fear.

When the intent to control is present, it becomes increasingly difficult for leadership, responsibility and spirituality to function. When the intent to control becomes intimidation, it undermines intention, undermines the well-being of the circle by breaking the social net of contracts and destroying the power of covenants to hold the heart-space of the group together. If someone or something starts to intimate the circle, a series of symptoms show up.

1. Symptoms of trouble.

(1) People stop being vulnerable. People try to avoid emotional risk or exposure. Even though the form of sharing may remain intact, in verbal camouflage people sound like they're saying something significant, but they aren't really revealing anything. Things appear the same, but don't feel the same.

(2) Anyone crossing the transaction or challenging the situation is immediately intimidated. The show of force is excessive—much greater than is appropriate or even necessary. Its purpose is simply to exhibit power and to scare people away from confrontation.

(3) People stop being themselves; everyone goes into placating behavior. People react to intimidation in different ways: denial, passivity, rationalization, bargaining, anything they can think of to smooth over the surface.

(4) People retreat from everyone in the circle, not only from the one carrying the negative charge. The interconnections that bind you togeth-

er seem to vanish. Everyone is isolated in their adaptive behavior and withdrawal, incapable of unifying to make a thoughtful response or take action. Synergy disappears; people go into shock and fear. Suddenly the circle's reliable energy is gone.

(5) *The circle feels charged with underlying energies which cannot be explained by what's occurring on the social level.* You and others are waiting for the other shoe to drop, and may not even know why.

(6) *The negative energy is looking for its positive pole, and the group is looking for a lightning rod.* You may feel drawn toward confrontation by this energetic attraction, compelled to dissipate the energy or watch as another person in the circle suddenly clicks into the magnetism. When someone breaks circle energy, *other* people get weird, begin doing strange things that draw attention away from the person who is holding the negative charge.

When any or all of these signals are apparent, the three principles must be put to work among the MAJORITY of members in order to reinstate PeerSpirit. Remember—leadership rotates, responsibility is shared, and ultimate reliance is spiritual. Even if you haven't figured out yet what is happening, stay present. If you "leave" in your mind, you cannot protect yourself or help group process. Provide backing for the one taking the brunt of it. Hold on to your heartspace. Call for silence or some other spiritual intervention. Physically withdraw from abuse or potential violence—and invite others to do the same. Remember the group contracts and apply them—immediately and unswervingly.

If you don't feel empowered, don't feel that you can live the three principles, then this is a circle in trouble. These situations can be terrifying. Take some quiet space, either within the circle, or by taking time out. Each circle member needs time to ask: *Has my own ego or unconscious material gotten in the way here? Am I railroading something the circle doesn't want? What's the focus, the thing I want to resolve? Is this possible? How do I finish this moment in a way that restores the circle?*

When the circle is shattering, don't expect to feel cool as a cucumber. There's a reason you are afraid—intimidation is at work. If you and others confront the issue, you will need to assess what's really happening:

- Who or what is controlling the circle?
- Who or what is respecting the circle?
- Who is the carrier of discordant energy?

- Is it me?
- What is a non-ego manner of confrontation?
- What kind of support do I need? How will I elicit it?
- Am I prepared to lose the circle if the confrontation doesn't work?

If you decide to confront a situation, prepare to be confronted in return. The more you can stay out of your ego, the less you will get hooked into power plays. If you do not have the support of the circle, then you cannot "save" it.

Circling is an extremely ancient form which has weathered many challenges. A shattered circle has the potential to come together again, but you cannot regather it by yourself. Who is still aligned with the circle? Ask for help. If this circle's life is still intact, it will come through the shattering stronger than before. If not, take care of yourself. Leave and reform the circle in a safer setting.

2. Respectful practices. One way of keeping the balance of a circle is to practice respect for each other. If people feel safe and know they will be held in decent regard, the circle will feel harmonious.

It is respectful to walk into a circle and observe boundaries. The body needs a level of trust as much as the mind does. There are several practices of touch that help sustain the circle. You need to consider how and in what ways you are comfortable participating. Men and women, many with histories of physical or sexual abuse, have different understandings about touch as manipulation or domination. This is an area where asking, showing respect and a little healthy hesitation help establish trust.

(1) Eye contact and sound. At the beginning of the circle, be silent, look at each other, listen. Listen to your own inner self. Listen to the center. Touch down. Center down. Come into your body with some stretching exercises or deep breathing. Hum, sing, chant. "OM" is said to be the sound of the universe. It has a special resonance when sounded in a group. Or choose another word—'cir-cle' will do, or "I-you-we" repeated slowly over and over.

Songs create a wonderful link within circle experience and keep people connected to the circle while it's not in session. Many chants and simple rounds are composed for circles or create your own. Days later, in the shower, in the car, there is this little tune circling around in your mind.

(2) Heart Drumming. The drum is a circle. The drum is a universal instrument which has always been in the circle and comes to us from First Culture. You don't actually need a drum to try drumming. The body is covered with skin, like a drum head, and makes a pleasant resonating thump when played. Thighs and calves are satisfying to slap gently. Lub-dub-dub, or 1-2-3-4 are basic rhythms.

Drumming is a good way to re-establish harmony after time away. Playing off one another's rhythms, following first one person then another, coming into shared beat, losing it, laughing, refocusing—all bring the circle together in a profound way.

(3) Touching. Hands are powerful tools in a circle. With or without actually touching palm to palm, you can pass energy in a ring, ground energy beneath you, extend hands into the center, or reach out and pull energy in. You can pull energy down from the sky or send it spiraling upward.

While you are learning your personal and collective levels of comfort, ask before touching someone with your hands. Tell people how and if you like to be touched. People who are comfortable with their bodies and intuitive in how they reach out for others may think this conversation is unnecessary; others, who have been invaded in the past, may be thankful to have the topic raised. Always assume there is a wide range of comfort and personal history in every circle.

When something happens in the circle that touches your heart, be literal about it—touch your heart. There is a place on our bodies, in the center of the breastbone, that is called the high heart, the spiritual heart. This point is the source of compassion, empathy, and the ability to release heart energy. Stroke this part of the body gently, especially when you are aware of tender emotions. It can be a great comfort for someone who is in a vulnerable state to see others with their hands on their hearts as a gesture of communion. Heart touching is non-intrusive; it simply lets someone know they are not isolated in their feeling or insight. This helps the speaker remember to touch their own heart, to be tender toward their own emotions and experiences.

(4) Backing. One way of being touched that can feel literally and symbolically supportive is *backing*. You have probably used the

phrase, "Would you back me up on this?" or "I could use your back-ing..."

In the circle, backing has several variations: the idea is to liter-ally stand or sit behind someone and touch their back, *upon direct request*. Putting your palm flat against a person's spine, resting the heel of the palm between the shoulder blades and extending the fin-gers upwards is a subtle way to provide meaningful touch in a public setting or business environment. Even simply standing right behind someone, not touching, and sending energy through the palms or good wishes through your high heart will have an impact.

If you are in a circle setting which is more informal or where people are comfortable with touch, *upon direct request* you may back someone by scooting your torso behind them, arms and legs making a kind of chair, and letting them lean against you. Both of you remain facing into the group, engaged with the whole circle. This kind of backing provides tremendous support and is usually considered non-intrusive because it allows both people to stay in equal relationship to each other and to the circle.

Circle members may request this kind of backing when some-one is having an emotional response and doesn't want to leave the circle; when two people engaged in conflict resolution ask for physi-cal support while they talk through an issue; when someone wants a little extra energy in the middle of a meeting; or just because it's a wonderful supportive gesture.

FOUR STAGES OF A CIRCLE'S LIFE

A circle has a natural life span—four stages that occur as the circle moves through time, *and* in the course of every meeting. How the four stages occur in the microcosm of a single meeting indicate how the four stages are progressing in the macrocosm of the circle's life span.

1. Building trust. Trust is developed by creating a structure which every member may count on and a history of respectful inter-action. Everything discussed so far in sustaining the PeerSpirit circle builds trust.

Circles may meet weekly or once a year. Between meetings people have experiences which impact their willingness and ability to be present to the group. People mature, change their minds, meet individually, and find resolutions to issues outside council. At each meeting, people need to greet each other again and check out the level of trust. The group needs to know what is being brought back to the circle by each member.

When the circle regathers, trust is re-established as people restate their relationship to each other and to the group's intent and purpose. The following questions need to be answered to re-establish trust.

- Are you still who I think you are?
- Are we still in the kind of relationship I think we are in?
- Are you still trustworthy? Am I still trustworthy?
- Is this circle still heading in the direction I think it is?
- Is there anything I need to clear up, internally or with some one else, in order to be fully present here?

The check-in that fosters the re-establishment of trust includes words, eye contact, body language, and touch. As you re-enter the circle, practice being aware of your reactions and interactions with others on all these levels.

Trust is also built by a track record of doing tasks well together, a confidence that comes from treating each other respectfully, solving problems, holding focus, and moving forward to carry out intent. People are energized by accomplishing what they have contracted with each other to do.

2. Carrying out intent. Intent needs to be re-established and acknowledged on a meeting-by-meeting basis. Deviation from intent needs to be discussed and negotiated.

Carrying out intent is an exhilarating phase of the circle's life. Group process is carried along by its own momentum. The circle's definition of "success" combines the respect with which you treat each other and the accomplishment of tangible, concrete, and measurable goals. While engaging in carrying out intent, a new set of questions arises:

- How can I tell if we are following intent?
- What would a reasonable goal look like for this meeting?
- What would a reasonable goal look like for carrying out our overall plan?
- How does the balance of leadership, responsibility, and spirit feel during this "work phase" of the circle?
- Are my personal priorities and circle priorities still aligned?
- Has my understanding changed? What is our covenant now?
- What's exciting about all of this? What's scary?

Accomplishing intent brings with it stress, excitement, celebrations and group cohesion. This is the circle at its greatest triumph—working together and building a sense of comradeship in the accomplishment.

3. Recontracting. This is the time to acknowledge that something has been accomplished and there is a void in direction: *Now what?* Recontracting can be a vulnerable time in the course of a circle meeting or in the life span of the circle itself. The drive to fulfill purpose may still be running high, or there may be a let down in energy after an event has occurred or a goal reached.

This is a time when some people may want to leave the circle. Their direction or priorities have taken them elsewhere, they need to move on, commitments have changed, personality clashes have developed, or someone wants to start another circle. This is a time when others may want to define a new purpose and pursue the next accomplishment. It's helpful if each member can be clear and not unduly influenced by others or by their own nostalgic attachments to the group.

• What do I really want to do?
• What is my energy and time and commitment now?
• What will the group do next time it gathers?
• Do I want to take on another task?
• Who wants to go? Who wants to stay? Who wants to join?

However the circle proceeds—toward the next meeting or toward the next cycle of commitment—new contracts need to be set in place to provide the foundation for continued action. Recontracting is a literal process. It draws the circle back into council to reshape, redirect, and restate its collective energy. This is a time when people need to step forward again, take on responsibilities, or shift their role and relationship to the group. It is a time for careful listening, with detachment and an open heart.

In circle, energy is an invisible, working member of the group. It has been called upon in a sacred manner and we are reminded of its presence through ritual, guardianship, council and silence. When recontracting, pay attention to this energy—notice it within and around you.

4. Letting go. No matter how dynamic and successful a circle is at continuing to find purpose, and no matter how committed its members, there will come a time to acknowledge the closing of the cycle. There are circles that meet for a week—such as seminars and annual gatherings. Others meet for a few months—such as task forces and planning groups. Some circles meet for years—book clubs or social action or environmental groups, consciousness raising or spirituality circles.

Letting go is a time of grief and celebration—two sides of a spinning coin. A dynamic circle is a significant presence in your life. Prepare for grief, expect it, talk about it in council, have the courage to say goodbye in whatever ways fit you and the circle. In ordinary settings, or during times of celebration, people may forget that grief will also be present. Monitor sudden impulses toward irritation or withdrawal and ask yourself if grief is perhaps the real emotion.

Letting go, whether of one meeting or a long-term experience, is a time when ritual helps. Ritual provides a container for handling your emotions. Through ritual's symbolism, ordinary actions are infused with spiritual presence and we remember to honor the mystery of the circle. Some form of ritual will develop in how your circle gathers, conducts itself, and parts. Leave-taking needs simply to be acknowledged so that everyone knows when the meeting is over or when the circle is complete.

In leave-taking a circle, there are practical details and contracts that balance the heart energy.

- What conversation does the group need to have to honor itself?
- What do we want to do with the artifacts created: the log book, the altar/basket and other tangible records of our experience?
- What guidelines of confidentiality do we still want observed?
- How does each member respect the learning process here?
- Is there a ritual for closing that we want to design?
- What are the friendships, or potential friendships, we've discovered, and what contracts do we want to make for meeting outside the circle?

Wherever you may be in the life span of your circle,
blessings to you.
May your circle open and disperse,
and its heartspace remain unbroken.

Christina Baldwin

BIOGRAPHY

Christina Baldwin has taught journal writing seminars internationally for over twenty years, and contributed two classic books to this field. Her first book, *One to One: Self-Understanding through Journal Writing* (M. Evans, 1977, 1991) is a ground-breaking document that has remained in continuous print. Her best-selling book, *Life's Companion: Journal Writing as a Spiritual Quest* (Bantam 1990) takes the art of writing and expands it into spiritual practice.

She has been committed to helping people free up their lives through the introspection and raised consciousness of working with their own life stories, and has conducted all her teaching in circles. In the early 1990s, she began exploring how to help people bridge from introspection and consciousness to social action using the circle as the primary source of support. This exploration led to the concepts presented in this book.

She holds a bachelor's degree from Macalester College, St. Paul, Minnesota, and a master's degree from Columbia Pacific University, San Rafael, California. She has been a self-employed voyager, pushing at the edge of the culture to incorporate the values of new consciousness. She is now located in the state of Washington, in a business partnership called PeerSpirit™. She and her partner, author/educator Ann Linnea, chose this location for its international accessibility.

In setting after setting, when the circle has been used as the primary organizational tool, she has seen the principles and concepts of this book flourish between people, leading to empowerment, accomplishment, and community. She firmly believes that the introduction of the circle will contribute to societal transformation.

Ms. Baldwin is available for speaking engagements, seminars, and consultation to the circle. Please contact PeerSpirit, Box 550, Langley, WA 98260/ USA, tel: 206-321-8404. NOTE: after 1/15/95 the telephone area code will become 360.

Cover Art

The cover art for this book is an original painting by visionary artist Susan Seddon Boulet. Having seen the basket-centered altar in Christina Baldwin's own circle work, Susan felt drawn to the imagery of a "basket of creation contained within a circle of stones."

The painting represents the nature of our circumstances. We are in darkness and in light. We are held within the web of life. We are calling the circle out of mystery, combining the ancient and the modern, the past and the future. We are facing each other—young and old, male and female, all races and groups. The symbol of the world itself is the unifying focus that rides in all our minds. How may we love the world? How might we respect life? What qualities are we willing to seek in ourselves and each other that bring us into circle again?

In the midst of our questioning, at the rim of the circle, we are sheltered by the everlasting stones. The circle holds. We are cut through with possibility.

Susan Boulet's work is distributed by Pomegranate Press.

CIRCLE TALK

Circle Talk is a way of speaking to each other at a deeper level of conversation than we usually do in social interaction. People may at first feel awkward using this language, but as we understand that being in a circle is a consecrated way of being together, the language, the ritual and form begin to flow more easily.

Altar	is the common word designating the table, cloth or area set aside to hold items we have chosen to display in the sacred center of the circle.
Attention	is spiritual alertness; a state of acute awareness in which we listen from the heart, without interrupting. When we listen attentively, we open our minds to what is being said at the moment and are not distracted by planning our response or statement while others are talking.
Backing	is the physical support of one member of the circle by another, where, upon request, one person sits or stands behind another and offers literal physical support.
Calling a Circle	means to issue an invitation for people to convene within a circle. Circles may be called for any number of purposes, to accomplish any number of tasks, large or small. When we call a circle, we create the environment where honest talk and respectful listening may occur.
Checking In	is self-inventory, without commentary. Usually check-in occurs near the beginning of a circle meeting so everyone may speak and be heard. A talking piece may be passed once around the circle, then placed in the center to be picked up if anyone has more to share.

Circle

is a mutually-supportive group convened for a specific purpose. It is a gathering held literally in circular form, in which members share responsibility for what happens in the group. It is a mechanism of self-empowerment in which leadership rotates, responsibility is shared, and the group relies on Spirit to hold and focus energy.

Circular Change

is a shift from power-based, individual control, or from top-down, hierarchical control, to community action based on honest discussion and consensus. Members discover, define, and follow the path with heart.

Circle Consciousness

is the living dynamic of the circle; the amalgam of personal energy with group energy. When we become personally conscious, we awaken to the possibility that groups may also become conscious.

Citizen

is a member of a group, state or nation who grants allegiance to certain principles of governance, *and in exchange*, is invited to participate in defining the group's direction and maintaining its values.

Citizen of the Circle

is a person who practices the principles of PeerSpirit circling.

Community

is the extension of relationship from the personal to the collective and the potential outgrowth of many forms of circling. *Community* is the sense that there exists a group of people who know you well, and whom you trust. They keep track of you, your goals and dreams and whereabouts, and you track their goals, dreams and whereabouts.

Compassion

is the art of "suffering with." It is not suffering *for*, the taking on of another's pain. It is the realization that pain and confusion are not exclusive, that people may cry together as well as laugh together.

Conflict Resolution

is the settlement of a disagreement in a respectful way that honors differing viewpoints and opinions and works toward a loving compromise without blaming or shaming those involved in the conflict; it is agreement through negotiation.

Consecrated Space is space that is acknowledged as special; "sacred" space where everyone's willingness to listen dwells.

Consensus is the process of coming to agreement by everyone. To reach *consensus*, people talk through an idea, a direction, a decision, until everyone present is able to agree on the action to be taken. This does not mean one person gives in, but discussion continues until all points of view have been shared, aired, and a *new vision* develops that takes everyone's contributions into account and creates something that was not in anyone's mind when the discussion began.

Contract is the articulated and agreed-upon guidelines which govern the circle, the ways people interact, the things they expect from the experience, the things they do not invest, as well as the things they do invest. See also Circle Guidelines.

Council is a group of people assembled for a deliberate purpose with the goal of acting in partnership. In *council*, a facilitator may guide discussion, while each member of the circle is given equal and uninterrupted time in which to contribute; or in peer council, the talking piece designates the speaker and facilitation is held by the group as a whole.

Covenant is the deeper, spiritual level of understanding between people who have made a contract, who meet with clear intent. The *covenant* in circling is often a commitment for two or more people to offer each other the best of their clarity and to defer to spiritual guidance when confused.

Descent is the necessary and worthwhile journey through darkness into light; the exploration of our shadow selves where we grieve, forgive, and finally transform and heal into our higher spiritual selves.

Empowerment	it is the power gathered from the energy of the circle that gives us the strength to act in harmony with our spiritual selves. In a circle, *empowerment* does not mean power *over,* it calls on power within and invites us to unilaterally share our power.
Facilitation	is the act of assisting the circle to realize its purpose. *Facilitation* is the result of shared leadership. A *facilitator* is a guide, more than a leader.
First Culture	is where we are rooted; the flowering of human community based on the campfire and the council, where the circle flourished in kinship-based tribal groups across the globe. *First culture* groups use the circle to combine governing council with spiritual counsel.
Second Culture	is the place Western society now finds itself. Second culture is a "triangle culture," a hierarchy in which power is concentrated at the top and imposed upon those at the bottom.
Third Culture	is the realm of the possible; an amalgam of the past and present where our ancient and intuitive knowledge may combine with our present experience to create a society where each person is empowered and encouraged to make the offering they have been born to make.
Group Process	is the way that commitment, contract, and intention are carried out during gatherings of the circle. The healthiness of any circle's *group process* is dependent upon the ability and willingness of the group members to think about their actions, to notice whether they are currently contributing what needs to get done, to take responsibility for staying out of the way of *group process* when their input isn't needed, and contributing when their input is needed.

Group/Circle *Guidelines*	are the contracts, or clarifying statements, that govern social interaction in a PeerSpirit circle. See also Contracts.
Heart Connection	is a listening point between the small self and the Sacred; a balance between receiving and offering. Heart connection may be experienced internally as a deep sense of well-being, and may be experienced interpersonally with another person, or non-human being as a communion beyond words, a spiritual link.
Hierarchical *Leadership*	is the delineation between leader and follower; between management and employee; between teacher and student. Someone knows something and passes it on to someone who doesn't know. Authority or power is located with the one who knows and passes on information, direction or decision.
Hierarchy	is a structure designed for running things from the top down. It is very efficient for types of production and in situations where skill is required at the top to provide learning, safety, or successful completion of a complex task. It tends to focus on outcome rather than process.
Holding Council	is an intentional coming together—a meeting held with agreed-upon parameters and procedures in which the respectful exchange of ideas takes place.
Intention	is the clarification of the reasons for this particular circle. *Intention* is like the mission statement of a circle. "This circle is called to support..." or "this circle is called to provide..." *Intention* is the verbal transmission of the idea for the circle.
Longing	is the energy that ignites a need in us for change, for movement.

Negotiation   is the process of talking something through until it is well understood, and action is agreed upon. *Negotiation* is kept going by the willingness of people to keep asking the next question.

Patriarchy   is the power-based, hierarchical model that operates at the core of Second Culture. Hierarchy is an operational structure; patriarchy is a system that uses hierarchy to accomplish its own ends. In patriarchy, the "father" is the supreme authority in the family, clan, or tribe. In Second Culture, this authority has been granted to men in general, who are viewed as having authority over women, children, business, government, and religion.

Peer Leadership   is a forum of shared responsibility in which members in a circle volunteer to provide certain things which the circle needs. The leadership floats between people according to the contracts made, according to the structures which have been defined by the group.

PeerSpirit Circling   is a form of circling that is carried out with intent, with clearly stated contracts, and with the inclusion and acceptance of spiritual direction.

Perseverance   is the commitment to stay awake, to battle our inertia, our lethargy, our desire for avoidance.

Relationship   is connection based on exchange, interaction, and mutual acknowledgment of each other's presence.

Reliance on Spirit   is the third of the Three Principles of PeerSpirit circling. *Reliance on Spirit* is the commitment within the group to call upon some mysterious inner/outer element to guide the overall intention and direction of the group.

Rim   is the edge of the circle, where those who participate in a circle gathering take their places to exchange ideas of the heart and mind openly and honestly, in an atmosphere of spiritual equality. "Holding the rim" is a way of stating that we are present and attentive in the circle.

Ritual is any action we do with intent to keep the channel open; the transformation of ordinary action into symbolic action. *Ritual* in the circle is the way we invite collective wisdom and acknowledge spiritual center.

Rotating Leadership is the first of the Three Principles of PeerSpirit circling. *Rotating leadership* means that every person helps the circle function by assuming small increments of leadership that carry forward the group's purpose. In PeerSpirit circling, leadership occurs when we listen as well as when we talk. Rotating leadership invites shared responsibility.

Sacred/Spirit means whatever *you* mean by the words *you* use for God, god/us or Spirit, the Holy One, the Creator, the Mystery.

Sacred Center is a place of raw energy, located metaphorically in the center of the circle. Each person draws upon this energy as needed, and contributes as needed. The way people usually acknowledge the presence of *sacred center* in their circling is by placing some representative symbol important for their group in the middle of the circle and by creating rituals that open and close and maintain the circle's commitment to using the center as the resting point in group process.

Second Culture see *First Culture*

Shared Responsibility is the second of the Three Principles of PeerSpirit circling. *Shared Responsibility* means that each person pays attention to the social, emotional, and spiritual elements of the circle and works to sustain a respectful environment. *Shared responsibility* means to pay attention, to be sensitive to what others need in terms of support, to think before speaking, to take time to consider the consequences of action and to ask for help in setting direction.

**Speaking from
the Heart**   is communicating beyond ego, taking the risk to let others know us on a spiritual level, not only as social beings.

Spiritual Practice   is an action we do with intent to discover the sources of spiritual guidance and to help make us conscious of our relationship to Spirit.

Spirituality   is the desire to make the daily patterns of how we live sacred. *Spirituality* is a drive to integrate all the realities we are capable of perceiving from hope to despair, from ecstasy to anguish, and to bring this range of human experience into a framework that helps us make sense of our lives.

Synergy   is the attraction to a particular circle, group of people, or idea that occurs when "the call" is clear; synergy is an experience of harmony established between intention and action.

Talking Piece   is any object designated to grant the person holding it the right to speak without interruption. It needs to be an object comfortable to the setting of a circle that reflects the personality of the group.

Third Culture: see *First Culture*

Three Principles   are the basic structure of PeerSpirit circling. They consist of rotating leadership, shared responsibility, reliance on Spirit.

Tribe   is a group of people united by common ancestry, custom, religion or place. In circle talk, a *tribe* may also be a group of people who come together to create these commonalties.

CIRCLE BOOK SOURCES AND RESOURCES

This bibliography represents some of the cultural context inside which the circle is reawakening. It is drastically incomplete, but offers a partial map for putting your own journey into circle. The joy in each of these books is that many of them also contain a bibliography, and so we may explore the information, stories, histories and possibilities that lead many writers and thinkers in considering the foundations for Third Culture and the coming of a new age for humankind.

...I have claimed the altar. In ancient times there was an altar in every room of the home. The home was where spirit lived.
—Tsultrin Allione

Lighting a candle is a symbolic gesture, often linked with the preservation of the soul—a small light in the darkness, the fire in the center of our circle.
—From "A Way to Begin", found in *The Box*, created by The Térma Company

Ceremonies and Rituals:

Cahill, Sedona and Halpern, Joshua. *The Ceremonial Circle.* San Francisco: Harper, 1990. A practical and inspirational guide for creating ceremony and ritual for "all those who dance in the circle." The book also includes interviews with well-known ceremonialists like Starhawk, Vicki Noble and others.

Eclipse. *The Moon in Hand.* Portland, ME: Astarte Shell Press, 1991. A lovely book of rituals and meditations that has as its focus the wheel of the Four Directions—the magic circle of life.

Paladin, Lynda S. *Ceremonies for Change.* Walpole, NH: Stillpoint Publishing, 1991. When Paladin's husband died, she created a special ceremony to scatted his "cremains." This experience opened a door for her into the use of symbol and ceremony to celebrate and note life changes. In this book, she teaches others how to create ceremonies—an act she calls her "giveaway."

Starhawk. *The Spiral Dance.* San Francisco: Harper & Row, 1979. An exploration of the Goddess religion and a wealth of information on ritual and ceremony.

Starkhawk. *Truth or Dare.* San Francisco: Harper & Row, 1987. Through ritual, myth, story and symbolism, Starhawk examines the nature of power. In her poetic and informative style, she shows how to exercise power-with instead of power-over. Her examples of ritual and ceremony are particularly useful for circle work.

Térma Company. *The Box.* Santa Fe, NM: The Térma Company, 1992. Everything you need to take a spiritual journey, deep and lasting. *The Box* contains an altar cloth, candles, seeds, and books for each stage of inner exploration. *The Box* is an active process designed to help participant/readers heal themselves and the world. It is designed for circle work and serves as an excellent tool for calling a circle together, working through the clarification *The Box* provides, and then setting intention for continuing the circle with a goal in mind.

All things are connected like the blood which unites one family.
           —Chief Seattle

Cultural Perspectives:

NOTE: *We are a global people, global seekers, trying to find our way to renewed culture and spirituality. People raised in one tradition may feel drawn to other traditions in this search. We need to remember and respect that in spite of the ravages of the last 5,000 years, indigenous peoples have held the remaining wisdom of First Culture, the source that is common for us all. We need to approach this search with respect for those who have been carrying this wisdom for us.*

Arrien, Angeles. *Four-Fold Way*. San Francisco: Harper, 1993. A sensitive, cross-cultural approach to studying shamanic teachings of indigenous people and how this wisdom can lead us to wholeness.

Bancroft, Anne. *Origins of the Sacred.* London and New York: Arkana, 1987. The subtitle of this book is, *The Spiritual Journey in Western Tradition,* a fine look at the European indigenous roots of spirituality among the Celtic, Nordic, and Greco-Roman roots that predate Christianity.

Dreher, Diane. *The Tao of Peace.* New York: Donald I. Fine, Inc., 1990. This book explores the *Tao Te Ching* as a practical path of reflection and cooperation. Each chapter opens with quote from the *Tao* which can be used as a theme for meditation and closes with an affirmation.

Eaton, Evelyn. *The Shaman and the Medicine Wheel.* Wheaton, IL: Theosophical Publishing House, 1982. Eaton is a Metis Medicine Woman of the Bear Medicine Tribe and the Deer Tribe who shares her inner journey around the medicine wheel.

Foster, Steven and Meredith Little. *Roaring of the Sacred River.* New York: Prentice Hall Press, 1989. Wonderful resource, particularly for those interested in the Native American vision quest and wilderness rites.

Macy, Joanna. *World as Lover, World as Self.* Berkely, CA: Parallax Press, 1991. A beautiful collection of talks and essays that apply Buddhist philosophy to every-day living as active citizens in a shared world.

Underwood, Paula. *The Walking People: A Native American Oral History.* Georgetown, TX: A Tribe of Two Press, 1993. This ancient oral history, handed down with meticulous care through five generations of Ms. Underwood's family, stretches back over thousands of years of human experience and shows us the possibilities of effective survival in a changing circumstance. It is part of the Past is Prologue (PIP) Educational Program based on Learning Stones handed down in the same oral tradition. Personally, I think it is one of the most important spiritual documents of our time.

I need to be with people who are in longing with their lives.
                                        —Ann Linnea

Workplace and Everyday Life:

Fox, Matthew. *The Reinvention of Work.* San Francisco: Harper, 1994. Fox explores how our souls have been separated from work and offers ways to reintegrate a "new vision of livelihood."

Sher, Barbara and Annie Gottlieb. *Teamworks!* New York: Warner Books, 1989. A process for garnering unconditional support through the formation of teams in the workplace.

Sinetar, Marsha. **Ordinary People as Monks and Mystics.** New York: Paulist Press, 1986. In this classic study, Sinetar explores the ways people are striving to make sense in their lives.

The dust of exploded beliefs may make a fine sunset.
                        —Geofrey Madan

The Spiritual Context:

Baldwin, Christina. **Life's Companion: Journal Writing as a Spiritual Quest.** New York: Bantam Books, 1990. This book establishes writing as a spiritual practice.

Eisler, Riane. **The Chalice and the Blade: Our History, Our Future.** San Francisco: HarperCollins, 1987. An intense look at 40,000 years of human history. This book is the basis for much understanding of original culture, hierarchical culture and a model for coming into a partnership culture.

Eisler, Riane and David Loye. **The Partnership Way.** San Francisco: HarperCollins, 1990. This is the practical workbook for understanding how to move into a partnership way of viewing the world. It is designed for group study and provides a good way for a circle to gather, educate itself and decide what further functions it would like to have.

Fox, Matthew. **The Coming of the Cosmic Christ: The Healing of Mother Earth and the Birth of a Global Renaissance.** San Francisco: Harper & Row, 1988. Fox, like so many who meet in circles all over the world, calls for a metanoia, a change of mind. "When a civilization is without a cosmology it is not only cosmically violent, but cosmically lonely and depressed," writes Fox. It is time, he says, to move from the historical Jesus to the quest for the "Cosmic Christ," an inclusive sacred wisdom.

LaChapelle, Delores. **Sacred Land, Sacred Sex: Rapture of the Deep.** Durango, CO: Kivaki Press, 1992. This book is as broad a look at how we live on the planet and with each other as the title implies.

Osborn, Diane K., ed. **A Joseph Campbell Companion.** New York: Harper Collins, 1991. This is a beautiful and useful little book of Campbell wisdom that intertwines his own words with the words of those he studied and respected.

Sellner, Edward C. *Mentoring.* Notre Dame, IN: Ave Maria Press, 1990. A good historical and practical guide on spiritual mentoring and the importance of becoming a "soul friend."

Térma Company. *The Box.* See full listing under *Ceremonies and Ritual.*

Every day is a god, each day is a god, and holiness holds forth in time.
—Annie Dillard

Each being is sacred—meaning that each has inherent value that cannot be ranked in a hierarchy or compared to the value of another being.
—Starhawk

Women's Spiritual Perspective:

Gadon, Elinor. *The Once and Future Goddess.* San Francisco: Harper & Row, 1989. This book can single-handedly educate the reader in the history and hope of the goddess tradition. Gadon has done tremendous historical research and relates it to modern imagery and emerging art and spirituality. Her selected bibliography will keep you going to the library and the bookstore for the next five years.

Harris, Maria. *Dance of the Spirit.* New York: Bantam, 1989. An insightful book that explores the seven steps of women's spirituality and discusses the meaning and movement of each step that forms the spiritual dance.

Murdock, Maureen. *The Heroine's Journey.* Boston: Shambhala, 1990. This book traces the heroine's journey and serves as a guide for those who are on a path to discover their complete spiritual selves.

Noble, Vicki. *Shakti Woman.* San Francisco: Harper, 1991. Riane Eisler describes this book aptly. "It is a passionate call for women to reconnect with our goddess heritage and reclaim our ancient powers of healing before it is too late for ourselves and our Mother Earth."

Noble, Vicki, ed. *Uncoiling the Snake.* San Francisco: Harper, 1993. "Uncoiling the Snake," writes Vicki Noble, "refers to the deep, hidden structure behind things and the sacred patterns to which shamans in all cultures attune themselves." This is an anthology of stories, poems, pictures and essays that inform and celebrate women's power to heal.

Spretnak, Charlene, ed. *The Politics of Women's Spirituality.* New York: Anchor Doubleday, 1982. This is an important and eclectic collection of essays on the rise of spiritual power within the feminist movement.

Does this path have a heart? If it does, the path is good; if it doesn't, it is of no use.
—Carlos Castanedas

Men's Spiritual Perspective:

Hudson, Frederic. *The Adult Years: Mastering the Art of Self-Renewal.* San Francisco: Jossey-Bass, 1991.

Liebman, Wayne. *Tending the Fire: The Ritual Men's Group.* St. Paul, MN: Ally Press, 1991. A small book with much guidance for men wishing to understand and reform council.

We know ourselves to be made from this earth. We know this earth is made from our bodies. For we see ourselves. And we are nature. We are nature seeing nature. We are nature with a concept of nature. Nature weeping. Nature speaking of nature to nature.
—Susan Griffin

Connecting With the Earth:

Badiner, Allan Hunt, ed. *Dharma Gaia.* Berkeley, CA: Parallax Press, 1990. Essays on Buddhism and ecological consciousness. Inspires and encourages readers to connect and work together to save the Earth and ourselves.

Gore, Al. *Earth in the Balance: Ecology and the Human Spirit.* New York: Houghton, Mifflin Co., 1992. A comprehensive discussion of global environmental issues. Gore expertly explores the connection between spirituality and environmental activism.

Halifax, Joan. *The Fruitful Darkness.* San Francisco: HarperSanFrancisco, 1993. This is a personal account of Halifax's spiritual journey and reconnection to the earth.

Hynes, Patricia H. *Earth Right.* Rocklin, CA: Prima Publishing & Communications, 1990. A hands-on resource book and guide to reclaim our earth. After explaining environmental problems in a nontechnical way, Hynes offers creative ideas for action and resources for further information. She offers hope.

Linnea, Ann. *Superior Spirit: One Woman's Journey Sea Kayaking Lake Superior.* New York: Little, Brown & Company, 1995. A story of how one woman uses incredible physical adventure to transform her life and connect with The Sacred.

Roberts, Elizabeth and Elias Amidon, ed. *Earth Prayers.* San Francisco: Harper, 1991. An amazing compilation of prayers, poems and words of wisdom that may enhance any circle gathering by invoking a connective, loving spirit.

Seed, John, et al. *Thinking Like a Mountain.* Santa Cruz, CA. New Society Publishers, 1988. A collection of essays, meditations and writings to help people connect with the Earth and establish a council of all beings.

I think, at a child's birth, if a mother could ask a fairy godmother to endow it with the most useful gift, that gift should be curiosity.
—Eleanor Roosevelt

Circling With Children:

Gibbs, Jeanne. *Tribes.* Santa Rosa, CA: Center Source Publications, 1987. (Her revised edition is entitled *Tribes: A New Way of Learning Together,* 1994.) Since 1987 when Gibbs first described this process for social development and cooperative learning, tribal circles have been flourishing in classrooms. These books and her curriculum training apply the circle in school settings.

Linnea, Ann, (under the name Schimpf) et al. *Teaching Kids to Love the Earth.* Duluth, MN: Pfeifer-Hamilton, 1991. 186 activities, leading children through a Sense of Wonder Circle comprised of curiosity, exploration, discovery, sharing and passion. A nationally award winning educational tool for teachers, parents and others working with children.

Milord, Susan. *Hands Around the World.* Charlotte, VT: Williamson Publishing, 1992. 365 ways for children to learn about other cultures and connect with other children around the world. Her ideas are empowering, creative and fun.

If you don't have turbulence, nothing moves.
       —Jeanette Picard (first woman balloon pilot)

Conflict Resolution and Circle Skills:

Eisler, Riane and David Loye. *The Partnership Way.* See full listing under *Spiritual Context.*

Fisher, Roger and William Ury. *Getting to Yes: Negotiating Agreement Without Giving In.* New York: Penguin Books, 1983. A bestseller that might help resolve conflicts in your circle when they arise.

Johnson, Robert A. *Owning Your Own Shadow.* San Francisco: Harper, 1991. "The fire of transformation and the flower of rebirth are one and the same," writes Johnson. Owning one's shadow is a necessary step in reclaiming ourselves—putting ourselves back together again so we might, in turn, heal our fractured world.

Sheeran, Michael J. *Beyond Majority Rule.* Philadelphia, PA: Religious Society of Friends, 1991. Quakers have been meeting in circles and operating through consensus since the 1600s. Sheeran traces the Friends' tradition of religious decision making and its applicability in contemporary society.

Starhawk. *Dreaming the Dark.* Boston: Beacon Press, 1982. This is groundbreaking work on the structure, dynamics and spirituality of the circle. It is the philosophical basis for her novel, *The Fifth Sacred Thing* (see full listing under fiction).

Zimmerman, Jack and Virginia Coyle. *Speaking From the Heart: The Council Press.* Ojai, CA: The Ojai Foundation, to be published in 1995.

We must be the change we wish to see in the world.
                              —Mahatma Ghandi

*Never doubt that a small group of thoughtful, committed people can change the
world. Indeed it's the only thing that ever has.*
                              —Margaret Mead

Building Third Culture:

Eisler, Riane. *The Chalice and the Blade.* San Francisco: HarperCollins, 1987.
A ground-breaking re-examination of human society from a "gender-holis-
tic" perspective and an exploration of how we may more effectively intervene in our own cultural evolution. This is a study of possibility, of "cultural
transformation."

Eisler, Riane and David Loye. *The Partnership Way.* San Francisco:
HarperCollins, 1990. A companion book to *The Chalice and the Blade.* Offers
ideas, information and exercises to help implement global transformation.

Etzioni, Amitai. *The Spirit of Community.* New York: Crown Publishers,
Inc., 1993. Etzioni maintains that we have many rights as individuals but he
reminds us that we have responsibilities too. This book explains the
Communitarian movement—a movement that seeks to move society from
me to we.

Ferguson, Marilyn. *The Aquarian Conspiracy.* Los Angeles: Tarcher,
Houghton, Mifflin Company, 1980. Fifteen years ago, Marilyn Ferguson
wrote about an irrevocable shift that was beginning to overtake us—a turn-
about in the consciousness that was beginning to seize certain individuals.

Kyle, David T. *Human Robots and Holy Mechanics: Reclaiming Our Souls
in a Machine World .* Newberg, OR: Swan Raven & Company, 1993. "The
adventure of another kind of life and world that emerges from a new imagining is growing in many of us," writes Kyle. His "epiphanal community"—a group of individuals who have a common insight—is a circle. His
book is a careful analysis of Second Culture and offers a path onward to
evolving a new culture

Montuori, Alfonso and Isabella Conti. *From Power to Partnership.* San
Franciso: Harper, 1993. Using Eisler's *The Chalice and the Blade* as a guide, the
authors explore other ways to work and learn cooperatively.

Peck, M. Scott. *The Different Drum: Community Making and Peace.* New York: Simon & Schuster, Inc., 1987. A challenge to move beyond individualism into connection—an earnest plea to recreate community.

Stories that Point the Way:

LeGuin, Ursula. *Always Coming Home.* 1985. New York: Bantam, 1987. In this "archeology of the future" LeGuin creates a whole culture for us to consider: maps, songs, mythology, and history that is yet to come to pass.

Starhawk. *The Fifth Sacred Thing.* New York: Bantam, 1993. Set in the early years of the 21st century, the circle is used as the governance of a Third Culture enclave in the Bay Area. Much good teaching woven into a gripping story.

Underwood, Paula. *The Walking People: A Native American Oral History.* See full listing under *Cultural Perspectives.*

Other Resources:

Angeles, Arrien. *The TAROT Handbook.* Sonoma, CA: Arcus Publishing Company, 1987. This guide, based on the classic Thoth Deck, is a most comprehensive, cross-cultural and persmission-giving guide to Tarot.

Borden, Barbara. *Dare to Drum.* San Anselmo, CA: Cloud 9 Productions, to be published in 1995. This autobiographical piece tells the story of one woman learning to drum, and through the drum, learning to listen to, contribute to, and hold the hearbeat of the world and all her peoples. Her recordings are available through Cloud 9 Productions.

Newman, Naomi. *Snake Talk: Urgent Massages from the Mother.* San Francisco, CA: Traveling Jewish Theater, 1991. This one-woman performance piece, available on audio cassette, video cassette and in live performance, is Newman's exploration of the "Triple Goddess, in the voices of Else, the poet, Rife, the Jewish immigrant mother, and a street crone who calls herself The Hag." A beautiful tour de force.

Noble, Vicki. *Motherpeace: A Way to the Goddess Through Myth, Art, and Tarot.* San Francisco, CA: Harper, 1983. This book accompanies the

Motherpeace Tarot deck, putting the cards in a goddess tradition.

Read, Donna. *Goddess Remembered.* Los Angeles, CA: distributed by Direct Cinema Ltd., 1990.

____. *The Burning Times.* Los Angeles, CA: distributed by Direct Cinema Ltd., 1990.

____. *Full Circle.* Los Angeles, CA: distributed by Direct Cinema Ltd., 1993. These video documentaries are Read's *Women and Spirituality* trilogy, an exploration of the history, repression and resurgence of the women's spirituality movement.

Waulen, James. *Voyager Tarot.* Carmel, CA: Merrill-West Publishing, 1989. Another modern look at this ancient tradition. This voyager deck and book are richly cross cultural and a good way for men to enter into the cards.

PeerSpirit™
In Service to the Circle

PeerSpirit is a partnership dedicated to bringing the circle into the culture. We form a circle around the belief that by rotating leadership, sharing responsibility, and attending to Sacred, people may align their lives with their own dreams, social awareness, and spiritual values and respond to the pressing needs of the earth, its people and creatures.

Three internationally known seminars—*Calling for Change, Tenfold*™ and *Women and the Planet*—form the core services of PeerSpirit.

- *Calling for Change* is a training session in circle and council skills designed to be used by groups in businesses, civic organizations, churches, temples, schools, and private settings. The program walks participants through intention setting and provides background support and consultation for groups of people who have identified areas or issues of change. *Calling for Change* helps people make the circle a relevant and effective reorganization tool. It may be introduced as a one day workshop and/or form the basis for ongoing consulting between PeerSpirit and the group.

- *Tenfold* is a culture-changing, life-changing process for mid-life women who are ready to integrate spirituality, insight and worldly achievement. The process begins with a two and a half day seminar that provides focus and teaches council holding skills. At the end of the seminar participants are invited into a contractual, time-limited support circle, self-guided on the principles of peer spirit. Support for *Tenfold* groups includes networking across state, provincial and national boundaries.

- *Women and the Planet* is a three to seven day experience of circle and community offered in retreat and wilderness settings. Its purpose is to provide time away from the ordinary routine, to provide a common basis of support and intention for ongoing groups, and to return women to their home communities with confident council skills. This circle calls women into a renewed understanding of the connection between ourselves and the planet, to tap into planetary wisdom as the wellspring for social action and personal change.

Founders, Christina Baldwin and Ann Linnea, and other facilitators, trainers and colleagues offer a variety of consultation services to the circle. Our mission is to extend the work of council and circle to women, men, and mixed groups, and to form a collegial consortium of individuals and businesses which work in coordination to bring forth Third Culture values.

Information on this work may be obtained by contacting:

PeerSpirit
P. O. Box 550
Langley, WA 98260 USA
Tel: 206 321-8404

(**NOTE**: After January 15, 1995, the area code will change to 360).

ACKNOWLEDGEMENTS

Just as the circle has been through many mutations making its way through Second Culture, so has this book. In Minneapolis, on Whidbey, and along the road 1992-94, during a time of intense personal change and professional realignment, writing was an arduous and exciting process of spinning raw experience into story, concept, and understanding. I could not have made this journey—literally or on the page—without the assistance and companionship of many people. My deepest thanks will occur hand to hand and heart to heart as this book passes into the circles where it belongs; but I want to offer some public expression, the way one leaves a cairn of rocks piled on the beach, or flowers tucked in the limb of a tree to signify that someone walked by with heart.

In its first evolution, this book was to be called "Everyday Ceremonies," and was acquired by the same editor at Bantam who brought out *Life's Companion*. In the summer of 1992, every time I went into a bookstore it seemed another book on ceremony and ritual had just been released. We agreed to not duplicate what was already being done by other writers, and I set off to discover my next topic. For that initial trust, and for letting the book go when that seemed in its best interest, I thank editor Linda Gross, at Bantam New Age. In August 1992, I went to my first Women's Alliance Camp and encountered the circle at a whole new level. This story is described more fully in the book, but I want to thank Charlotte Kelly, founding director of WA, and Olivia Turner, Camp Director 1993, as well as the wonderful staff, facilitators, and women in the camp communities. The staff circles at camp have been rich places for my own personal development and participation. In Minnesota, Cynthia Orange served as my research editor, first in our exploration of ceremony and ritual, and later in putting the circle into context. Evidence of her contribution remains in the glossary and bibliography. I am deeply grateful for her willingness to shift her role as the book shifted, and her steady support.

In 1993, readers of the early versions of the book helped me better understand what I was trying to accomplish. For their critique and ability to vision the whole from its early jigsaw pieces, I thank Barbara Borden, Barbara Bowen, Carol Dilfer, and Ann Linnea. Thank you to Jo Spiller for channeling Moses and making other prophesies when I needed to hear them. And thanks to the great synergism of the world for countless conversations that transmuted their way into the fabric of the book.

I tried out ideas and discovered people's readiness to hold circle in wonderful places, large and small: Hollyhock, Interface, MorningStar, Omega, Split Rock, WinterMoon, Wolfridge ELC, Women's Alliance and other sites. I want to thank the Taos writing circles at Mabel Dodge Luhan House in both 1993 and 1994 for their rich contributions and friendships and acknowledge the women in many Tenfold™ circles for their brave peer spirit. Thank you to the people who told me their stories, and allowed them to be used here. Some names and circumstances have been changed in the longer scenarios, but they remain true to the spirit of those experiences. I am especially grateful to the people whose relationship to the circle is shared in the chapter on citizenship: Jeanne Gibbs, Hilary Mackay and Shelly Wine, Al Singer, Jo Spiller, Charlaine Tolkein.

Thank you to all the people who took me in, Macintosh PowerBook tucked in my backpack, and let me set up shop for a few days of writing interlude in the midst of much travel and teaching. This book is richer for all the places it has incubated. A special thank you to Blue and Phil Lenox for lending me their house and view of Puget Sound. Thanks to the circles in Minnesota which let me go, especially the Split Rock Reunion Group for modeling the switch from facilitation to peer leadership with such grace. And thanks to the circles in Washington, Oregon, California and British Columbia for inviting me to come—especially the friendship of Barbara Borden and Naomi Newman, women of deep council, great heart and big medicine.

In the winter of 1994, my brother Carl, my sister-in-law Colleen, and my niece Erin took me into their home in ways that we are no longer easily accustomed to. After several months of rewriting at the kitchen table, I asked Colleen to "please read the stories and anecdotes of our family life, see how they fit into context and let me know if you are willing to be part of the circle in this way." Their willingness to stand in place for hundreds of thousands of Carl-Colleen-Erin-s is a gift beyond measure to this book. I thank them for this generosity.

While I was writing, I often felt as though "the circle" was surrounding me, trying to get through my preconceived notions and conditioning to a place where I could simply see the possibilities. In the final stages of rewriting, editing, and production this position shifted: the book called its own circle and I became a participant along the rim. This was a stunning switch, initiated by my meeting David Kyle and reading his fine book, *Human Robots and Holy Mechanics*. Here was my brother/mind, a man thinking about the social context in which the circle will arise. I am deeply glad to have joined his publishing company and a circle of kindred spirits in bringing out this book. *Calling the Circle* is walking its talk in how it comes into the world. I hold the rim with much thankfulness to David Kyle and Patt Lind-Kyle of Swan•Raven & Company, Pam Meyer and Brian Crissey of Blue Water Publishing, and the circle alive in this publishing consortium. Amy Owen, Denise Twiggs, designer Marcia Barrentine. Thank you, Parvati Markus, editor extraordinaire, artist Susan Seddon Boulet, and others who helped this book make passage. And I am ever grateful for the steady, deepening presence of Ann Linnea, partner in our business PeerSpirit, sister in the circle, dear friend.

The Box: Remembering the Gift

It is the continuing work of life: of learning to trust that the universe is unfolding exactly as it should, no matter how it looks to us; learning to appreciate that each of us has a part in nurturing this interconnected whole and healing it where it is torn; discovering what our individual contribution can be, then giving ourselves fully to it...We may have forgotten that all of us have something important to give...

(Book of Reconciliation, *p.40, quote from Mirabai Bush*)

All of us have something to give and the ability to make a difference. We all have a gift to remember. *The Box: Remembering the Gift* is a collection of self-guiding materials which take an individual or group through an inner/outer journey of discovery, deepening communication and inspiring responses to the challenges of our times.

The Box grew out of ten years of circle gatherings—gatherings which mixed scientists with indigenous medicine people, poets and educators with theater people and social activists. The desire to share the wisdom that emerged from these experiences led to the concept of a tool kit which could be used to explore and integrate ideas and visions, spiritual and ceremonial traditions and the wisdom of the wilderness. The resulting compilation of text and art, teaching, healing and ecological tools was put together by a collaborative group, guided by the process of council.

The journey of *The Box* begins with the creation of sacred space in office, home or classroom. It unfolds according to a carefully orchestrated sequence of explorations, pilgrimages, and exercises, culminating in a rite of passage that focuses on one's own pivotal life questions. It encourages a commitment to service and compassionate action in the world. By exploring the parallels between our own personal wounds and the wounds of the planet, a mutual and simultaneous healing can take place.

The pace of the adventure is determined by the participants and could take six months to a year or more to complete. *The Box* is being used in schools, salons, study groups, prisons and churches and by major corporations and individuals from all walks of life. It is helping very diverse groups of people awaken to life as a purposeful, sacred journey.

Like *Calling the Circle, The Box* advocates the concepts of PeerSpirit—shared responsibility, rotating leadership and a reliance on spirit. *Calling the Circle* is a valuable resource and guide for *Box* journeyers, furthering the teachings on council, helping people reconnect with each other at a profound level and strengthening community.

> *Being able to turn to oneself and examine where we are, creatively and mindfully, is a way to stay whole. So often when we engage in the world, we lose ourselves to the point of confusion and internal chaos. Rather than going back and forth about what to do or what not to do, the pros and cons of any particular issue, we can access the wisdom of the circle...*

(Book of Reconciliation, *p.22*)

· For further information on *The Box: Remembering the Gift,* contact:

The Térma Company
P. O. Box 5495
Santa Fe, NM   87502

phone: (800) 793-9395
fax: (505) 988-4982

ORDER FORM

Books and Tapes available through Swan•Raven & Co.   **1-800-366-0264**

      or write to: Swan•Raven & Co.
                    P. O. Box 726
                    Newberg, OR   97132

Life's Companion: Journal Writing as a Spiritual Quest $11.95
      by Christina Baldwin

Companion Meditations, 3 cassette set $25.00
      by Christina Baldwin

Sunrise, Sunset, cassette tape $10.00
      by Christina Baldwin

One to One: Self Understanding through Journal Writing $9.95
      by Christina Baldwin

Human Robots and Holy Mechanics $14.95
      by David T. Kyle

When Sleeping Beauty Wakes Up $14.95
      by Patt Lind-Kyle

Ritual: Power, Healing and Community $12.95
      by Malidoma Somé

PEERSPIRIT PRODUCTS   **202-321-8404**

      or write to: PeerSpirit
                    P. O. Box 550
                    Langley, WA   98260

Guide to PeerSpirit Circling   1-4 copies $3.50
                            5-10 copies $3.25
                            10+ copies $3.00

Books by Ann Linnea

Teaching Kids to Love the Earth $14.95

(Watch for *Superior Spirit*, Little Brown, spring 1995)

(NOTE: After January 15, 1995, the area code will change to 360.)

Two internationally known seminars—*Women and the Planet* and *Tenfold*™—form the core business of PeerSpirit. Christina Baldwin, Ann Linnea and other facilitators, trainers and colleagues offer a variety of consultation services to the circle.